PENGUIN BO

DAY OF MY D

Martin Boyd was born in Switzerland in 1893 of Anglo-Australian parents. He was brought to Australia when six months old where the Boyd family made impressive contributions to the artistic and intellectual life. At the outbreak of the First World War he travelled to England and joined an English regiment and later the Royal Flying Corps. In 1948, at the height of his literary success, he returned to Australia to make a permanent home near Berwick.

Most of his novels maintain an Anglo-Australian theme and are based on his preoccupation with his own family. Martin Boyd moved to Rome in 1957 and lived there till his death in June 1972.

BY MARTIN BOYD

FICTION

Love Gods (1925)
Brangane: A Memoir (1926)
The Montforts (1928, revised edition, 1963)
Scandal of Spring (1934)
The Lemon Farm (1935)
The Picnic (1937)
Night of the Party (1938)
Nuns in Jeopardy (1940)
Lucinda Brayford (1946, revised edition, 1954)
Such Pleasure (1949)

THE LANGTON QUARTET (in reading order)

The Cardboard Crown (1952, revised edition, 1964)
A Difficult Young Man (1955)
Outbreak of Love (1957)
When Blackbirds Sing (1962)

The Tea-Time of Love (1969)

AUTOBIOGRAPHIES

A Single Flame (1939)
Day of My Delight: An Anglo-Australian Memoir (1965)

NON-FICTION
Much Else in Italy: A Subjective Travel Book (1958)

CHILDREN'S NOVEL
The Painted Princess: A Fairy Story (1936)

MARTIN BOYD

DAY OF MY DELIGHT

An Anglo-Australian memoir

PENGUIN BOOKS

Penguin Books Australia Ltd,
487 Maroondah Highway, P.O. Box 257
Ringwood, Victoria, 3134, Australia
Penguin Books Ltd,
Harmondsworth, Middlesex, England
40 West 23rd Street, New York, N.Y. 10010, U.S.A.
Penguin Books Canada Ltd,
2801 John Street, Markham, Ontario, Canada L3R 1B4
Penguin Books (N.Z.) Ltd,
182-190 Wairau Road, Auckland 10, New Zealand

First published 1965 by Lansdowne Press
Published in Penguin, 1986

Offset from the Lansdowne edition
Made and printed in Melbourne
by The Dominion Press-Hedges and Bell

CIP

Boyd, Martin, 1893-1972
Day of my delight.

ISBN 0 14 008716 8.

1. Boyd, Martin, 1893-1972 – Biography. 2. Novelists,
Australian – Biography. I. Title.

A823'.2

CONTENTS

continued

CONTENTS

continued

*"And was the day of my delight
As pure and perfect as I say?"*

IN MEMORIAM

Apologia

In 1938 I BEGAN A NOVEL on the theme that the standards which we are taught when young are not observed by the authorities of our adult life. I was using my own life to provide the plot. When I spoke to a friend of the difficulty of doing this, she said: "Why don't you write a straight-out autobiography?"

I replied that my life was not of public interest. She pointed out that a pantryboy had recently published his autobiography, and added: "Any honest autobiography is of interest. It is all human evidence."

I agreed that this was true, and I wrote my book in the first person. It may seem unduly egoistic to write two auto-biographies in a lifetime, but the 1938 book only deals with two-thirds of my life, leaving out my later development. Also, as many people appearing in it were still alive, I had to invent one or two fictional characters to record their sayings. In it too were a few factual errors, due to my not having verified what I had been told as a child.

In Australia in recent years there have been written various articles and essays, identifying my fiction with my family, but inaccurately. I have deliberately created this confusion, to avoid libelling the innocent. Now all those who might have been hurt are dead, and I shall give the real names of the people whom I mention. It may be of interest to readers who value the social history in my novels, to be informed of its source.

Since, in my life-long search for the non-existent abiding city, I have come to live in Rome, all my previous life seems remote, as it is unrelated to my present environment. Because of this I have tended to write of people who are still alive and flourishing, as if they were no longer of this world. To do so is necessary for the artistic unity of my book, and I hope that they will forgive it.

I have written as much about my times as about my life; but how an individual reacts to his times is part of the human evidence which justifies an autobiography.

Thackeray's daughter, Lady Ritchie, said that the faults in our nature are only lacunae, and that it is the good within us which is our essential self. This positive attitude to life is against the mood of today, when only the evil is admitted to be real, though there are signs that this mood is beginning to change. The command of the sages is that we should know ourselves, and I believe that the purpose of life is to discover this essential self, freed from the lacunae. Therefore the only human evidence of any value, is of the extent to which we have been able to do this, or perhaps of how we might have done it. Or, if even this is too great a claim to make, of how the times in which we have lived have helped or hindered the process.

This may rather over-emphasise what is serious in my book, which, after all, is only the account of my life. In that life there has been much that is frivolous. A true picture must give a proportion of this, and I have not repudiated anything that is human.

M.B.

EMIGRANT BABY

"Samedi 10 Juin. S.Landry. Minnie not very well. I went for a walk and bought a bottle of eau-de-cologne, a chess-board and three cakes for the children. Minnie came down to déjeuner and had some fish that the Russian officer caught. Her baby born at twenty-five minutes past four in the afternoon. She has a sage-femme who speaks English, and a nurse who speaks German and French, and likes them very well. Everyone asked very kindly after her. Mrs. Hay-Gordon came back from Brunnen today. Played bezique with her in the evening."

Over half a century later I discovered this account of my birth in my grandmother's diaries. The year of the entry was 1893, and the family were in Switzerland.

My grandmother then went to Paris but came back to Lucerne for my christening. She wrote "The baby smiles a great deal when spoken to", also that I "behaved very nicely" at the christening; that I had a Venetian lace cap; and that a French lady gave me a bouquet. In the evening they all went to the Casino.

In Australia the land boom was bursting, and after living for some years at Penleigh in Wiltshire they were returning home to face comparative ruin. They did not hurry, but took

CHAPTER I

five months to travel from Lucerne to Brindisi, via Milan, Florence, Rome and Naples. In Rome I was taken by my nurse to be aired on the Spanish Steps, where at seventy-two I still air myself occasionally. At Brindisi my grandmother wrote:

"19 Novembre. Dimanche. Ste. Elisabeth. The *Arcadia* came in at eight o'clock this morning. I bought a fan, some silk caps and a picture and we all went on board before luncheon. Last time I was here I had some chocolate in the hotel with Mr. Rudyard Kipling."

On that day, at five months old, I ceased to be a European, at any rate physically, and for the next twelve years lived on the shores of Port Phillip Bay.

The earliest thing I remember was my mulberry juice spilling down the well. With my two elder brothers I had squeezed mulberries to make a drink, and the glass which held my share fell over, and the red juice dripped through the boarded well-cover where I had placed it, into the black echoing hollow. I wept, blaming God and my parents for this irreparable loss, believing that they should have arranged a world wherein such a happening was impossible.

My other early memories also hint at my temperament. The beach was edged by a belt of tea-trees and a line of shingle. We ran about barefoot, and when we went down to bathe I used to stand at the edge of the shingle and wail: "Carry me over the stones."

Once my brothers had become involved with some larrikins —a larrikin is a young Australian rowdy—and in their company had broken a neighbour's window. Although we were seldom punished, my father thought this occasion demanded a beating. He cut a tea-tree switch and sent for my brothers. I went into his studio with them, and when I saw the switch, in a passion I flung myself at him and broke it. My father laughed, explained that he had no designs on me, and went out to get another switch.

2

These things happened when I was about five. I had a nurse called Daisy. I believed that the popular song was written about her, and wondered how soon she would have a bicycle made for two.

Once at luncheon my father mentioned the socialists. I asked what they were. My father told me with a kind of banter that they were people who would take away everyone's money so that we should all have to live at a level of drab uniformity. Though only seven, I exploded with indignation. My father was amused and said: "I see you are a little conservative."

I had terrifying dreams in which I was chased by a kind of minotaur.

At about the same time my father mentioned that the Chief of our family had been executed after the 'Forty-five, and I declared myself a Jacobite. Fifteen years later, when entering the army, I had to swear allegiance to George V, I was unable to deny my childhood's allegiance, and only muttered.

When I was nine I was knocked senseless by a cricket ball and took a dislike to the game.

Before my grandparents died we occasionally felt the stress of poverty, but I ignored my mother's economical suggestions and refused to travel other than first class.

As we are said to change every seven years, I may complacently repudiate the child I then was.

For about eight years, until I was thirteen, we lived at Sandringham, near Melbourne. Apart from a few shops round the railway station, there were then only half a dozen scattered houses. We had the undisturbed use of a mile of golden beach, and tea-tree covered cliffs. An arcadian horse-tram trundled twice a day along the road to Black Rock and Beaumaris, and twice a day it went off the rails. Inland from our house was a tract of sandy scrub, covered with pink and white heath, prickly flowering shrubs, and small orchids called "donkey's ears" and "spiders" which they resembled.

In this sunny, aromatic world real poverty was unknown, excepting that of the extremely idle and feckless. There was no unemployment and there were no slums. War was the picturesque affliction of distant lands and times. The climate was that of the Riviera, only fresher. The income tax was sixpence in the pound, and in spite of this low taxation, any sick person with no money automatically received the best attention in the public hospitals. How did this happen when nowadays everyone has to pay what in a lifetime amounts to two or three thousand pounds into the National Health?

We grew up with the feeling that the adult world was entirely reasonable and secure. The only dangers to life were the natural menaces—snakes and sharks, centipedes, bulldog ants and scorpions. There could be no danger from the folly of human authority nor from mad economics.

We extracted a great deal of pleasure from our surroundings, but we did not think them paradise, not when we came out of the childish absorbed pleasure of the moment such as poking at the catfish and anemones in a rocky pool, or climbing like monkeys from branch to branch along the tea-tree on the cliff, or splashing into the limpid sea on a still, hot Australian morning.

We were made critical by our excursions into richer life. My mother's parents lived at Brighton, about three miles away, while my grandmother Boyd lived in St. Kilda, in a grey, gabled house set in a large garden and surrounded by fields. We were always conscious of living against the background of our relatives. The normal life seemed to us not the simple, adequate, well-warmed and nourished atmosphere of our own home, with its unsurpassed natural pleasures of sea and countryside, but one where money always was available for luxury. We were extremely fond of our parents and considered them just and kind, but subconsciously we may have blamed them for not providing us with a more opulent home.

They were entirely without snobbery, having escaped from the social life where it was an armour, and my mother was dismayed to find it rampant in her children.

It was not only the large houses, the several servants and richer food that made me so eager to visit my grandparents. I felt it an excursion into an altogether more secure world. Sandringham was arid and exposed. There were no trees but the stunted tea-tree, and few stretches of grass broke the waste of sandy scrub. Roses bloomed with difficulty in our garden. The greener lawns, the fatter buds, the damper, darker soil of the gardens in St. Kilda and Brighton satisfied in me some nostalgia for a fertile terrain. There was a field dotted with gum-trees which we passed on the way to Brighton, and which I regarded as the frontier of civilisation. It was not until I had spent some winters in England that I learnt to appreciate the beauties of a hot and arid coast.

My grandmother Boyd's house was called Glenfern, and still stands, shorn of its fields, at the corner of Inkerman Road and Hotham Street in East St. Kilda. The other houses in the neighbourhood were of the same kind, inhabited by judges and various kinds of early gentry. Glenfern was the first house in which I slept in Australia, but my grandmother was already a widow, and we did not go there so much as to our maternal grandmother's. When we did go, I felt that I had penetrated further into that civilisation of which we were on the outer fringe at Sandringham. It seemed to me to have more old-world dignity than most houses, and I know that there were some fine paintings and pieces of inherited eighteenth century furniture.

Not far away Judge Chomley lived at Woodlands. Three of his daughters were my close friends throughout my life. Although my father's brother had married their sister, the two younger were no blood relation to me. Also my mother's sister had married their cousin, and my grandfather's cousin their uncle. Because of all this, I called the eldest sister Aunt

Mary, and the two younger by their Christian names, Eileen and Aubrey.

They were in England for most of the years I was there, and when I came back to Melbourne in 1948 they too had returned. This parallel of experience gave us much the same view of the world at large, and in their company I had a unique feeling of being at home.

As far as I know I am the only one to put on record the kind of life led by these people, even if I have done it with a touch of levity. In the last century they were the "ruling class" in Victoria, and so have historical interest. Up to 1914 they still held the pre-eminence this had given them. Poor as we were, when my brother Penleigh read from some comic rules of etiquette in *Punch*: "People of assured position may spit their pips into the middle of the table" I did not question that I was entitled to exercise this privilege. Our sort were soon overshadowed by rich squatters, who since in turn have been overshadowed by rich business people.

My mother was commissioned to paint a picture of the Italianate mansion of one of the latter group, and there was an amused discussion as to whether she should accept an invitation to lunch with her patron.

Melba was engaged by a socially ambitious woman to sing at a reception. When asked her fee she said it would be five hundred guineas. The woman warned her: "I shall not expect you to mix with my guests."

"Oh," said Melba with relief. "Then it will only be two hundred and fifty."

My à Beckett grandparents' house was called Wilton, and was at Middle Brighton, nearer to Sandringham. In addition to this they had a country house, the Grange in the hills of Harkaway, a few miles north of Berwick. This was really their home, built forty years earlier when my grandparents were first married. Here their children spent their early youth, and to this simple house their thoughts turned nostalgically from different parts of the world, from Wiltshire manors and Riviera hotels. One of my mother's favourite arias was that from *Trovatore* "*Ai nostri monti*—Home to our mountains let us return", I believe because it expressed her longing for that happy home.

In my own childhood my grandmother seldom went there, probably not after her husband died. My eldest brother Gilbert was thrown from his pony and killed there when I was two years old, which must have affected her attitude to the place. My last visit in her lifetime was when I was five, though this house was to have an important influence on my life and my work. It is the "Westhill" of the Langton novels.

My mother's married sisters, besides other relatives, all lived within a few miles of Wilton, and we were as familiar with our cousins as with our brothers. When we went for holidays to Tasmania half the cousins came too, which tended to give us the feeling that the world was entirely populated by our relatives.

This was the stage on which I played my early life, brightly lit and self-contained, but with the awareness of a backcloth painted with dim mediaeval motifs, blending with Victoriana, and elusively glimpsed in occasional remarks dropped by my elders.

It is not in the mood of today to refer to one's origins. It is thought more admirable to give the impression of being a new creation, sprung suddenly from nowhere, and this would be a beautiful thing to do if one was a new creation. But ordinary men cannot assume a Virgin Birth.

If I am to provide human evidence, I must also admit the tendencies in my blood, and the colouring given to my mind by the images in the backcloth. Readers who are not interested in hereditary influences may prefer to skip the following chapter.

THE BACKCLOTH

MY FATHER'S FAMILY WERE IRISH, but of Scottish origin, being a cadet branch of the Boyds of Kilmarnock, who took a turbulent part in history from Bannockburn to Culloden and were frequently beheaded. The last of these grim occasions was on Tower Hill after the 'Forty-five, of which my father had told me, producing an immediate colouration of my mind. The temperament of the family is indicated by an entry in the Kilmarnock pedigree: "Contrary to the traditions of his House, his lordship supported the existing government."

In the eighteenth century my father's more immediate antecedents acquired property in County Mayo, and were entered in the cathedral register at Killala as "Boyd of Crosspatrick Esquire". Nearly all the younger sons were soldiers, except one William, who became a doctor and was knighted at Castlebar in 1785, and my father's uncle Alexander, who became Treasurer-General at Corfu. My paternal great-grandfather held military appointments at Gibraltar and Corfu, and also for a short time Sydney, so that everyone of my eight great-grandparents was at some time in Australia, and for four generations we have been used to the sun. One of my father's great-grandmothers was a Swift, a relative of the dean's, but this was the only faint creative link on his father's side.

I think that the strong artistic impulse in our family, now spreading to the fourth generation, though stirred into activity by my mother, has its origin in a cluster of talented Kirby's, a Suffolk family who were my father's maternal ancestors. John Kirby, a topographer, wrote a book called *The Suffolk Traveller*, a detailed record of the whole county. He and four of his children and grandchildren have separate entries in the *Encyclopaedia Britannica*. One of his sons, Joshua, was an architectural painter, and the friend of Hogarth, Reynolds, and Gainsborough. His friendship with the latter was so close that they were buried side by side in Kew churchyard. He published among other works a book or perspective, for which George III wrote the preface.

Joshua's brother William married Lucy Medowe of Witnesham Hall, Suffolk, an amateur naturalist who trained her son William and her daughter Lucy to see the beauty in the small and intimate life of nature. William's accidental finding of a beautiful insect made him decide to study entomology. He was a clergyman and held two livings, but "his chief aim in life was to trace the benevolence and wisdom of the Creator in his works". He discovered one hundred and fifty-three specimens of wild bees in his parish of Barham, and "founded the new insect order of Strepsiptera". His sister Lucy was a talented painter and also delighted in the paintings of birds and fauna. Joshua's daughter Sarah Trimmer was an authoress and a friend of Dr. Johnson, and one of her sons was a geologist who delighted in the beauty of rocks and minerals. One of her daughters was governess, confidante and valued counseller in her escapades to Georgina, Duchess of Devonshire.

I mention these Kirbys at length, as they all seem to have had this impulse to find truth in the beauty of nature, which if it does not return to the artist, art itself will die in ridicule.

Incidentally, Joshua Kirby, in his portrait by Gainsborough in the National Portrait Gallery, has the same kind of face as my father and my nephew Arthur. Lucy, sister of the Reverend William, married Dominicus de Guzman, who was said to be of the same family as St. Dominic, and also to have bequeathed to us passions which were evident in my brother Merric.

The second Lucy also gave her name to her daughter and this custom continued for five more generations. With the name went certain paintings and furnishings, some of which my father's sister Lucy (called Aunt Lily) the last in the succession, gave to me.

My grandfather John Theodore Boyd, who came to Victoria as Military Secretary to an early Governor, eloped with the sixth Lucy. My grandfather à Beckett also eloped, with a more considerable heiress, which may have something to do with the dislike of constraint which was felt by my brothers and myself.

He was of an old Wiltshire family, the à Becketts of Littleton by West Lavington, and of Penleigh near Westbury. They had held the former manor in the male line since 1440, and in the female since 1185. They were generally regarded as the kinsmen of St. Thomas, and when his tomb was opened in Canterbury Cathedral, my grandfather's cousin was one of the few invited to be present.

My mother's great-grandfather William, the ninth in generation to have this Christian name, was a lawyer with a passionate hatred of injustice, which may account for the fact that eight of his descendants became judges. This also in turn may account for the blind looming judges and the sense of their doom in my nephew David's paintings. Though there was no legal blood in my father's family, one of his brothers married a judge's daughter, and one of his sisters, christened Lucy de Guzman after her Kirby ancestress, and one of the most kindly influences of our childhood, married

10

Judge Gurner. My father's other sister married a son of Dr.
Mahaffy of Trinity College, Dublin. He was High Commissioner of Fiji, where he captured a black and mother-of-
pearl headhunting canoe which is in the Melbourne National
Gallery. These inconsequent facts may be slightly confusing
but Dr. Mahaffy and his son's headhunting canoe made a
surrealist corner among the mediaevalisms on my backcloth.
It is an even stranger juxtaposition to recall that Rupert
Brooke stayed with my aunt in Fiji, and shocked her by
coming to dinner in his bedroom slippers.

It is only fair to my parents to state that they did not stuff
our minds with the past. I was the only one allergic to it and
I do not know how I picked it up as they seldom mentioned
it; but they did talk a good deal about Europe, and about
Penleigh House, where they had lived in the years before I
was born.

To return to the ninth William. He was a man of great
reforming energy. With Lord Brougham he helped to found
the Law Society, and he was instrumental in bringing about
the repeal of the Window Tax. This is the delightful thing
of which my mother's family, if they were given to pride,
might most worthily be proud, that one of them let the sunlight return into ten thousand homes.

He had four sons. The eldest, the tenth William, became
Chief Justice of Victoria, and was my mother's grandfather.
Two of his brothers followed him to Australia. One, Thomas,
who became a member of the Legislative Council and a
Minister of the Crown, was the father of one of the eight
judges and grandfather of another. Arthur, the third brother,
having fought for Queen Isabella in Spain and been
three times decorated, became a doctor, married an Elwin of
Norfolk and settled in Sydney. The fourth, Gilbert Abbott à
Beckett, remained in England. I was told that while still at
Westminster he edited a magazine describing the arrival of
prominent people in Hell. He was with Thackeray one of

the founders of *Punch*, also a leader-writer to the *Times*, and author of the *Comic History of England*. An Eton boy told me that his dame found him reading the above book and dressed him down severely for reading a work that made light of the noble history of his country. She may have been right as, though harmless in intention, it may have been the first drop of that dreary spate of "debunking" books, which give the impression that the literary world is composed entirely of people competing desperately in the search for some figure who has bestowed immense benefit on mankind, in poetry or fine painting, or in liberating the oppressed and healing the sick, so that they can show him up as a squalid and shifty charlatan.

Although we were only cousins and on the other side of the world, the *Punch* tradition affected us strongly. We had to cherish the absurd when we saw it in order to scarify it with ridicule, like breeding pheasants to shoot them. This characteristic was stronger in Gilbert's sons and grandsons, who continued to have some connection with *Punch*.

Sir William, my mother's grandfather, wrote some Gothic poems and a travel book, which I find sympathetic, as he only wanted to see what he thought beautiful or meaningful. An old stone on which some famous person had once sat was of no interest to him. This travel book was dedicated to Sir Alfred Stephen, Chief Justice of New South Wales and Virginia Woolf's grandfather. I mention this because her name in this connection also seems slightly surrealistic.

I have now finished with the more remote dead. On the stage itself were some who were soon to fade into the back-cloth, but who were then still alive, notably our grandfather, the eleventh William, who was very much so. As I have drawn highly coloured portraits of him in my novels, for which the basis was largely the malicious gossip of more conventional relatives to whom he was antipathetic, I shall try to make amends here. I have even used the basis of his character, and made it fictional by adding misdemeanours of which he was innocent, such as the affair with Hetty in *The Cardboard Crown*. I had been told that he could not resist attractive women, and thought it tidier to concentrate the magnetism in Hetty. In him the family wit was genuine and he also had the excessive, easily wounded sensibility which was another family characteristic. He thought that only himself was vulnerable and had little idea of the pain he inflicted with his savage *mots*. He may have thought, as I find myself apt to think, that if a retort is really funny it is not wounding, that the wound is healed by the laughter. My relatives played to excess the game of scoring off each other, with little more malicious intention than people play croquet. I was terrified of my grandfather. He used to chase my brothers round the house with a driving whip. To the one he caught he gave sixpence. I did not realise that this affectation of ferocity was a game.

On the night of his elopement he brought his wife to Bishopscourt, on the Eastern Hill of Melbourne, which his father then rented, a scene which I have also travestied in *The Cardboard Crown*.

Our grandmother brought the family a large and increasing fortune, which if undivided would now be worth millions. My mother said that she also bestowed on us what mental stability we possessed. She gave eager encouragement to any creative effort, and in England and on the Continent her cultural horizons were wide and interesting. I have used her diaries in my Langton novels, inserting whole passages unchanged, except those necessary to the fictional romance. People who have read the first of these books have remarked on the fine character of the heroine, so largely my grandmother.

Her husband, although he had no need to earn his living,

13

was far from idle. He took an active interest in the development of the new country, and became a member of the Legislative Council, and a Minister of the Crown. He combined with this an interest in horses and heraldry. His smoking-room was lined with red and gold books of genealogical reference. He thought himself important as the head of his family. His yellow-wheeled four-in-hand drag and the other carriages were freely splashed with his escutcheon. He was clever with horses, and used to drive them in odd formations, such as one leading, two in the second row, and three behind. He could drop the reins and control the horses by speaking to them.

His personal vanity and his preoccupation with his ancestry, like his savage wit, were an armour deliberately assumed to protect his too soft and sensitive core. He did not belong to his period, and disliked the bourgeois society of Melbourne, with its exaggerated snobbery of wealth. He was generous to the unfortunate, and one used to see at Wilton unsuccessful musicians whom he brought there to play out-of-the-way instruments with him. He is said to have asked in a music shop: "Have you any shawms?"

He was groping for enlightenment and used to attend every possible kind of religious service. He could subscribe to no single creed because of his regard for truth. Hatred of a lie was perhaps the most striking characteristic of my relatives. My mother could not frame a social excuse because of it. My grandmother would reiterate to anyone who tried to explain why he had failed to keep his word: "Yes, but you *said* . . ."

Grandfather à Beckett barely lived into the new century. My grandfather Boyd died in the year before I was born. He left a reputation of legendary chivalry, and in the front of a prayer book at home was pasted his obituary notice, which compared him with Colonel Newcome, so that he was in my backcloth from the beginning. Occasionally other figures in it achieved a clearer outline, as when an old Aunt Brigid in County Mayo died and left my aunts minute legacies; or when my mother read out from a letter from England the odd sentence: "Cousin Coo was knighted and died." The two processes were linked in my childish mind.

TASMANIAN HOLIDAY

WHEN MY PARENTS were feeling exceptionally poor they used to let our house at Sandringham, which was near the golf-links, and we all went to Tasmania, a form of economy which we enjoyed.

When I was ten my eldest surviving brother had pneumonia. My mother, who was very religious, could not bear to see the lopping off of her sons, and although my brother's temperature reached 105 degrees, she prayed to such effect that his life was saved. The doctor was bewildered at his survival.

Although the champagne came from Wilton to keep my brother alive, his illness was very expensive, and after it we had to go to Tasmania for a year. My father had a small yacht in which he used to cruise round the rivers of Tasmania with my brothers. Once I went with them, but I was too young for my brothers, and I used to go ashore with my father. He would stop for so long talking to yachtsmen and fishermen that I became inexpressibly bored, and asked to go back to join my mother in Melbourne. A few years later I used to drive round with him in the country, when he would pull up and talk to the farmers. This enabled me to read the whole of Scott's novels, one of which I always brought in my pocket, and sitting in an Australian dogcart, soaked my mind in mediaevalism.

On the Tasmanian trip after my brother's illness, my father was so hard up that he had to sell his yacht, but my grandmother bought it and gave it back to him. This strengthened my belief that a benevolent power would always remedy misfortune. She came over to Tasmania for that summer with her two unmarried sons, two other married daughters and their half-dozen children. Our clan used to flood hotels and we filled two large drags when we went on excursions. There used to be family rows as my richer cousins expected the best rooms in hotels, although they paid no more for them.

One of the events of the Tasmanian season was a fête at a place called the Bower, half-way up Mount Wellington. Staying at the hotel was a socially ambitious woman who afterwards married a peer. I read sixty years later in my grandmother's diaries that she was sitting talking about antique china to this woman while I was sprawling on the floor, playing with dominoes at their feet. I must admit that I have used aspects of the character of this lady in a novel, and have also turned my grandmother's life into a work of fiction. What would they have done if they had known what was to germinate in the head of the small boy at their feet? Would they have smacked me on account?

Sir Harry Allen, a professor at the Melbourne University, was at the Bower with his wife and three daughters. Every night at bedtime the latter used to sing a hymn in their room, but they were remarkably erudite, and Biddy, a few years younger than myself, asked me: "Who is your favourite character in French history?" I was dumb with shame, as I had imagined that all history was English.

Another woman in Hobart had a mother or grandmother whose gardener in the early days had run away to join the bushrangers. He held up a coach in which she was travelling.

When he put his head in the window and said: "Hands up!" she exclaimed: "How dare you, James?" He replied: "Sorry mum, I didn't know it was you", and rode away.

On an earlier holiday in Tasmania, when I was seven, I was taken to see Captain Dumaresque of Mount Ireh, who was then a hundred years old. So it is possible that I have spoken to someone who was born in the eighteenth century.

As I grew older, Tasmania, to which this was my last visit as a child, became part of the backcloth. It had more feeling of history than Victoria. Many of the houses were Georgian and the villages, woods and orchards along the River Derwent were very picturesque. The ruined church of the convict settlement at Port Arthur was the Australian equivalent of Glastonbury.

While we were in Tasmania, Penleigh and I went to Hutchins School in Hobart. I think that Merric was then at an agricultural college, where he was more or less tortured for his noble eccentricities. We lived at Bellerive and went to school by ferry steamers. On the way we passed a group of young hooligans who used to throw stones at us. We sailed a great deal in my father's yacht, when we used to fish with a spinner for black-backed salmon. At Bellerive, in a little inlet between some rocks, I taught myself to swim, though previous efforts to teach me by instructing me in the correct antics had failed. This illustrates one of the basic facts of my nature, that I am more intuitive than intellectual.

Shortly after this year in Tasmania my grandmother became ill. I was puzzled and resentful that on our visits to Wilton she no longer greeted us with friendly interest, nor gave us presents, but lay listless on a sofa. She had been to us the fount from which all blessings flowed. Everything to do with her had been interesting and pleasurable. In the drawing-room at Wilton was a cabinet full of curiosities from all parts of Europe. Beneath the crystal chandelier were two marble cupids fighting over a heart. These fascinating objects were for me an extension of her personality. When she was under her last anaesthetic she recited the twenty-third psalm in Italian.

Before I finish with these influences of my boyhood, I must include those of my parents, particularly of my mother.

Where I have written of her hitherto, I have over-emphasised the religious side of her nature, which was more evident towards the end of her life, in which she had great anxieties and sorrows. She always had this preoccupation with religion, but in her youth it was accompanied by a normal love of pleasure. In fact I think for all her life she had a greater love of one kind of pleasure than most people, that of any kind of artistic creation, whether in a serious work, or in the ephemeral adornment of ordinary living, such as the decoration of a dinner table, or the invention of a new dish. In the year before I was born she had lived mostly in France, and had acquired a knowledge of French cooking. She made a puppet theatre in which with the help of our governess she performed *Red Riding Hood* and *The Three Bears*. At one of our parties a child was carried out screaming when the wolf gobbled up the grandmother. I was thinking of her when I wrote of Diana in *Outbreak of Love* "all the artistry she had used to make the details of their lives charming". Once she said to me: "If you don't want your food, don't eat it. It's better to throw it away than to make yourself sick." This hardly supports the puritan parent, stuffing tapioca pudding down reluctant throats.

She painted the four seasons in a wide frieze round the dining-room at Yarra Glen. This was painted out fifty years later by the farmer who then owned the house. A similar fate threatens the murals painted by Arthur at the Grange.

I do not think that the puritanism which I have exaggerated became so evident until later in her life, when she felt that any extravagance was wicked when such a large proportion of humanity had not even enough food.

One critic said that a character in *The Picnic* (a novel I dislike), a genteel Australian woman with an anxiety to admire the correct forms of culture, was drawn from my mother, to whom she had as much resemblance as Mr. Collins, Jane Austen's tame curate, had to Savonarola.

Even earlier, at Penleigh, she was horrified at the poverty of the villagers, which had no equal in Australia, and in my grandmother's diaries there are frequent references to her taking them food and wine.

In later life she cared little for her appearance. Once at Yarra Glen when she was going to a rare luncheon party, as she came out of the door the man who was driving her exclaimed: "Lor, mum, you do look a lady when you're dressed up." She disliked formal social functions of any kind, so that they came to have for us the enhanced value of a thing forbidden. She thought that we should be contented with the simple natural pleasures provided by our ponies and orchard and river. I do not think it unfair to say that the worst Australian characteristic is a reverence for money, and for the artificial social distinctions created by its possession in any quantity. My mother was repelled by this and anxious to keep us uncontaminated. If she had labelled a thing bad, no threat of ridicule or disaster could make her compromise with it, nor would any obstacle deter her from her pursuit of what she had labelled good, but she was as indulgent to us as was compatible with this integrity.

She also had her share of the family wit and could annihilate what she thought absurd. A fair portion of my parents' joint income was set aside as my mother's personal allowance. She gave half of this to charity, and the other half she spent in indulgence of her children. She tried to protect us from folly and misfortune, and if we fell into them, to obviate the consequences. She thought nothing of her importance as an individual, only of the welfare of the group in which she found herself.

My relations with my father were polite and amiable, but we were never close friends. During my schooldays we had few interests in common; though I think it was my approval which decided him to buy our farm at Yarra Glen. He was always absolutely just, and both our parents were generous to us beyond their means, and continued to be so throughout their lives.

These were my influences until I was about twelve or thirteen. They made me believe that reason had only to be stated to find a hearing, that God was the witness of my smallest act, and also that there was no incompatibility between this and a life of absolute pleasure, as my mother was often at pains to draw my attention to her father's wisdom and kindness; while it did not occur to me that it was admirable to work for one's living. Neither of my grandfathers had worked, my maternal uncles did not work, and if my father's brothers worked I have no idea what they did. My father, although he was an artist, gave an impression of leisure, and was responsible to no one for his time or effort.

In an article in an English weekly I read recently: "Before 1914 it was not thought dishonourable for a man with a private income to do no work." On the contrary it was thought dishonourable if he did, and now it would be more than ever dishonourable, as he would most likely be depriving another man of the means of livelihood. What proportion of jobs are of benefit to humanity? A great many are harmful, the vast horde of superfluous bureaucrats for example; or the advertisers of harmful medicines and sterilised foods. There is no cut-and-dried morality about this. Also, it is not really true to say my relatives did not work. My grandfather à Beckett was always doing something for the public benefit. He blazed the road from the coast into the Dandenong Ranges, part of which is called by his name. He was a magistrate as well as a member of parliament and a Minister of the Crown. His sons were magistrates and conscientiously fulfilled their duties as country gentlemen. My father was a serious painter, and managed his farm. It did not produce much revenue, but it paid the wages of the farmhands and fed his family. He also helped others as far as his limited means would allow.

When I hear from others of their treatment as boys, I am amazed at the benevolent enlightenment of my own up-bringing. It was reasonable that I should believe that the voice of authority was the voice of the Good.

When I was thirteen I was tormented by sexual desires and for six months or so my mind seethed with erotic images. Then I was confirmed at school and my eroticism was sublimated. The devil, if this instinct is the devil, left me for a number of years and I went through my schooldays vaguely aware that there was such a thing as sex, but quite untroubled by its urgency.

LEARNING THE MYTHS

AFTER OUR WILTON GRANDMOTHER'S DEATH my parents had more money, and a year or two later when "Grannie at Glenfern" died, again a little more, and when a great-grandmother died a little more still. They sold our house at Sandringham and bought a farm at Yarra Glen, about thirty miles from Melbourne. This was at first intended to provide a livelihood for Merric, but instead of a farmhand he employed a valet, while the thistles grew in the field. I went up with my father to look at the condition of the place, and shared his disgust. In spite of my religious and aesthetic preoccupations, I have the instincts of a farmer.

Merric was not to be blamed. He had none of the farming instincts, except that he liked galloping on horses. He was restless, passionate and full of creative impulses that had not yet found the means of expression. He was the victim of the belief held in Australia in those days that if a boy did not fit into any niche, he should be "put on the land". In Ireland he and his uncles would have automatically been sent into the army, though that would have been far from his *métier*.

It was a great benefit to me that he abandoned Yarra Glen, as we all went to live there, and the feeling which my mother had for the Grange I have for this place. Our house was on the banks of the Yarra, which ran through a valley eight miles wide, bounded on one side by the mountains of Healesville, and on the other by the Christmas Hills.

I spent all my school holidays at Yarra Glen. I had no sense of deprivation during my schooldays, as our life was not contrasted with that of more affluent relatives. My parents considered themselves very poor, and like most artists lived a picnic kind of life, but we had advantages which nowadays in England are the prerogative of the rich. We had our own ponies, and a mile and a half of river frontage with a private bathing-place. There was hunting and rough shooting and fishing if we wanted it. The fruit and cream were unlimited, and after dinner we could go into the orchard and stuff ourselves with peaches from the standard trees. Roses bloomed in mid-winter, when the river banks were a blaze of yellow wattle, and the house smelt pleasantly of burning gum logs. I spent my holidays bathing and riding. Leisure and freedom were unrestricted. As long as we were not out riding after dark we could do as we pleased.

A boy who had been ill came up to convalesce with us, and in exchange left us with a family catchword. He helped himself with excessive liberality to cream saying: "It is good for me."

At Kincraig, a mile and a half away on the hill, lived a Scottish family who had been rich before the boom, and had laid out a beautiful garden round their house, with flights of cypress-planted steps and a long soft-carpeted avenue of pines. Their tennis court was surrounded by vines of passionfruit entwined with jasmine and climbing tea-roses. In the autumn the medlars and chestnuts in their orchards achieved a brilliance of colour that is rarely seen in the north.

The Rosses were extraordinarily kind to me, and if I was bored at home I would ride off and spend the day with them, staying uninvited to all meals. From their terrace there was a view of eight miles across the valley to the hills of

Lilydale, which were generally opalescent mauve and gold in the evening light. Across the river were vineyards, planted in early Victorian days by a Swiss baron, where they made a good claret. Once I was shown over the place by a young man who told me that he was a teetotaller, but that he became tipsy from the fumes whenever he had to clean out the enormous vats. Beyond the vineyards was Madame Melba's house, where she came back regularly from the homage of Europe to help her native land, but she was not given a free ticket to the Yarra Glen Agricultural Show lest the local bigwigs should be jealous. Penleigh was then learning to paint at the Melbourne Gallery, and he used to bring student friends to stay with us, among them Willy McInnes and Frank Crozier, an artist of fine sensibility, whose work I think is too little known. We drove out on sketching expeditions when we would boil the billy over a fire of gum twigs. If we took our luncheon we grilled chops on the forked end of a stick. My father, my mother, my brother, and myself and any visitor would all sketch, and afterwards appraise each other's work. Sketching for us was as normal an activity as breathing. It was not until I came to England that I was made to feel that it was either conceited or indecently self-revealing to offer one's work for criticism.

We did a great deal of impromptu acting, and would often break out into charades. A cousin whom I met in Vienna thirty years later tried to recall to me a scene at Yarra Glen when my brother and myself staggered across a field pretending to be stewards carrying plates on a ship, but which I had forgotten as this sort of thing was so usual with us.

The natural beauties of the countryside were all enhanced for me by poetic interpretations. When at school I read of the hedgerows above Tintern Abbey, I thought of a row of overgrown hawthorns below the Kincraig garden, and I remember one still autumn morning riding slowly down the hill above the railway station, and dreaming that "the little lines of sportive wood run wild" that divided the paddocks were close to the banks of the Wye.

Ruskin said that perfect beauty was found in man's work tempered by nature. I enjoyed nature more when it was tempered by man's work, and I responded with all my being to the few fragments of traditional culture that marked the landscape. The view from Kincraig was more attractive to me because of a Gothic memorial to M. de Castella in the foreground. Any tinge of the traditional excited me. Even the arrangement of a cheap altar, with ugly brass ornaments, linked me to the aspirations of mediaeval saints and poets.

I think that I was happier at Yarra Glen than I have been at any other time in my life. The country was beautiful in itself, and my imagination clothed it with poetic significance. More than this, the landscape and the friendly people, though delightful, were merely the prelude to a world that for me was full of hope.

When we moved to Yarra Glen the problem of my education became acute, and I was sent to Trinity Grammar School on Kew hill, about six miles from Melbourne. My parents chose this school, probably because the fees were less than at the larger schools, but also because of the character of the headmaster, George Merrick Long, afterwards Bishop of Bathurst and of Newcastle. They were indifferent to the fact that its status was less "public school" than that of Melbourne and Geelong, now the Australian Eton, which also are called "grammar schools". It was partly because although they considered themselves entirely Australian, they were too much of the early days to consider grades of this kind to be of any importance. I have only lately recognised that my parents had another characteristic—they had completely by-passed the industrial revolution. My father's family came from the agricultural west of Ireland to agricultural Australia, and their attitude in these matters was more eighteenth century. All the same there are public school virtues, and Canon Long, as he then was, was ardent to instil them into us in their finest essence.

Being a pioneer, he was far more enthusiastic for the public school virtues than he might have been in an English school. To resist the brute, to protect the weak, to work for the general good, to face the truth, these things were instilled into us and illustrated by every lesson in history, Latin, Greek and English literature. It was unthinkable to show fear or to let down a friend. It was perhaps only to be expected, after all this, that in the war our school had the largest percentage of casualties of all Australian schools.

But our headmaster was liberal, almost left, in his sympathies. There was no fagging, and there were not even compulsory games, in spite of which we beat all the schools of our size at cricket and football. He did not beat a boy if he thought reason would be effective. He drenched us in the sentiments of patriotism, and neither he nor his scholars were afflicted by any doubt that the British Empire was the most beneficent institution the world had yet seen, because it was the guardian and disseminator of the principle of freedom.

History was taught as the gradual evolution of the English people towards the state of individual liberty. The greatest heroes, Greek and English, were those who had resisted the tyrants. The implication of our headmaster's teaching was that now that particular struggle was over, and we were the inheritors of what had been gained by the death and agony of noble men. The days of corruption, tyranny, and misrule were far off, beyond the ocean and beyond the centuries. Our function was to build up the brave new world in our new country which was free of those dead evils. When he studied with us Wordsworth's sonnet on Milton, he read it as if only for its literary quality, as if no purifying influence could be needed for the fireside, the heroic wealth of hall and bower of present-day England.

When he read us Tennyson's "You ask me, why," he treated it as the presentation of an unthinkable contingency.

"You ask me, why, tho' ill at ease,
    Within this region I subsist,
    Whose spirits falter in the mist,
And languish for the purple seas?

It is the land that freemen till,
    That sober-suited Freedom chose,
    The land, where girt with friends or foes
A man may speak the thing he will;

A land of settled government,
    A land of just and old renown,
    Where Freedom slowly broadens down
From precedent to precedent:

Where faction seldom gathers head,
    But by degrees to fulness wrought,
    The strength of some diffusive thought
Hath time and space to work and spread.

Should banded unions persecute
    Opinion, and induce a time
    When single thought is civil crime,
And individual freedom mute;

Tho' Power should make from land to land
    The name of Britain trebly great—
    Tho' every channel of the State
Should fill and choke with golden sand—

Yet waft me from the harbour-mouth
    Wild wind. I seek a warmer sky,
    And I will see before I die
The palms and temples of the South."

I quote it here, not because it is so unfortunately apt today, except that instead of choking with golden sand we have to borrow money from Italy, but because it describes the moral and political mirror in which we were taught to see ourselves. Its lines were fixed forever in my mind as they caught my youthful imagination as reasonable and just.

From choice as well as obligation I soaked myself in the poetry of Tennyson. His cadences and those of Shakespeare formed the rhythms of my brain. I had read the whole of Shakespeare's works by the age of twelve. All the images awakened by my education were English and European. Tennyson filled my head with visions of English fields and gardens, but they were gardens where it was always afternoon. Round the sixth-form room were hung large photographs of Stratford-on-Avon and of famous cathedrals.

We were also, of course, taught the Christian religion. The headmaster wove its threads thickly into the historical pattern. Although he was High Church, it was the reformers whom he most admired. He caused us to believe that mankind, led by the Christian English-speaking peoples, was within sight of the final goal of its progress, and that with the nineteenth century, encouraged by the noble voices of Wordsworth, Arnold, and Tennyson, we had come round the last bend. Once he said to us: "Private speculation or the discoveries of science may lead you to doubt the truth of the Christian faith, but if you should be tempted to disbelieve, remember this, that many of the greatest and most intelligent men have been able to accept it." That seemed to me unanswerable. He also said: "Our boys' religion must be that of the knight and not that of the monk." This I repudi-

29

ated. To explain why I must turn a different light on my schooldays.

I was not, of course, between the ages of fourteen and nineteen simply a kind of sponge absorbing lofty sentiments and fine rhythms, though they were poured over me so perseveringly that they coloured all my integral parts.

When I was not lifted by the magic of beautiful words and the serious nobility of my headmaster's teaching into a realm of abstract virtue, I remained a greedy and lazy but not vicious human animal.

I was afraid when I went to school that I would be bullied and hurt, but I was greeted by a kindly matron, and put in a dormitory with half a dozen new boys nearly as nervous as myself. Our ideas of what school would be like had probably been formed by an extensive reading of *The Boy's Own Paper*, and *Chums*, augmented by books like *Tom Brown's Schooldays* and *The Hill*. We were all desperately anxious to behave in the correct public school fashion. If we had believed that this involved making incantations to Buddha or whipping ourselves with scorpions, we should have done these things. You can make a wretched, aspiring, vulnerable boy do anything if you tell him that it will bring him securely into identity with his species. We believed that it was correct to ask each other: "What's your father?" and to have a fight. The result of this was that during a "What's your father?" questionnaire in the dormitory, the boy who was the most hefty challenged me, who was the most frail, to a fight.

The next morning in the gymnasium with prefects keeping the ring, he began to batter my face. After the first round he asked if I had had enough, but although I loathed violence and saw no prospect of anything but more battering I believed it would be unthinkable to say "Yes" so I submitted to a continuation of the process until the prefects with a deprecating smile stopped the fight. At Eton a hundred years ago two boys were kept fighting all day, sustained by brandy, until one of them died, so I was comparatively fortunate.

On another occasion in the dormitory, when we were still quite young, someone suggested that we should all get into the same bed. At first I thought this contact matey and agreeable, but as no one had any idea beyond propinquity, and as it soon became oppressive I gave a grunt of discomfort. The boy who had suggested it was deeply wounded in his *amour propre* and muttered: "If you don't like it, why didn't you say so?" We fell apart and returned to our own beds. I was worried at having appeared prudish. This was the only sensual experiment I knew of at school. If we had been discovered we should have been expelled, and our subsequent lives spent under a cloud, though the incident had no more importance than if we had gone into a shop and bought a piece of indigestible pastry. As it was, two of those boys, including the one I offended, have their names on the Roll of Honour. They were killed at Gallipoli.

Although my life was so uniquely sheltered I was always conscious of the danger from the brute in my fellows. Like all my family I had a thin skull, so that sometimes on a scorching Australian morning I could hardly bear the dash from my house to the Big School. I was poor as a physical organism, and, in spite of my mother's careful supervision of our diet, my teeth were wretched, and I had at monthly intervals throughout the whole of my schooldays to submit to the tortures of the dentist's chair. I was not likely to become an admirer of the physically aggressive. When attention was drawn to my unboyish dislike of violence I was ashamed that I could not go about knocking out bullies, but generally it did not worry me much.

In spite of my completely unathletic nature and my exaggerated religious phase, I was accepted at school as a human equal, and was not unpopular, even with the athletes themselves, so well was the liberal principle established. The headmaster had a tendency to quick anger, which was only aroused by the suggestion of anything base. There was once a row when he kicked a rich man's son off the football field for playing some dirty trick, and it was thought he would have to resign. I thought he was quite right. Violence done in hot blood is not so unsympathetic to me as violence done in cold blood or for pleasure. A pre-arranged act of violence, whether judicial or otherwise, seems to me of the devil.

Nearly all my holidays I spent riding. Once or twice I followed the Yarra Glen and Lilydale Hunt. I loved the excitement of galloping in a body, but I was not in at the death, and do not know what effect the breaking up of the fox would have had on me. In one sense I am much tougher now than I was then, but I was able to witness a slaughter of animals which would now revolt me.

I was never flogged at school, though the principle of violence lurked near me. On one occasion a boy had not attended an important football match. The prefects were not allowed to give punishment, but in the evening before prep. they collected about thirty of us who were all ordered to give him a whack on the behind with a ruler. Whoever refused would receive the same treatment. Another boy and myself disliked this anticipation of Fascism, but we had not the physical courage to submit to thirty strokes, so we merely touched the boy's behind delicately with the ruler, and this was accepted as an "acceptance in principle" of the punishment. There are people who would be angered by this story of "soft" behaviour. They are those to whom the idea of the vindictive herd is satisfying, and who view any departure from a regulated animalism with suspicion.

A Cambridge undergraduate told me that at his college they did not think much of grammar school boys, as "they had not taken their beatings". This suggests that admission to learned circles or to good society is not secured by a scholarly mind or considerate manners, but by the ability to show a scarred behind.

When I was about fifteen a boy named Winsland arrived at the school. He was a little older than I was, and had just come out from England, where he had been at an Anglo-Catholic public school. I had been brought up to regard Catholicism as one of the major manifestations of evil. If we had Roman Catholic servants we naturally expected them to be thieves and liars. In spite of this I felt not only that Catholicism had the attraction of something forbidden, but I was also drawn towards its romantic mystery. I had the adolescent longing for ecstatic spiritual union with something outside myself, a longing which was sometimes made intolerable by the beauties of the natural world.

> "The earth, and every common sight,
> To me did seem
> Apparell'd in celestial light."

When I made my first communion I felt that I was united to a mystical lover, and all my teaching led me to believe that along that path I would arrive at heavenly bliss. The novels of Scott and the poetry of Tennyson encouraged this Gothic frame of mind. I dreamed of Sir Galahad pursuing the Holy Grail, though I could not understand why a pure heart gave him the strength of ten, as my own heart was pure, but I was not at all strong. Winsland caught me when I was groping towards emotional satisfaction, and turned my mind into a definitely Anglo-Catholic channel. He took me to sing Mass in a church in Melbourne where, for the first time, I heard plainsong. This music had an immediate effect on me. I felt that it expressed my own emotional rhythms and its quiet flow elevated me into another world. Winsland showed me photographs of stately churches and beautiful altars which made me long more than ever to go to England and lose myself in Gothic loveliness. I conceived the idea of becoming a monk, and wrote to the Abbot of Caldy, a newly-founded Anglican Benedictine monastery on the Welsh island, asking him if he would take me as a novice, so that afterwards I might return and found a monastery in Australia. He replied on very good quality, slightly scented paper, explaining that it was impossible for any promise to be made to a monk as to what his work should be. My mother, when I told her I had written, was worried but reasonable. She said: "It would be fatal for any of our family to stay confined in one place. Their whole nature is restless." She also told me that members of our family developed slowly. This seems to be true. Many of my relatives have spent their lives experimenting and changing their opinions until they only arrive at their final conclusions on the verge of the grave.

One evening when we were parting beneath an avenue of elm-trees, Winsland embraced me tenderly. My soul seemed to rise singing among the stars, and I felt myself a consecrated being, lifted high above all evil, which was perhaps not quite the effect that Winsland had intended.

When we returned after the next holidays, to my horror I heard him boasting that he had seduced the baker's daughter in his town. I had a quarrel with him in the dormitory and he half-suffocated me. I struggled free, and furious at being smothered flung a jerry at him. It hit his forehead, bounced off against the wall and fell clattering amid showers of chipped enamel. After this he took no further interest in my religious instruction and I cannot remember what happened to his Catholicism, except that I saw him four years later, coming out of a church.

There was another boy at school called Hart. He was an orphan and his guardian was the Mother Superior of a community of Anglican nuns. He was not very popular as he was highly conscientious, and he did not shave off his disfiguring black fluff. Once he had been the butt of some joke. I took his part and won his too earnest friendship. However, he took me to tea with the nuns, where I was allowed to attend vespers with candles and incense and to soak myself in Catholicism, while the nuns were friendly and delightful.

Hart was always correcting me for frivolity. I had bought and hung in the dormitory the reproduction of a picture called "The Ideal", by Frank Dicksee. It showed a brown and beautiful young man stretching his arms upwards towards an ethereal creature who was eluding him among soft and creamy clouds. It expressed perfectly the Tennysonian idea of the maiden passion for a maid. The spiritual aspiration was given a sensual form, and forgetting for the time my celibate intentions, I was deeply satisfied by this unity. Hart destroyed my picture and replaced it by a bad photograph of King George V, increasing my distate for Hanoverian monarchs.

I think that for all my religiosity I had a kind of cheerful colour in my personality which attracted Hart, who was essentially puritan, and felt it his duty to blot out in me the thing that attracted him.

Once a new master arrived from England. He told me to stand up and read something. When I did so he furiously told me to sit down. Apparently I had not a very "Australian" voice and he thought I was mocking him. When after class a boy told him I always talked like that he came to me and apologised.

The only correction of speech I had at home was when my mother told me not to say "photo" or to use any abbreviations. She also said that one should not use a word of French origin if there was an English one with the same meaning.

While I was at school a Colonel Riccardo was killed out hunting. His funeral procession, a mile long, passed not far from the school. His charger, bearing some part of his equipment, followed the hearse. We were allowed to go to see the procession, and we gathered that the manner of Colonel Riccardo's death had placed him among the great heroes of antiquity. Our school motto was "Viriliter Agite".

In my school years I was cut off from association with our clan, as Yarra Glen was not in their region. This gave me seven years sheltered from their astringent wit, when my roots could be put down undisturbed into the basic values of our civilisation. Beauty and truth, wisdom and goodness, if only caught in sudden vivid glimpses, appeared to me the normal food of adolescent minds. It must be exciting for a boy to discover chemical and other physical processes; but unless he also learns the truths that have formed the character of his race he is in a pitiable condition, squandering his diminishing capital of moral intelligence. As Traherne said: "Men do mightily wrong themselves when they refuse to be present in all ages, and neglect to see the beauty of all Kingdoms."

THE LIGHT THAT FAILED

ABOUT A YEAR BEFORE I left school, I was suddenly switched over from classics to English and history for my university entrance examination. The reason was my inability to understand a passage in Sophocles's *Ajax*, which made the classics master recommend the change to the headmaster. I am still puzzled by this, as I had gone happily through Xenophon and Aristophanes. However, it had an effect on my life, as I failed in my matriculation, not only in Australian history, but in English composition. When I returned to Melbourne in 1948 I was asked to give some lectures in English at the university, but modestly declined.

The immediate result of my failure was the decision that instead of the university I should go first to St. John's Theological College, of which the Warden was Dean Stephen, a scholarly clergyman with an air of imperturbable good breeding who, I think, must have been a cousin of Virginia Woolf's. His repeated maxim was, "After all it's character that counts."

The students consisted of about a dozen farmers' sons and clerks who had insufficient brains or money to go to the university, two or three missionaries who had come back to be educated before saving further Polynesian souls, and two or three graduates taking a course in theology. True to my life-long fate of never quite belonging to my environment I was the only one who had come there straight from school.

I imagined, now that I was among people whose lives were officially dedicated to the service of God, that cruelty, lust, meanness and stupidity would not be found within their gates, and that their sole concern would be to bring the Kingdom of Heaven on earth as quickly and efficiently as possible. I expected this to happen within five years, or ten at the most, just as nowadays young Communists expect to experience international brotherhood or butchery before they are thirty. I wrote the last sentence in 1938. Now in 1965 they still have the same expectation. I imagined that the students would obey implicitly all the Gospel precepts—that one cheek smitten they would turn the other, that they would expect no material reward for their ministry, and that they would be prepared to endure hardships and even destitution, should God require it of them in his service. I imagined that with people of this kind I was about to enjoy the mysteries of the spiritual life.

About a week after my arrival I was awakened in the middle of the night by a low groaning. When I opened my eyes I saw above me, bending over my bed, a row of hideous faces, dimly lit by the torches they were carrying. One was like the minotaur which years earlier at Sandringham had chased me in my nightmares. Coming from a warm, relaxed sleep, and not realising immediately that these masks concealed the innocuous faces of my fellow students, I was terrified, and when groaning "put him in the tomb" they carried me away to the initiation ceremonies in the gymnasium, my heart was still pounding. As far as I remember, after a mock trial, they stripped me and rubbed tar on my stomach. After this I was apparently a full member of their brotherhood, and fitted to study the nature of the Holy Trinity and the evidences of Christian truth.

One of the missionaries was much older than the other students. His name was Shaw, and he was generally called "Dad Shaw". He was treated with affection and half-amused respect. He knew he was a character and lived up to it. He always had a pipe in his mouth. His pipe was one of the institutions of the place and increased the affectionate respect in which he was held. It was then that I first realised the hypnotising effect of a pipe on any Anglo-Saxon people. A prime minister who clings to his pipe, whatever disastrous blunders he may commit, is with difficulty judged unsound. The same applies to an author who is always photographed with his pipe.

As a younger student, I had to share my study with another. With me was a young man of German parentage. The students might have been willing to go far to save the soul of a Polynesian, but a European foreigner in their midst, even a converted one, was only a fit object for ridicule and practical jokes. One evening when Zeigler and I were engrossed in the contemplation of divine mysteries, they decided to smoke us out, or rather to pickle us. They climbed on the roof and covered the chimney top with sacks, and then surrounded the place to prevent us from escaping.

There was no electricity in this part of the building and our studies were lighted by paraffin lamps. Zeigler was standing on a chair peering through a fanlight at our be-siegers. We were choking in the room filled with smoke. I suggested emptying the lamps over them. Zeigler demurred but I handed him up the lamps and he threw out a shower of paraffin. There was a furious mutter of moral indignation from below.

"Now let us buzz through the door," I said. We suddenly flung open the door and dashed through the disconcerted students into the night. A manhunt began, and being a natural escapist, I collected pyjamas and a toothbrush and went off to spend the night at the George Hotel in St. Kilda.

When next day I gave this explanation of my disappearance it was far too simple to be believed.

It appears that I was not scrupulous in my choice of weapons, but I was absolutely benevolent in my attitude towards my associates and loathed to hurt anyone. If I was gratuitously attacked I was obliged to retaliate with what means my physique demanded. It is easy for the six-foot-two, thick-muscled thug to say: "Why don't you use your fists?"

A youth of my own age, who for some reason had been sent out from England to enter the Church, arrived at the college. He had laughing eyes, a pleasantly sensual mouth, floppy hair, and a quaint accent. I found him delightful and thought that he would be a comrade with whom I might explore the Kingdom of Heaven, but to my distress I found he was a Protestant. He made jokes about the Catholic mysteries and, even worse, took pleasure in quoting the obscene passages in the Bible. When there was a day's retreat at the college, during which complete silence was ordered, he drew me aside to whisper and snigger in corners. The barriers of religion inhibited our friendship, especially as he believed with the other students that the good, though it must be preached in season, should not be allowed to interfere with the course of daily life, with the natural impulses of brutality, the fun of improper conversation, and the all-important design of acquiring preferment and property. My mother had taught me that one must apply belief one had accepted. I began to realise that the Church did not provide the atmosphere where this was possible, and also how little, mentally and physically, I was fitted for heroic moral freedom.

Lying about in the students' rooms were various three-penny booklets with titles such as *Before the Altar*, *Is Incense Legal?* and *Personal Purity*. In one of the latter variety I found almost explicit instructions how to accomplish those vices of whose existence I had hitherto been only

dimly aware as of practices which brought their addicts to
the lunatic asylum. I remember catching sight of my face in
the glass and being surprised at its touch of adolescent
beauty, as I had always disliked my own face, particularly
my profile when I saw it in the glass in the tailor's fitting-
room. Now I felt the longing for some caress, to express my
body in some gesture of love. All my sublimation, my search
for self-realisation in beauty and religion and romantic
friendship came sinking down like a deflated balloon, and in
its place rose the urgent pagan body. This was bound to
happen sooner or later, but its immediate cause was the reading of one of those filthy little ecclesiastical books on purity.

It is true that only the pure in heart see God, or rather
that those who are concerned with the release of the body
are less likely to be anxious about the release of the spirit.
The half-mystical, half-sensuous exaltation I had experienced—once most intensely when I served the Midnight
Mass in the nuns' chapel—no longer lifted up my heart. The
devil having left me for six years returned with vigour to the
attack. My reveries were no longer of Fra Angelico heavens,
but of woodland streams and seductive nymphs. My desires
were still more absorbed into the imagination than intent on
action. I still wanted them coloured with poetry. My religion
had been largely a desire for beauty, combined with a genuine wish to see the good prevail, but less concerned with
abstract truth, knowing unconsciously that the last was better
expressed in myth and symbol than in exact statement. My
animal desires were, heaven knows, genuine enough, but I
had to clothe them with classical imagery, which seemed to
spring fully developed into my mind, though I had of course
been absorbing it for years from Virgil and Catullus. If I
gave myself up to erotic imagination, behind myself and the
impersonal female was always some grassy bank of asphodel,
or a broken temple gleaming above a wine-dark sea.

It seemed to me, now that my desire was no longer set exclusively on the Kingdom of Heaven, and my imagination was full of sin, that it would be an impossible hypocrisy to enter the Church. I cannot remember whether I was so simple as to imagine that the other students' souls were as candid as the angels', but I was not given to judging people unless their misdemeanours injured myself.

My time at St. John's was a kind of waning of the Middle Ages in my mind. They had coloured my whole being and remained in my system, but dormant for the time being. It was a kind of cooling-off chamber from Trinity, with no positive influence of its own.

At last I went to the dean and told him I did not think that I had a vocation. In a disinterested but urbane voice he asked me what I meant. I did not know, but thought that he would understand his own idiom. Our brief discussion was at cross purposes, but the result was unaffected by it. After sitting for an examination in which I gained the highest place in Liturgiology and the lowest in Christian Evidences, I went down to see my parents, who were in Melbourne, to tell them that I was not going to be a clergyman. My father was out, but my mother was at home and, though she said little, was deeply distressed. I had not thought of this part of my apostasy. Young people see what they want to do at the moment and leave out of consideration the remoter effects of their actions, and the wounds they may inflict on others.

I sold my expensive theological books, for which my parents had paid, and went up to Yarra Glen. Canon Hughes, a pioneer of Anglo-Catholicism in Australia, was conducting a mission in the village. He had a genial way of bundling people into religion. He was tall and rubicund. He had a rich wife, and was fond of good food, art, and music. I saw him nearly every day during this fortnight, and under his cheerful influence began to regret my turning back from the plough, though he did not mention it nor reproach me.

He made me hold a lighted candle at the baptism of a girl as old as myself, and then for a caprice, in the middle of the service, made me her godfather.

Yarra Glen was at its best. I remember it as a place of perpetual sunlight—sunlight on the distant hills, sunlight filtering through the vines and nectarine trees that enclosed the veranda, and through the wattle branches on the river bank, though there were other days, in winter when the mists did not lift from the valley, and in summer when whoever crossed the fields was pursued by a crowd of flies, which settled in black patches on his back, and the sky was orange with the smoke of bushfires.

After my escapist's fortnight in which I basked in the golden days and in the urbane conversation of Canon Hughes, my father came up for the week-end. I drove to the station to meet him. We treated each other with our usual reserved politeness, and my flight from the theological college was not mentioned. I continued my ecclesiastical dalliance while my father spent his time going over the farm and sketching. In the evening he went out to shoot duck.

On Sunday night he said to me: "You can't stay up here indefinitely. You'll have to do something." I agreed politely. My father said: "You had better come back to Melbourne with me tomorrow."

"What train are you going by?" I asked. He said the evening train would do.

In Melbourne, my mother had a talk with me and asked me what I would like to do. She suggested that I might like to be an architect. I leapt at the idea. Within two or three days she had arranged for me to be articled to one of the well-known architectural firms in Melbourne. When I interviewed the senior partner he said: "Are you sure that you will stick to architecture—or will you get tired of that too?" I assured him that I would stick to it—and probably I should have done so if there had been no war.

A few years later, a fellow subaltern and I were talking about our lives hitherto. He said: "You seem to have spent your whole time throwing away your opportunities." I was startled and thought: "Am I as big a fool as that?" I was, but it was inevitable.

BACK TO THE CLAN

THERE WAS ANOTHER AUXILIARY INFLUENCE detaching me from St. John's. The college was one of the old-fashioned houses in East St. Kilda, extended with studies, lecture rooms and a chapel, and was in the region inhabited from the early days by my relatives. Glenfern was only half a mile away, and closer still was St. Margaret's, where lived a cousin of my mother's, Theyre à Beckett Weigall, then a K.C. and later another High Court judge. He had married a daughter of Sir Robert Hamilton, a Governor of Tasmania, and formerly Chief Secretary for Ireland. Mrs. Weigall was related to the Macaulays and Trevelyans and had exchanged *mots* with Dr. Mahaffy across the dinner-table at Dublin Castle. She brought a powerful access of culture to the family which, combined with à Beckett wit, made the household formidable but fascinating to me. I have travestied it slightly in *Outbreak of Love* but I hope not unkindly, as for the next two years the three daughters were the delight of my life. They were the first girls of my own age whom I had met since we moved to Yarra Glen, as my sister Helen was some years younger than myself, and could not act as a link with her school friends. They have remained my close friends ever since. If we meet after a gap of ten or twenty

45

years, we take up the conversation, if not in subject, in tone and idiom where we left it off. They dispelled rapidly the lingering shades of Gothic twilight.

Their seclusion from vulgar contacts was emphasised by an enormous hedge surrounding their delightful garden, where low hedges and brick paths led to a wide and shaded lawn which suggested Surrey or Kent more than Australia. In this household the family wit was embellished with erudite allusions, and the dinner-table flashed with repartee. They were accused of snobbishness, unjustly, as they were free from the Melbourne obsession with wealth, though they were faintly intrigued by rank. All they demanded of their friends was culture and vivacity. I had not much culture and was unable to recognise quotations from Rochefoucauld or Talleyrand, but I was supercharged with vivacity and my naïveté amused them. When I began to know them well they had just returned from England, where they had seen Nijinsky at Covent Garden, had stayed in historic houses, and paced conscientiously the miles of the Louvre and the Uffizi. To me they came trailing clouds of glory.

Once while I was still at St. John's, a Cambridge don on a world tour, who seemed to exude European culture, made a slighting reference to the Church. I thought he was ignorant to speak in this way of one of the major contributors to the Western mind, while illogically wanting to free myself from associations which I felt were a barrier between me and the bright world in which my cousins moved.

On one occasion I ignored the barrier, and slipped out of the college to attend the Melbourne Club Ball, from which savage dogs could not have separated me. It was held in the St. Kilda Town Hall, transformed into a fairyland. A huge autumn tree had been brought into the hall and its golden leaves entirely hid the ceiling. Powdered footmen held silken ropes making a passage through which the guests entered to greet their hosts. Lord Denman was then Governor-General, and was there with his aides-de-camp, their evening coats with gold buttons and coloured lapels, while Lady Denman's bodice was almost solid with diamonds. This was my first grown-up dance, and gave me the expectation that, poor and unknown though I was, it was the kind of world in which I would naturally move; especially as my cousins from St. Margaret's, the two younger Chomleys and many other relatives were present.

After Sunday luncheon at St. John's Mrs. Stephen generally asked two or three of the students to coffee in her drawing-room. On the following Sunday I was one of these. She mentioned that at the ball a young friend of hers had danced with a Mr. Boyd and asked if he was a relative of mine. I had to admit he was myself, and consequently that I had broken the college rules. The dean ignored this, which strengthened my belief that gentlemen observed a meticulous code. I had made this admission as his guest, and he could take no action.

I met the two elder Weigall girls, Marian (generally called Mim) and Nancy most often at the house of Edward à Beckett, who was a kind of universal uncle, as many who were quite unrelated to him called him Uncle Ted. Joan the youngest daughter, who later married Daryl Lindsay, was still at school and I think inclined less than her sisters to accept the tradition of à Beckett wit. I believe that she and her young brother Theyre once carried out a solemn ritual burning of *Punch*. If so, she was ungrateful, as she shows its influence in her comic history of African exploration, *In Darkest Tondelayo*, which contains one of the best collections of malapropisms in the English language. Also she drops casual pearls of concise expression, some of which I have picked up and used in my novels.

As a young man Cousin Ted had been an artist, but had lost an eye after an attack of smallpox, which he caught in London in a hansom which had just been used for a smallpox patient. His culture was of the 'nineties, though he was too naturally right-thinking to be decadent. When later I sent him my novels he tore out the indelicate pages before lending them to his lady friends. His hobbies were his garden and his house. He was always buying new curtains and carpets in his search for soft effects of colour, but he was reluctant to buy new clothes, as he said he might die before he could wear them out. In 1914 he was over seventy, but he lived to be ninety, when he was killed riding his tricycle to read to the blind, which he had done twice a week for more than fifty years, with the exception of his annual *villegiatura*, a fortnight with us at Yarra Glen, and a fortnight with his brother Sir Thomas à Beckett, the judge, who had a house at Portsea from which he bathed naked at dawn. A lawyer told me that this judge could arrive at the essential issue of a case more quickly than any other he had known. When Cousin Ted came to visit us he brought a present for everyone, including the stable-boy, whose name was Lorenzo. A year or so before he died, having recovered from a serious illness, he wrote to me and complained: "Now I shall have to go through the whole beastly business again." His drawing-room walls were covered with my parents' watercolours, and all his tea-cups were exquisite, of different patterns. In his dining-room he sat on a mild form of throne carved with a huge family shield. His house smelt of lavender.

Every Sunday afternoon he was at home to his friends, who flocked to see him. One of his habituées was not popular with the others, and when he knew she was coming he would ring up his favourites and say: "My dear, I shall be delighted if you come, but the wrong end of the magnet will be here." His comment on a florid Spanish shawl bought by a rather mousey niece was "Charming, my dear, you look like a Methodist Carmen."

I always went to his tea-parties, not only because, with an

air of lofty amusement, he revealed to me the Beardsley-Swinburne motifs, and laughed with uproarious contempt at any hiatus he found in my own culture, but because there I met my cousins from St. Margaret's, who might ask me back to Sunday supper, where we played intellectual games, did charades, and argued with bright, hilarious repartee. I used to bring him my designs to criticise, and cubist pictures which I had painted to provoke his vivacious contempt for my generation and all its works. He was short, fat, and bald, and he would posture grotesquely up and down his drawing-room, caricaturing modern dancing.

I have made open and shameless use of him in my novels, exaggerating, but not much, his raciness of language. He said of a young nephew; "He could be quite a good musician, but he has debauched himself with that bloody jazz." I have also understated his endless acts of kindness. For half a century he must have given pleasure, comfort, solace and entertainment to a great number of people, and if anyone in his modest circumstances can do better than that, I have yet to hear what it is. He gave back a hundred talents for his ten.

Always his sisters, Cousin Minnie, the grandmother of Mim and Nancy, and Cousin Lizzie came to tea, and had their special chairs and special tea-cups. Cousin Minnie's sister-in-law was a niece of the Duke of Wellington and a daughter of one of the great houses of England. This made her appear historically interesting to me when she quoted what Lady Rose had written to her last week. Cousin Lizzie had a son in England, a radical, and when she quoted what he had written to her there was a pained silence. They had no understanding of politics, but to them a radical was little less than a criminal. Both these ladies wore black dresses, black mantles, and black bonnets trimmed with white lace. They spent the afternoon crocheting white lace mats, and discussing the births, marriages, and legacies of their numerous relatives.

Before I leave this period I must record one or two happenings in my immediate family.

Merric, while we were still at Yarra Glen, wrote announcing his engagement. My mother hurried off to Melbourne to see his fiancée, expecting from his quixotic nature that it might be some distressed chorus girl whom he was rescuing, or a Mexican or a Maori, or anything but a respectable Australian girl. I remember standing by her dressing-table where, on her return, she was taking off her hat, and her exclamation: "Thank Heaven she's a lady."

She was in fact quite a lady, being one of the military family of Gough. She had four relatives who were V.C's and I think she should have been the fifth to gain that honour. The marriage was what Cousin Ted called "unfinancial" and my sister-in-law spent forty years as the strength and stay of her husband and children, the former filled with creative passion, and desperately anxious to provide for his family, but with an unaccountable aversion to making any work of art when once he had been told that it was saleable. At least this is what dealers in Melbourne have told me. He was the first person in Australia to cast individual hand-made pottery and to bake it himself. He worked harder than any of our family, in fact harder than anyone I have known, sitting up all night attending to his kiln, with the added mental strain of anxiety as to the result of the burning, which finally injured his health; and for all this he had a negligible reward. In his obituary notice he was described as "the father of Australian pottery".

His sons have remedied this situation, but with all their army antecedents, the military spirit has deserted them, perhaps exhausted. One, a private soldier, did not like the washing quarters provided, and used the general's bathroom.

Finally they were all packed off to painting camouflage, and the companions they left said: "The Boids have flown."

My brother Penleigh when studying in Paris married a Brisbane girl, Edith Anderson, daughter of the Minister of Education in Queensland. Her eldest son, with far less military blood than his cousins, won the D.F.C. with bar in the war. The second son Robin is the architect.

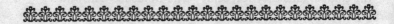

THE DARKENING SKY

MIM, WITH WHOM I USED MOST TO DISCUSS the prospects of a brave new world, was inclined to sympathise with Cousin Lizzie and thought she was unfairly treated by the others. On the Sunday afternoon after the assassination of the Archduke Ferdinand we came in from the garden and found the black bonnets nodding with indignation, and Cousin Ted looking unusually serious and irritated. Cousin Lizzie said: "I tell you there will be war within three weeks."

This was a remarkable forecast for a woman of nearly eighty, made in a remote colony, when even Sir Edward Grey and the Kaiser apparently had no idea that it would eventuate.

I was immeasurably depressed. Everyone seemed to think some glorious picnic had begun, and one which was made more enjoyable by the ingredient of moral indignation. My adolescent belief that I should have to go and fight if England were attacked by Germany had been overlain by my aesthetic preoccupations and all my optimism for the brave new world. It was difficult to drag it up from under these things. I heard women talking of their sons who were longing to get to the front, and who were afraid that the war would be over before they arrived. I could not understand their attitude. The idea of maiming and killing other men, who like myself would simply be acting under orders, was nearly as repellent to me as being killed or injured myself. In an argument with my father about the war he told me that I was "curiously constituted" because I did not enjoy the prospect of fighting.

I remember on a beautiful summer evening walking with Mim along a country road near Warrandyte and saying that if a party of Germans were to turn the corner, and if they were in uniform, it would be my duty to try to kill them, and how senseless and bestial was the whole idea. If one was obliged to go, there was nothing else to be done, but I could not see the attraction of living in filth, of shooting and being shot. To talk of the war as if it were a hurdle race at school, or a run with the Yarra Glen and Lilydale hounds seemed to me the depth of brutal imbecility.

To my relief I found that no one expected me to go. A doctor cousin said the idea was fantastic. The war was remote from Australia, and at the beginning people only expected the more virile and adventurous type of youth, which I obviously was not, to volunteer, as for the Boer War, and they expected it to be over even before these arrived in Flanders. Then it was announced by the recruiting authorities that no one would be taken who had a dental plate, from which I suffered. I was relieved again that the onus of deciding was no longer on me, and I then declared my pacifist views with an easy mind. I mostly made myself tiresome at Cousin Ted's on Sunday afternoon, where the "wrong end of the magnet" tried to shame me into the army, and horrible middle-aged men wished they were young again. I was far more ashamed of my dental plate than of my pacifism, and gave no excuse for staying at home. Cousin Ted said: "As I am unable to go to the war myself, I don't feel that I have the right to advise anyone else to go."

He had a carved two-headed eagle in his hall. At the

outbreak of war he had the heads amputated and replaced by a fleur-de-lys.

I went to the local cinema with a friend who turned insolently away from a kindly old German musician for whom she had always had a friendly greeting.

I had lost sight of the idea of the England of Richard Grenville and Wordsworth and Tennyson, in peril of her life. Then one evening, coming home in the train, I read that the recruiting authorities had removed the embargo on men with my particular disability, and my mind leaping to extremes, I thought: "That is my sentence of death."

The next day I told my parents that I was going to enlist, and in the evening I went to the recruiting station in the basement of the Melbourne Town Hall. I was passed fit, but when they found I was born in Switzerland they would not enlist me until further inquiries had been made.

In the meantime, one of my uncles-by-marriage, who had thought me a worm as a child, did me a supremely good turn. He told my parents that I would not survive the life of an Australian private, and that I should go to England and get a commission among people "of my own class". In Australia there was no direct access to commissioned rank.

It was the end of August 1915 before I left Australia. My architect employer kept me to finish the working drawings of a huge warehouse, which I was sufficiently advanced to do unaided. Also I had to wait a few weeks for a berth in a liner.

When I left my mother she had already spent nearly a year lying on a sofa, and it was another year before she was up and about again. Her body seemed too frail to bear the sorrows that had come upon her, but her spirit was strong. There are some lives in which the pattern of tragedy and affliction is evident, and the scientists are still children until they have discovered the cause of this. It cannot all be put down to individual psychology. It was nothing to do with my mother's psychology that when on a fine afternoon she stopped the wagonette to walk across a field to the house, she was met on arrival with the corpse of her beautiful and brilliantly promising eldest boy, who in that ten minutes had been thrown from the pony on which he had been riding beside her.

I left on the *Miltiades*, an Aberdeen liner that went round by the Cape. I had a great many presents of articles which were supposed to be of use at the front. An aunt gave me a money belt, stuffed with golden sovereigns, the last of which, the last gold coin I ever possessed, I gave with unintentional symbolism to a prostitute in London. My parents gave me everything they could and opened an account for me at a bank in London.

On the ship I became friendly with a young man named Lord whom I had known as a child, but who had since been to one of the famous English public schools. He enjoyed telling me about England, and in which areas of London it was possible to live and where to have one's clothes made. Most of the young men on the ship spent their time reading *Infantry Training*. I read Max Beerbohm's *Zuleika Dobson* which had been given me by Mim, and pored over Mrs. Carruthers's Baedeker. Mrs. Carruthers and her son, a youth of about twenty, who was also on his way to the war, were very consciously gentle-people. Mrs. Carruthers as well as Lord told me about London, and talked a lot about nice people and nice neighbourhoods. "The part about Knightsbridge" she most preferred. She described herself as "upper middle class"—a term I had not heard before. But she could be friendly and amusing, and in a certain dress she said: "I feel like Rosie Rapture, the pride of the beauty chorus." There was a very attractive Danish couple on the ship, who were avoided as German spies.

Older but more innocent than either of them, I listened to Lord and Carruthers talking about women. Carruthers was chaste in fact and intention, not from moral scruples, but because, as he said: "I couldn't bear to have a paid woman messing me about."

Lord startled me by talking not only of women but of boys with equally interested appraisement. I expressed surprise and he told me of the prevalence of pederasty among public-school boys, sailors, and Egyptians. I thought this rather more funny than shocking and said: "Then really it's quite virtuous just to go with a woman."

We called at Durban and Capetown, where some South Africans joined us, young men who had been in the campaign in German South-West. The ship had at one time been cut in half and lengthened, and a dummy funnel had been added for the sake of appearance. Its spacious gloom, reached from the boat-deck, made a rendezvous for lovers. Carruthers said that one heard sensual chuckles coming from it at night. "Sensual chuckles in the dummy funnel" became a stock phrase with us.

The ship rolled lazily northwards through a sweltering ocean. I felt as if I were suspended between two incarnations. Part of me had died in Port Phillip Bay. The past and the future were dreams, and the only reality was this ship, where from Mrs. Carruthers and Lord I gleaned brief glimpses of the life to come. The life on the ship had a curious unreality, with the lazy games under the awnings; the pseudo-smart people from the tropics who talked of sahibs and tiffin; the bogus spy and his lovely wife; the slight excitement of flying-fish; the pock-marked and bejewelled woman at my table who complained about the perfectly good food; and at night the queer phenomenon of sensual chuckles in the dummy funnel. It was unlike anything I had known hitherto.

At concerts the third officer, who had a broken nose and a tenor voice, used to sing very sweet songs, which stirred my still adolescent longings. He sang about a girl who was brown and bright and made for love, and about another whose two grey eyes and two white arms were waiting for him. In the evening, when before dinner I lay in my bath of warm sea-water, with the sub-tropical sun streaming through the skylight, I thought sensuously of the impersonal acquiescent girl waiting for me somewhere.

We called at Tenerife, my first contact since infancy with an old civilisation. The water was bluer in the shadows of the boats that came out to meet the ship, and more opalescent than I had ever seen it in Australia. The golden-brown Spaniards dived from the bridge for coins. One could see them deep down, like fishes in the clear water. I went ashore with Carruthers. We visited the bull-ring, the cathedral, where there was a flag captured from Nelson, and then drove up the hill to luncheon in an hotel garden. The cobbled streets and the crumbling walls, all this sun-drenched antiquity, filled me with delight.

Lord had gone off with a Rhodes scholar to the brothel. In the evening in my cabin they were describing, for the benefit of Carruthers, their afternoon's experience. Lord said: "I didn't do anything. She was too much like a cow."

He had, however, bought some obscene postcards. I looked at them and they affronted my imagination. I had not thought that it would be like that. Those leering men and black-stockinged women bore no relationship to my dreams of the nymphs in the olive groves.

On the last four days of the voyage there was the chance of our being torpedoed, and some people did not dress for dinner, though I could see no particular argument against being drowned in a dinner-suit. I was very anxious not to be torpedoed, as one of the consolations for coming to the war was that I would see England before I died.

THE BACKCLOTH BECOMES
TANGIBLE

I LANDED AT PLYMOUTH and spent two or three days walk-ing about Devon and Somerset to get myself into good condition after the seven weeks on the ship. I saw the cathe-drals of Exeter and Wells and the ruins of Glastonbury. At last the backcloth had become solid and tangible. For fifteen years my imagination had been historically stimulated, and when for the first time I visited the scenes of the ancient dramas, their beauty and significance struck me more forcibly than they could ever have done if I had grown up amongst them. A young man is more likely to fall in love with a girl whose face is strange to him, than with one who has always lived next door. In every cathedral and church and inn the remembered pages of John Richard Green leapt to brilliant life.

My anchorage in London was my aunt's house in Bays-water, near Notting Hill Gate. She was my mother's sister and had married her second cousin Charles Chomley, the son of Cousin Lizzie, who read from his radical letters at Cousin Ted's Sunday tea-parties. I believe there was some anxiety about the possible offspring of this union, that the family eccentricity might be exaggerated beyond reason, but their children seemed more sane than those of us with exogamous parents.

Their hospitality was amazing. During the war their beautiful Louis Seize drawing-room was always full of visiting Australians, relatives and soldiers, high and low, from General Monash to private soldiers. At one stage a slightly eccentric Irish peeress dined there every night, first ringing up and asking the parlourmaid what there was for dinner. She was so amusing that this custom was tolerated. I took all this as a matter of course, though I was grateful and fond of my aunt, who had a sensibility very like my own, but less protected by young male selfishness. Inevitably she had to make unsympathetic contacts, sometimes with pushing people who mistook her gentleness for humility. If they could have heard her concise summing up of their characters they would have been startled. I have used some of her sayings in my novels, such as her rebuke to a woman who wanted to evict a tipsy cottager: "I do not think it is our place to administer adversity"—the superb irony of which, however, was above her hearer's comprehension. At last living in a flat in what had formerly been her home, all but one of her children dispersed to Australia and America, and another war begun, she said: "I cannot put out a tendril of thought in any direction." But her thoughts often dwelt on the Grange and the mountains to which she would so gladly have returned.

I went to stay for a few days in Suffolk with Mary Brett, one of my playmate cousins of our Wilton childhood. She had married Humphrey Clegg, a cavalry major. The day after my arrival there was a shoot, but I had never owned a pair of knickerbocker breeches. When I came down to breakfast in an ordinary Harris tweed suit with trousers, he said: "Good God" and lent me a pair of his own, which were enormous. They laughed at me, but they were so friendly that I did not mind. There were masses of game, but I had never cared much for shooting and had never shot driven birds, so that my bag for the day was one partridge. However, they were quite pleased that I had not shot a beater. After standing about all day behind damp hedges, I could not warm myself up again, as I am sorry to mention that the bath water was not very hot. There was a dinner party in the evening. After swallowing a little turbot and champagne I muttered an apology, hurried down the long, panelled room, and was noisily sick just outside the door. When I came down later they called me "The wild man from Borneo" and taught me to play poker. At intervals on both sides of the world for the next twenty years, some relative would fling up at me a wildly exaggerated account of my début among the landed gentry.

I had other connections in London. I went to see Cousin Em, the widow of Cousin Coo, on whom knighthood had had such a lethal effect. She claimed to be the only woman to whom Lord Kitchener had given his photograph. She also told me that when she was having tea with him out of doors in Egypt, he picked up the ants crawling over the table and ate them, saying: "Formic acid, very good for you." When I told Mim this she was more surprised that there were ants on the table than that he ate them.

As Cousin Em died in 1923 leaving no family, I was able to put her undisguised into my novels, living where she actually lived in Brompton Square.

The three daughters of Judge Chomley had settled in Chelsea, and Mary Clegg took a house in Sloane Court, while I also had introductions to people who were unrelated to me. At the time this seemed quite natural to me, but I realise now how fortunate I was, and how different and miserable my life would have been, as a solitary young Australian in London.

One of my connections told a Mrs. Allgood that I was a worthy object of hospitality, and she wrote asking me to dine. Accepting this invitation, I drew on myself countless good fortunes.

Mrs. Allgood was the wife of a naval captain who belonged to a Northumbrian family of land-owners and himself had a place near Wark-on-Tyne. She was in many ways a typical fox-hunting country gentlewoman, but was entirely free from the brusque rudeness and insolence of which the more stupid of these can be capable, and of which my father had told me some gross examples from when he was hunting in Wiltshire. She was however absolutely direct, with a lively sense of fun, and very good taste in the arts, furniture and food. All these things made her an extremely sympathetic companion, especially as there was no grain of bourgeois pretension or stuffiness in her make-up.

She had taken a house behind Buckingham Gate, to be near the Admiralty where Captain Allgood had an appointment during the war. When I went to dine I was enchanted by the little house. I put it into *When Blackbirds Sing* as Sylvia's "toy palace". It had a kind of Renaissance richness which I had never seen before in such a small house, or in fact at that time anywhere. There were Italian mirrors, eighteenth century furniture and beautiful fabrics.

Her cousin Aubrey Waterfield was there on the night I went to dine. He was an artist of great distinction, who lived in Italy, where he had a castle inland from La Spezia, which is described in *Castle in Italy*, the memoirs of his wife Lina Duff Gordon. At the Slade he was admittedly one of the three most brilliant pupils, the other two being Orpen and Augustus John. Living abroad probably prevented his work gaining the recognition it deserved. Also it had another obstacle to modern recognition. It was aristocratic, luminous, direct, and full of grace. This meeting had more significance for me than I could realise at the time; his sons, his sister and her children were to become my valued friends for a lifetime.

CHAPTER VIII

After dinner we were looking at a large reproduction of Botticelli's "Primavera". Aubrey Waterfield commented on the central figure, a pregnant young woman. He said that we were wrong to think a woman's body disfigured by pregnancy, and that we should see the natural rounded curves as beautiful. I had been used to hearing art criticism from childhood, but this was the first time I had heard it tinged with philosophy, and this gave me a faint sense of expanding intelligence.

Although I came to know his family so well, to my great regret I only met him again two or three times, and each time I had the sense of his true culture, which is a feeling for the art of the ages, not merely an academic knowledge of it.

One of my relatives gave me a letter to a colonel in the War Office, who was fretful in manner and looked like one of the mourners in "The Burial of Count Orgaz". He asked hurriedly: "What d'you want, temporary commission?" as if he would give me anything reasonable if only I would state my demand quickly. I said I suppose so, and he took me along to Captain "Plum" Warner's room, and muttering: "Mr Boyd—wants temporary commission", he left me there. Captain Warner, the cricketer, was even more fretful than the colonel. He asked me if I had had any military training. I said "No", not dreaming that a few years in an Australian school cadet corps would count with the War Office as military training. This misunderstanding probably saved my life, as I heard later that if I had said "Yes" I would have been given a commission on the spot, packed off to a regiment, and would have been fighting in France in a month. As it was Captain Warner gave me a note to take to the Inns of Court O.T.C.

In the autumn of 1915 the Inns of Court still suggested amateur soldiering for the sons of gentlemen, though its ranks were becoming diluted with other types. In my first months of training I lived in a residential club in Seymour

62

Street and paraded on Hampstead Heath at about half-past nine. If it rained we adjourned to a Y.M.C.A. tent, where some volunteer waitresses used to sing to us popular songs.

After we had paraded, the company commander would give the eclectic instructions for the day: "Sergeant Leffmann will take No. 1 Platoon to Boadicea's Grave for plane-tabling." Another platoon would be sent to Jack Straw's Castle or to the Spaniards on a sketching expedition.

One morning after parade on Hampstead Heath, we were told that members of the Inns of Court O.T.C. had been seen in the company of undesirable women, and that commissions would be refused to men who spoke to women "to whom they had not been introduced socially".

In the last ten years enough has been written about sex and war to last the human race for another ten thousand, so I shall make no further contribution to the tales of lust and butchery, but shall only mention what is obscene or murderous when it has some bearing on my own development. It is enough to say of the result of this decision that it was extremely unsatisfactory. I had expected some revelation of beauty, but it was matter-of-fact and mechanical.

The leisurely training of the Inns of Court was interrupted one day by the appearance of Lord French on Hampstead Heath. He sat on his horse and watched us acidly. Shortly afterwards we were inspected by Sir Frances Lloyd, Provost Marshal of London, who was apoplectic at our amateurish appearance. After this inspection we were made to realise that the war was serious. We were packed off to join the main battalion at Berkhampstead.

When the train, full of troops, drew into Berkhampstead Station I heard a most frightful sound, like the scream of an angry cat. It was the battalion sergeant-major, imported from the regular army, giving an order. The first requirement in a recruit seems to be a terror of authority and this voice was evidently cultivated to induce it. Later my colonel used to pull faces at the men up for orders.

I spent a fortnight's hell in learning musketry drill from a sergeant who had been a board-school master. I do not know how many times a day he called me a syphilitic bastard. I toyed with the idea of shooting him, and believe that I would have if I could have done so with impunity. My wish to be revenged on him lasted for two or three years.

After this fortnight I enjoyed myself for the rest of the summer. I lost the sense of being a misfit and experienced the satisfaction of the young Fascist or Communist, the release from intellectual responsibility, and the sense of unity or comradeship with young men whose problems, appetites, and sufferings, even whose clothes, were the same as his own. Although we had no intellectual responsibility, we had intellectual freedom which is denied the Fascist, so that our unity was not that of common stupidity.

We did route marches and night operations in the beautiful woods round Ashridge and on the high downs above Tring. A fellow cadet, whom I met fifty years later, told me that I used to stop on route marches and pick flowers. I saw my first English spring unfold in these lovely places. A luminous pool of bluebells in Ashridge Park startled me with their colour when I was deploying through the trees in some mimic attack. Later, one summer morning, I was on a before-breakfast run with my company. Through the woods on either side of the lane was that filtering light and misty stillness which precedes a hot summer day. I felt that this green, intimate country and these young men running beside me were the environment and the associates for which I had been seeking all my life.

We were able to choose the regiment to which we were gazetted, if we could persuade the colonel to take us. I travelled down to Crowborough for an interview. When the colonel saw my middle name on my card he asked if I was any relation to Pat à Beckett, a cousin of my mother's who had married Norah, a daughter of the second Earl Kitchener. When I said that I was, he said he was a close friend of this cousin and accepted me at once.

He was a German from Düsseldorf, but had been to Eton, and most of his subalterns came from there or from similar schools. He was the father of Oliver Messel, and grandfather of Anthony Armstrong-Jones, whose marriage to Princess Margaret would have gratified him enormously, but sadly he did not live to see it.

I joined the regiment at Crowborough at the beginning of September. At first the colonel was very nice to me, I gathered on account of my cousin's wife. I became friendly with an engaging and light-minded young Harrovian who was always in trouble. One night at a drinking party he expressed with ribald naïveté the urgency of his desires. He was too natural to be indecent and I was amused, but the next morning he came to me and apologised.

One of the company commanders was an amazingly Elizabethan yeoman named Buss. On Christmas Day he went home to his manor-farm to a gargantuan dinner which began at 3.30 in the afternoon. He had one eye and sang "Uncle Tom Cobbleigh" in the mess after dinner, whereas the colonel had the astonishing moral courage to sing Schubert's songs in German. Buss was rollicking, hearty, unfastidious, and the *bête noir* of the colonel. He was my company commander and I thought him delightful and that it would be easy to follow him gaily into battle. One day I was on a Court of Inquiry beginning at 2.30. I had been out on night operations with Buss and did not return till 2.20. I was hungry, unshaven, and covered with mud. I was late for the Court of Inquiry. Major Whatman, another Etonian, the second in command, asked me what the devil I meant by being late. I explained I had been on night operations with Captain Buss. "Don't answer me back," he roared. We proceeded in constraint with the business of the court, which was to sort out old uniforms. In the evening before dinner Major Whatman courteously drew my attention to an illustration in the *Tatler* and offered me a sherry. The distinction between the officer on parade and in the mess was clearly pointed.

I was put on a draft to go to India, but I developed an illness which was never clearly diagnosed, but which I think was typhoid and the draft sailed without me. The ship was torpedoed and they were all drowned, including Captain Buss.

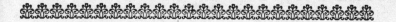

A BLESSING

WHEN I WAS CONVALESCENT Mrs. Allgood wrote to her cousin Mrs. Ramsay, Aubrey Waterfield's sister, who invited me to stay. The Ramsays were then living at Dane Court near Eastry in Kent, the home of the Rice family, which they rented. This was a mellow early eighteenth century manor-house but with traces of older periods inside. The panelling at the head of the main staircase was Henry VII. It was now autumn and the leaves were red and gold.

At Dane Court I felt that at last I had walked completely into the backcloth. I had never before been in a house which had so much acquired its unified character throughout the ages. It was peaceful and beautiful and yet essentially a country house. Indoors at night with the curtains drawn, one was still conscious that outside were meadows and woods. I felt that I was in my spiritual home. This feeling was increased when after tea three little girls came into the drawing-room. They were shy, but with amused and lively eyes. Being born under the sign of the Heavenly Twins I like children and by about eleven o'clock the next morning when I intruded into their schoolroom, we had become friends for life, in fact, not merely as a figure of speech. I played uproarious games with them, and in the evening Mrs.

67

Ramsay played the *Indian Love Lyrics* or songs from *Bric-à-Brac* on the piano while we made an orchestration with the fireirons.

In addition to this Mr. and Mrs. Ramsay were extraordinarily kind to me, and this kindness was not merely "war work" entertaining a sick soldier, but lasted all their lives.

In addition to this, they were the sort of people I expected the older generation to be, responsible, generous and just. Mr. Ramsay had much the same country interests and attitudes as my father. Like him he showed peace and good-will to those whom he thought worthy of it, but those whom he did not had better look out, though he was made tolerant by his belief that a man must act according to his nature.

Mrs. Ramsay revealed to me the life of the county families from within, and in its best aspects. My parents had lived that life at Penleigh, and although they had referred to it so much during my childhood, and had inherited the virtues of the good land-owner, their attitude had been rather one of detachment and even criticism. Also my mother was too overwhelmed by the poverty of the farm labourers to respond fully to the pleasures of English country life. She was happier in France, where the artistry in life accorded with her own nature. This may be why, though I loved England, my first impulse was always to get on to the Continent.

One morning, when I was chasing the children down the stairs, a colonel and his adjutant, without ringing the doorbell, stalked into the hall. The colonel said to me: "Where's your father?" I wish I had replied: "In Australia, sir" but I only explained that I was a guest. He ticked me off for wearing stockings instead of puttees. He refrained from going upstairs to see if I wore khaki pyjamas, and said he wanted to camp his troops in the park.

This insolence was only a mild forecast of what the military can do when they gain control of a country, especially when they are no longer directed by gentlemen. During the second war some military operation was being conducted in an area which included a village, the inhabitants of which were warned to stay in their houses, or they would be shot. A couple who had not received this warning went out into their garden. A screaming neurotic lieutenant ran down the street, yelling at his men: "Shoot! Shoot!"

Since the war the bombing practice on Salisbury Plain has caused the plaster to fall from the ceilings of the houses of West Lavington, including presumably the manor-house of Littleton.

Imber, a picturesque village with an ancient church containing a crusader's tomb, one of the sights within reach of Penleigh, was taken over for practice in street fighting, and after the war, continued to be held by the War Office for this purpose. The evacuated villagers were allowed to return once a year to a service in their church, but last year it was judged too unsafe, and those who fought and bled "for home and country" are no longer allowed near the home they left. Some moral rot seems to have seeped into the soul of the English people, that they have acquiesced in the almost general disfigurement of their land not from an enemy, but from their own rulers. They are now to be compelled to submit to "supersonic bangs" from aeroplanes, which break their windows, and cause cows and brood mares to give birth to abortions.

It was painful to leave the heaven of Dane Court to return to army life. On the way back to Tonbridge I had to pass through Canterbury. The Ramsays were friends of the Archbishop and Mrs. Davidson, to whom Mrs. Ramsay mentioned that I was a co-lateral descendant of St. Thomas, and I suppose because I was also a soldier I was invited to luncheon at the Old Palace.

For twenty minutes or so before luncheon I was entertained by Mrs. Davidson and her sister, who were lively and friendly. We were alone in a large drawing-room, but when we went in to luncheon a great many deans and their wives appeared. The palace at Canterbury seemed to be like a large and rather austere hotel for the higher ranks of the clergy. I got this impression from the conversation between Mrs. Davidson and a secretary. The archbishop came in last. He looked at me between his drooping Yorkshire terrier eyebrows, and asked me questions about Lowther Clarke, the Archbishop of Melbourne.

After luncheon he took me into his study where he spoke about the war. He said that he had been down the whole length of the Western Front and that Kitchener told him that he was the only civilian who had made this excursion. He was evidently proud of this. Then he said: "I wish I was your age, so that I could go too."

I was amazed. The idea that soon I might have to lead men to jab Germans in the stomach with their bayonets, to kick them in the genitals, to shoot them like rats with my revolver, was beginning to weigh on my mind. To hear the man in whom I vaguely imagined was accumulated the holiness of the Anglican Church, whose hands were the channel of the Holy Ghost, express a regret that he could not join in the sport struck me as horrible. I suppose I expected to hear some infinite wisdom or paternal grief.

After the war he said that it should have stopped at this time, the end of 1916. G. M. Trevelyan said the same thing after the war. Why did they not say it at the time, and back up Lord Lansdowne? They might have saved Europe from Lloyd George's "knock-out blow" under which it staggered for twenty years, and finally collapsed into suicidal anarchy.

It has long been known that the Emperor Carl offered the most reasonable and humane peace terms, but Lloyd George rejected them, as if there were an armistice "it might be difficult to get the nations fighting again". It is now known also that the Kaiser was anxious for peace from 1916 onwards.

I have written elsewhere of the vile treachery of our "national heroes" to the human race, and only mention here that I was half aware of it all through this period, otherwise my character was becoming full of lacunae.

The archbishop next asked me to kneel at a prie-dieu. He then put his hand on my head and at some length blessed me. After that he said good-bye and detailed a secretary to show me over the cathedral. Mrs. Davidson invited me to come and see them at Lambeth, but foolishly I did not go.

In the afternoon I went back to join my regiment in West Kent. In the evening the colonel asked me to dine at his table. He was very amiable to me. Half-way through dinner he asked me if any of my relatives of the group he knew were then in London. I said only one. The colonel asked me which one. I had referred to Cousin Em which put me in a dilemma as it was a crime to mention religion, politics, or a woman's name in the mess. I was dumb, felt ridiculous, and then thought: "Well, it's his own fault for asking me" and blurted out her name.

The colonel turned his back on me and did not speak to me again for the rest of dinner. He may, of course, have thought that I was referring to his friend's wife who was abroad, and that I was not only lying, but did not know the difference between a knight's wife and an earl's daughter, which would have shocked him as much as my breach of mess etiquette. It occurred to me that I might appease him by mentioning that I had lunched that day with the Archbishop of Canterbury— but it did not seem worth while. At the beginning of January I was on a draft for France.

PLEASURE AND DEATH

THERE WAS MORE POINT in 1938 than there is now in writing of my war experience. Since then horrors beyond imagining and outside the range of any crimes of history have been inflicted on humanity by its rulers, and what I say would be negligible in comparison. Also I have put most of it into *When Blackbirds Sing*, though the hero of that book has no resemblance to myself. But as one of the excuses for this autobiography is to make a contribution, however slight, to "human evidence" and to give the effect of experience on character, and as the war must undoubtedly have had a considerable effect on me, I shall put down some of my more vivid memories, even though, as in life, a proportion of them may be trivial.

On the night before I left England I was driving through the darkened streets to the Grosvenor Hotel, where I slept to be in time for the morning train, when a horse lorry came out of a side street and the shaft went clean through the door of the taxi, missing me by inches. I took this as a good omen.

With two or three other subalterns from my depot, I was dumped at about three in the afternoon at a railway siding near Calais. It was cold and wet. The name Calais had always suggested to me the English queen and the six burghers, and Bloody Mary's broken heart, and Wordsworth's sonnet, but here there was nothing to see beyond sheds and cinders and a lot of railway line, gleaming under the grey sky. At last we entrained for Étaples. The local Nord trains were never very luxurious. During the war, with their broken glass and bedraggled seats, they were like trains in hell. It took us several hours to make the short journey to Étaples. Someone found a candle-end and stuck it in its own grease on the window ledge. It flickered dismally in the draught, and went out when at rare intervals the train jolted forward. I was excited at being in France and peered greedily out at the dark flat countryside. I had always looked forward to going to France as to a supreme experience. As I strained my eyes at the broken windows it was as if some youth who had dreamed of, but never met a woman, had at last been confronted with a bald and toothless hag.

We arrived at Étaples at midnight, and the next day we had to march out with our draft of men to the Bull-ring, a place with quite as unpleasant memories as the front line. The Bull-ring was a part of the huge sand dunes across the river from Le Touquet. We marched out there against a biting wind, on ground that had been frozen for weeks. We were handed out gas-masks while a flustered captain shouted, unheard against the wind, how they were to be tested and worn. The bewildered men were then herded into a pitch-dark tunnel dug in the sand, where the gas was two or three hundred times as strong as it would ever be in the open. It penetrated our masks as we stumbled choking through the dark. A man fell over and was trodden on by those pushing behind him. It was rumoured that a man a day was killed through carelessness at the Bull-ring. This must be an exaggeration, but the worst aspect of a war is not the danger of wounds and death from the enemy, but the submission of one's body and soul to brutes and fools in authority.

CHAPTER X

After a few days at Étaples I was sent to join the first (regular) battalion of my regiment at the front. With two or three other subalterns and a draft of men we set out in a semi-derelict train for Béthune. It was snowing, and it took us from eight in the morning till dusk to make the short journey. When the train stopped the men got out. It all somehow suggested a journey in the Middle Ages, particularly to me, to whom snow was unfamiliar, as were the ancient farms and churches we passed, and the French names on the railway stations.

After a few days I was sent off with a guide to the trenches. For a while we walked along an open road. Nowhere around us was anything left standing. One or two broken tree-trunks stood up from the snow. A chink of light came from the basement of a shattered house. My guide with relief descended into the communication trench, which was called Piccadilly or Savile Row.

I felt a mixture of curiosity and depression, but also rather grand at being at last in the trenches. Occasionally a shell whined and exploded, but not near at hand, and now and then a Very light hung in the air and shed its sickly light on the snow-covered ground. Later, I had to censor letters, and I found that nearly all the new arrivals felt grand at being in the line, though none of them appeared to have any enthusiasm for the war. Certainly my own depression and hatred of the whole condition of this wrecked countryside were greater than my curiosity or sense of grandeur, and I had no "spirit of the offensive", nor had any of the men. Their courage was that of endurance.

At last we reached the front line. I lifted a piece of sacking, descended some steps, and entered the dug-out which was "A" company headquarters. It was about fifty yards from the German front line. Brown, my company commander, and his only other subaltern were just about to dine at a table illuminated by two candles stuck in bottles. They were expecting me, and an extra place was laid. We had fried sole, pork chops with vegetables, apple tart and cream, a hot cheese savoury, white wine, Vichy water, whisky, and coffee. This meal was prepared behind a sacking curtain by the two officers' servants, who were named appropriately Butler and Pantry. Brown was correct, efficient, and gentlemanly. He was killed in April while I was on a Lewis-gun course.

God tempered the war, but not the weather to my shorn, pacifist, nature. For the first three months my battalion was in a very quiet sector of the line, but the cold was intense in that 1916-17 winter. For three weeks there was a black frost. Apart from the desultory shellfire to which one became accustomed, there was little more than the discomfort of living underground and of the nightly two-hour watches to make one realise that there was a war. Occasionally one had to duck while machine-gun bullets rattled along the parapet. One morning "B" company had to do a raid to capture some specimen prisoners. I saw the walking wounded coming back down the communication trench. They were still wrapped in sheets they had worn to make themselves inconspicuous in the snow. Some were bleeding, with broken arms and bandaged heads. One man glanced at me with pain-drawn eyes. It was my first glimpse of the accumulated agony of the war.

Up till about the end of March we held the line peacefully. Our battalion did a week in the front line, a week in the second line, and a week in reserve, in one of the semi-shattered villages. No palace could ever seem as luxurious as the back bedroom of a miner's cottage on the first night out of the line.

I was sent on a course to a château near Béthune, the historic old town, which a year later was smashed to rubble. One evening with two fellow subalterns, I went there in search of women, strangely unsuccessful. The next morning a padre came to the château and held a communion service which my two companions attended. One said to me afterwards: "I like to go whoring on Saturday night and to communion on Sunday. It gives me a cosmopolitan feeling."

When I went back to the battalion Brown had been killed, and I inherited his servant Butler, who had been footman to the headmaster of Eton. Harvey James, an old Etonian actor, was now in command of my company. He was full of charm and courage, but he was too humane to be a satisfactory soldier. When, with his walking stick, his revolver, his gas-mask, and his Mills bombs in his pockets, he climbed up into the slimy, deathly trench for an afternoon tour of inspection, he turned and said:

"I shan't be long. If the vicar's wife calls tell her I'll be back to tea."

He was killed in April 1917, while making one of those noble gestures divorced from murderous intention, which are anachronisms in modern warfare.

A man named Wells, a year younger than myself, was then given command of the company. He had been wounded and had just returned to France. He was a regular, and very conscious of the fact. He felt it a disgrace that territorial officers should be drafted to the first battalion, and said so. In the line he was very timid, for which no one who had once been wounded could be blamed. My own courage I found depended almost entirely on my liver.

One morning the Germans put down a barrage of trench mortars a quarter of a mile to the right of our sector. They were mostly "minnies" which made a nerve-shattering "crump". My knees began to tremble and I had to go round a traverse to compose myself before giving orders. A few days later a barrage descended on our own bit of line. An aeroplane came flying low and dropped a bomb on the parapet which blew off my tin hat, just as I was trying to light a rocket. Stuff was flying everywhere. I felt exhilarated and began to laugh. Wells put his pale face up from the dug-out entrance and found me laughing and picking up my tin hat, which made him think I had iron nerves.

Though for a while I was his only subaltern, he stayed in the dug-out all night and would not take his share of the watch. In the daytime he complained that I slept too much.

One morning at "stand-to" the sun came up like a red orange, in an enamelled, unbroken sky. There were small field-flowers growing in no-man's-land and behind the trenches. The sun rising on this stricken land was beautiful, like a sunrise at sea. At five o'clock it was broad daylight and the men were relieved that we had passed the dangerous hour of another day. As the order to stand down was given a five-point-nine burst behind the trench. From five o'clock until eleven, every two minutes, one of these shells burst on the hundred yards of line held by our company. I was on watch for most of that time. Wells sat in the dug-out wondering nervously if this was the prelude to an attack. My own nervousness had become a sick dread. Every now and then a man came to me saying that so-and-so had been killed or wounded. A Lewis-gun section had been hit. I saw the men to whom I had been talking with forced cheerfulness a few minutes earlier, now hardly recognisable as human, their blood mixed with the earth under which they were buried. There was every possibility that the fatigue detailed to dig them out might soon be in the same condition. I walked about the hot, sunbaked trenches, thinking every time a shell burst: "Well, I'm alive for another two minutes", and wondering which way to go, not knowing whether I was walking towards or away from a danger spot. I had been in more dangerous situations, but in none that strained my nerves more than that six hours, when the leisure to think was combined with the certainty of the next explosion.

One day a subaltern was standing by the wire bunk where I was resting. He had his hair cropped and it stood up on his head like plush. I stroked it as I would a cat, and he was very cross, though there was no more intention behind my gesture than there would have been towards the cat. I think his reaction was sad, as this was the last caress of his life, his last human touch, a sort of viaticum. A day or two later he was killed by a stray shell, and I took his place on the leave roll, setting out at the beginning of July for ten days in England.

I went to stay with Mrs. Allgood in Buckingham Street. All through the war she was kind and delightful to me. She often put me up when I was in London, and took me to innumerable theatres and parties. When I returned to the trenches she came to see me off at Victoria by the cold early train; and when I was in France she sent me crystallised plums and lice-proof underclothes.

London all through the war was like a city at the height of its "season", the theatres thronged, the restaurants full of smart women and officers in uniform. But it was like a renascence banqueting-hall, where the screams from the torture chamber below were well muffled. It was as if those at home let themselves go, knowing that their frivolity was being expiated in the eyes of a savage god by the broken bodies of their brothers and sons, on that long thin line stretched across Flanders, the altar of Europe, dripping with human sacrifice. This may be thought emotional, yet the people who can keep a stiff upper lip while a new generation is slaughtered, will flounder in a swamp of bewildering sentimentality when some senile politician or general sinks to his overdue rest, as if Adonis himself had been slain in the flower of his youth.

I knew Leonard Outhwaite, the pacifist M.P. who was an Australian. His indignation at the slide back to barbarism made him savagely satirical at question time. He asked the responsible Minister if he was aware that an organisation was distributing pacifist literature from a certain address, which turned out to be that of the British and Foreign Bible

Society. When Lloyd George was speaking on his "knock-out blow", Mr. Outhwaite interjected: "It's murder", and Lloyd George was startled into silence.

During my ten days' leave I went to tea with Mr. Outhwaite on the terrace of the House of Commons, where he introduced me to John Burns, Lynch, Josiah Wedgwood, and a few other radicals. In the evening I went to dine with the Goughs, cousins of Merric's wife, in a grand house off Belgrave Square. After dinner Lord Gough began to speak of the iniquities of the land-taxers, and said: "Their leader is a clever young lawyer named Outhwaite." I did not admit that I had just had tea with him.

I am not sure that this was as cowardly as I thought it at the time. One need only accept the social discredit of unpopular views which one holds oneself, and I was instinctively against land tax, which as far as I could see, meant wiping out our own kind in favour of financiers.

At this time there was food rationing, and I asked Lady Gough if she was affected by it. She smiled and said: "Oh no, not in a nice house like this." There was a long dinner, with turkey and masses of cream sent from Ireland, while as at the Old Palace, Canterbury, quite a young-looking butler and footman waited at table. These people belonged to the generation to which a war abroad was not remarkable and could not be allowed to interfere with a dignified *ménage*. They were remote equally from pacifism and from the vulgarity of a knock-out blow. An old lady of this type on whom I once called at Portsmouth, when some marines appeared in the square, said: "Why are those men drilling there? There must be going to be a war with some foreign country."

About this time Siegfried Sassoon made his heroic protest against the futility of the war. How it was side-tracked is told by Robert Graves in *Good-bye to All That*. Robert Graves says that he realised the war was futile, but that one had to go on with it as one could not let down the regiment, the credit of the Welch Fusiliers being apparently of more importance than the future of Western civilisation.

Someone has written about the "mystique of war". What is the "mystique of war"? Is it some hideous atavistic need to compensate for one's pleasure in life by pouring out blood, but not one's own? Perhaps this is why Archbishop Davidson, being a religious man, wished he could go too. The word "peace" mentioned in any respectable company in London in the years 1914-18 had the same effect as the most obscene expletive.

Mrs. Allgood's house in Buckingham Street was next to Lord Northcliffe's and across the road was Joynson-Hicks, a brewer who wrecked the twenty years of labour by theologians and liturgiologists, which resulted in the 1927 Prayer Book; and who, within a few days of his signing the Kellogg Pact, made a speech in which he implied that it was all nonsense; and whose most conspicuous work as Home Secretary was to suppress that innocuous book: *The Well of Loneliness*. Mrs. Allgood once sat next to him at dinner and I believe gave him a *mauvais quart d'heure*.

Sometimes from my window I saw Northcliffe crossing the road, and wondered if it was my duty to shoot him, as I believed that with Beaverbrook and Lloyd George he wanted to prolong the war at all costs. My uncle Charles Chomley had also given me a hatred of him. A few years later when I was staying with the Ramsays, Dr. Donaldson, the Bishop of Salisbury, was also there. He told me that before Northcliffe you could believe anything you read in an English newspaper, but that Northcliffe "cooked the news to suit his views". So if I had shot him I would have been doing my country more service than by killing some unhappy young German peasant.

In the early 'twenties I saw Northcliffe again, when his megalomania was becoming obvious. He arrived at a large

luncheon to the Prime Minister of New Zealand when it was
nearly over, ignored everybody, made his speech, and
stalked out again. I am told that when he was dying he shot
his doctor in the head.

On the other side from Northcliffe's was the Lyttons'
house. Mrs. Lafone, Lady Lytton's sister, was a great friend
of Mrs. Allgood. Her husband was Commissioner of Police.
One morning while his motor car and chauffeur were waiting
at the door to take him to Scotland Yard, a young man
walked into the house, said "Good morning" pleasantly to
the housemaid whom he met on the stairs, cleared all the
jewellery out of Mrs. Lafone's bedroom, and walked out
again.

On this leave I also went to stay with that lady at whose
feet I had lain seventeen years earlier while she discussed old
china with my grandmother in the Bower Hotel on Mount
Wellington. She had a beautiful old cottage on a village
green in Essex, and certainly very good china and other fine
antiques. The summer days were perfect and peaceful, the
fields ripe with corn, and the hedgerows full of flowers. In
these brief days of leave the East Anglian countryside was
stamped unforgettably on my mind. Later associations increased its attraction, and when at last I was able to have a
place of my own, it was seven miles from Cambridge, and
that is the area of England where I feel most at home.

Shortly after I came back from leave our battalion did a
raid. Headquarters was anxious "to keep alive the spirit of
the offensive" which was a euphemism for "keep the blood-
lust simmering".

Two companies were to go over and two were to hold the
line. "A" company, luckily for me, was one of those detailed
to hold the line. On a fine Sunday evening, at about the time
the church bells were ringing in English villages across the
Channel, our guns, which may have been blessed by the
Bishop of London, let loose hell on the German trenches

opposite us. It was like a Guy Fawkes night in a thunder-
storm. Shrapnel fell in beautiful golden rain. The German
rockets, demanding retaliation, burst into stars. The din, of
course, was terrific. After a quarter of an hour of barrage,
and still under its cover, our men set off strolling in an
irregular line across no-man's-land. Another subaltern of
"A" company, named Diplock, of American extraction, and
myself stood watching the show. We saw odd men fall down,
knocked out by shellfire, making gaps in the straggling line.
We could not remain long as spectators as we had to bring in
the wounded. This was perfectly safe as the barrage had
stopped and there was no retaliation from the Germans.

At last the raiders returned, bringing a great many
prisoners. One of our subalterns who had been wounded in
the genitals was hysterical. He shouted that he wanted to
have another go at the bastards. He tried to climb out of the
trench, and I had to hang on to the tails of his tunic to stop
him from dashing back to the German lines.

When the prisoners came in I disgraced myself. They were
grinning with relief at coming out of the carnage alive, and
at being done with active service. They had only just come
from Russia, and were staggered at their first taste of the
Western Front. My own love of peace coming to the surface
at the sight of a smiling and now innocuous enemy, I
returned their smiles and said "Hullo" to them. Diplock
saw my criminal amiability and turned on me savagely. However, at the foot of the stairs into the tunnels, which the
prisoners descended, they had a more right-thinking reception. A machine-gun major concealed himself behind a
traverse and kicked each prisoner as he passed.

I felt slightly uneasy that I was curiously constituted. I
now realise that, not only in the eyes of God, but in those of
the Black Prince, the Chevalier Bayard, and the Greeks who
would spare the life of a beautiful youth in battle, I was
absolutely right.

There was an aftermath of gossip about the raid. Sergeant-Major X of "B" company had started out with seven prisoners and arrived with none. Apparently he had put Mills bombs down their trousers. Wells thought this very funny and everyone was inclined to be amused.

When we came out of the trenches we had a dinner to celebrate the raid, in which ninety of our men and a greater but unknown quantity of Germans had been killed. It occurred to no one that a Requiem Mass would be more appropriate.

Since we had been out of the line, Wells, to dissipate the effects of his timidity in the line and regain his prestige as company commander, had begun to pose as a martinet, and to emphasise his superiority as a regular. He said once to Dowling, my fellow subaltern, a quiet, cultivated young man: "I suppose you don't like your damned aristocratic company commander."

He also gave way to the resentment he felt towards me, presumably because he had treated me without consideration in the line, and it is a truism that the only people we are unable to forgive are those whom we have wronged.

Before dinner, the evening after the long march, Wells began to get drunk again. He had recently been for a week-end in Paris where he had spent fifty pounds on a woman he had chosen from a parade in a high-class brothel. Half-drunk he came into the farmhouse living-room which was our company mess, from his bedroom which adjoined it. He was wearing only his pants and he sat on the floor, waving the photograph of this woman, and shouting and singing obscenities. Butler, my servant, was laying the table. He must have found it very different from waiting on the headmaster of Eton.

In the midst of his revelry Wells called me a bastard. He probably meant it as a piece of Rabelaisian friendliness, almost as a gesture of forgiveness, but I still retained the adolescent idea that the epithet he had applied to me was an insult to my mother and demanded the honourable satisfaction of drawn blood. I thought that it was obligatory upon me to challenge Wells as it would be to pay a bill.

I went off to my billet and sent for Charlier. Charlier was half-Spanish. He was Roman Catholic and carried a banner in the local procession for the Assumption. He once asked me to dinner and taught me to play "slippery sam", at which I lost four pounds in half an hour. I liked him very much. I have always felt drawn towards swashbucklers who were not bullies. I thought he would be able to appreciate a point of honour. I then went out into a field and fired at leaves on a tree to test my aim. I thought, to console myself for this disagreeable duty: "If I have to try to kill a lot of Germans with whom I have no quarrel, I might at least have the satisfaction of shooting someone I detest."

I was not a bad shot with a revolver, if my hand was steady, and I once hit a piece of paper, four inches square, at fifty yards. But the colonel in chaff told me that I had the hand of a dipsomaniac.

Charlier sensed at once that I wanted him to take a challenge to Wells, and before coming to me went to Wells and persuaded him to come to my billet and apologise, which he did. I had to be satisfied, but I was a little disappointed in Charlier, feeling that he had confused a point of honour.

This naturally did not endear me any more to Wells. He told the adjutant that I was unsatisfactory, and the adjutant sent for me and ticked me off. He was a ranker, and his mind was quite uneducated. A man of intelligence would have seen that I was telling the truth when I said that there was no way in which I had neglected my duties. But his little pig's eyes showed no expression, and it was like being ticked off by an animal.

I felt life would become intolerable in the battalion, so I applied for transfer to the Flying Corps. But it was some weeks before I was interviewed, and there was a further interval before my application was accepted.

In spite of Wells I had some friends in the battalion, and I heard from a nurse who had a man from my platoon in her ward, that I was liked by the men. With Dowling my fellow subaltern I shared not only a dislike of Wells, but an interest in architecture. Swan, a gentle undergraduate from Queen's, Cambridge, who had intended to be a clergyman, but who was at the moment in charge of the Stokes mortar, used to talk to me wistfully about the beauty of boys. Swan was probably the bravest man in the regiment. His imagination did not conceal from him the reality of his situation, and he had mastered the fear it might have aroused. This is far greater courage than going raving mad and killing ten Germans with a trenching tool, but it does not gain honours.

There was a great deal of talk about lovely boys in the army, and Wells would smack his lips over the rosy cheeks of a subaltern fresh from Sandhurst, but this conversation was all, as it were, in inverted commas, and apart from a slightly chaffing flirtatious manner towards the young and blooming, there was no actual homosexuality as far as one was aware. In our regiment there were generally one or two good-looking second lieutenants attached to battalion headquarters to relieve with their naïve grace the tedium of a womanless world. One boasted to me that he had been kissed by a general. There was a private soldier, a very pretty boy with blue eyes and flaxen hair, who excited universal expressions of cupidity. He wore his identity disc on a silver bracelet. I had him as my runner but did not value the privilege, as he seemed to me grubby and unintelligent. Sergeant-Major X of "B" company, who had put seven bombs down the seven prisoners' trousers, in recognition of his enthusiastic prosecution of the war, was given a commission in the field. On the morning this came through, whoever went to tell him the good news, found him in bed with my flaxen-haired runner. This incident was related with less uneasy laughter than that of the seven dead prisoners.

Richard Aldington, in *Death of a Hero*, refers to the love which can exist between men who are comrades in battle. He writes rather as if he had discovered it, and as if some apology were needed for what was, after all, the motive power of Greek civilisation. It has nothing to do with effeminacy. It has to do with love of the highest when seen. It is difficult to speak of because it is linked up with those aspirations which are so idealistic that they can easily be made to appear ridiculous. It does not need a war for its manifestation, but it does need a concerted endeavour towards some selfless aim.

There was a subaltern named Hazelrigg with whom I enjoyed a brief friendship. One summer evening we were walking together across a harvest field near our billets. Some suggestion of home in the harvest field, our youthful unfocused desire for beauty stimulated by the loveliness of the evening, and our awareness of a mutual fate gave us a sense of romantic identity. We did not speak much, but we said that we would volunteer together for the next raid. This was a kind of vow of love till death. It may have a bogus Freudian explanation, but it was the same emotion that inspired the Greek heroes. At that moment life seemed to me noble and dangerous and beautiful. If I had known the Freudian explanation of my emotion which, thank God, I did not, I do not think its quality would have been less. We do not think a rose less beautiful because we know that the garden is manured.

I had left the battalion before we did another raid, so I did not mingle my blood with Hazelrigg's in no-man's-land. He was killed in September.

My application for the Flying Corps was accepted, but I had to go into the line again with the battalion. After luncheon on the last day out, a Gethsemane depression clothed everyone. We paraded before sunset for the march up to the line. A man was drunk in my platoon. To parade drunk on the night of a relief was punishable with death. In these matters I always evaded my "duty". Once I found a sentry asleep in the front line. To awaken him without letting him know that I knew he was asleep, I fired a Very light by his ear. This may not have spared him much, as later the unhappy youth was court-martialled and shot for running away, and it is possible that my Very light, fired by his ear, had done his nerves an injury. Australian soldiers were never shot for cowardice, and apparently this had no softening affect on their morale.

I now had to pretend that I did not notice that the soldier was drunk. The critical moment was when Wells came up to my platoon, as, if he had noticed it, he would certainly have sent him to be tried and shot. The sergeant-major, strangely enough, connived at my indiscipline. Sergeant-majors, as a rule, I found to be sadistic bullies, and when I look back at those I have known I seem to remember them all with small, pink pig's eyes. This sergeant-major I once saw kicking a conscripted conscientious objector, a pitiful sensitive boy who could hardly carry the weight of his pack and rifle. In the Myth he was Christ on the way to Calvary. Thirty years after this I saw in the Fitzwilliam Museum a painting by Diego de Sanchez in which a brutal soldier is punching Christ as He carries the Cross. It reminded me of something, but I could not think what it was. I only realise now, forty years later, that it was of the sergeant punching the conscientious objector as he carried his rifle. I shamefully did nothing about it, as I was then in disfavour with Wells and the adjutant, and although sergeant-majors are non-commissioned officers, they carried more weight with head-quarters than a second lieutenant. Every private soldier is treated as a potential criminal, with the result that there was nearly always someone up to company or battalion orders charged with some "crime" or other, particularly at the depot in England. The attitude of most of the men towards the war and the enemy was the attitude they might have towards a machine in which they had been caught. By 1917 no private soldier had the faintest idea what he was fighting for, so that the generals ordered more and more raids to keep the blood-lust simmering, and to try to key up the necessary hatred of the enemy, to whom the Tommies referred without rancour as "old Jerry". We were ordered to lecture our platoons on bayonet fighting and the spirit of offensive, to try and stir them to a vicious hatred of the Germans. I thought: "There is no escape from doing this filthy thing, so I will go the whole hog." In an old barn, built of thatch and clay and smelling of cows, I gave them a lurid and savage harangue on the delights of murder, on kicked genitals, and jabbed guts. Unless they cultivated these pleasures, the war for civilisation could not be brought to a successful conclusion.

When I had finished and they were dismissed, the men walked away in embarrassed silence, feeling that an attempt had been made to corrupt their core of human virtue.

Once when I was orderly officer, there was a man undergoing field punishment No. 1, which entailed being tied to a cart. I was expected to see him on my rounds, but the N.C.O. edged me away from the barn where he was supposed to be tied. At first I insisted, thinking that the man might be suffering, but then I realised that he was not tied up at all, and that there were certain human indignities demanded by the war machine, which the men would always resist when possible.

On the night of the relief, by taking his pack and rifle, I got my drunken man into the line undetected. At last he had practically to be carried through the battered communication trenches, where every now and then we had to halt our stumbling progress to murmur: "Pass it up when you're all up" in case the tail of the platoon was left and lost.

We took over a horrible line of trench, recently captured from the Germans, so that the entrances to the dug-outs faced the enemy shellfire, the reward of making an advance. There were two other subalterns besides myself, but we all had to be out all night as we were expecting a counter-attack. Wells alone stayed in the dug-out. One of the subalterns had just joined the battalion from Sandhurst. He was terrified. He used to tremble with fear and laugh at himself at the same time for being afraid. It was useless telling him that he would become accustomed to the war and that this was a particularly bad bit of trench. He went on trembling and said with fateful calm that he knew he would never become acclimatised. He was a charming and friendly youth. I think he was killed about a month later, when there was a battalion holocaust.

The other subaltern seemed to be going off his head. He had picked up a short round stick in the trench. He came to me in the middle of a hellish night and said: "Isn't this a funny little stick? Look at the little round holes it makes", and he jabbed it into the mud. There was an appalling smell from the dead bodies fixed on the wire, and our only food was bad ham.

The shellfire was intense. Our platoon was reduced to twenty-two men and then in one night to half that number. There was a nightmare atmosphere about that last fortnight I spent in the trenches. One man had found a German overcoat and rifle which he insisted on using. Life was too unpleasant to worry about minor eccentricities. A dog appeared suddenly on the parapet and was gone before I could shoot it, as one was ordered to do. The shellfire was almost a barrage for a whole night. I was peering over the parapet between two men of my Lewis-gun section. There was a blinding flash and explosion, it seemed about a yard ahead of us, and we were blown back into the trench. The men each side of me were hideously wounded in their faces.

I picked myself up, dazed but unhurt. Then I felt blood pouring from my ear, and thought: "Thank God I'm wounded, I'll get out of this now." But it turned out to be only a scratched ear bleeding disproportionately. At last we were due for relief. On the night when I led out the remnant of my platoon, headquarters sent a working party to repair the communication trench. "B" company, two platoons of "A" company and the working party came together in a jam at the entrance to the communication trench. We were stuck for twenty minutes. One shell in that group would have meant appalling confusion. After that final nervous strain I said good-bye to the trenches. I was the only officer who had survived neither killed nor wounded since the day I joined the battalion.

When I arrived in England I wrote politely to Wells, I think because this was the etiquette, like the pre-war custom of calling on a hostess after a dance. Wells wrote back disarmingly saying that I must think him a swine, which, in fact, I did.

The faithful Butler also wrote to me. He had been shockingly wounded and his letter began: "Dear Sir, I am now minus a nose." He too had caught the public school trick of referring semi-facetiously to what was a bitter human tragedy, the wreck of his earthly existence. It is a kind of courage, but ultimately it falsifies life.

While I was in the infantry I heard occasional talk about "the correct thing", though not so much from my fellow subalterns. I once listened to a conversation of this kind in a barber's shop in Béthune. One young officer was indignant that another had only given twopence as tip to a barber, not on the barber's behalf but because it was letting down the British Army. In the Inns of Court a proportion of our instruction was to make sure that temporary officers would behave as gentlemen. In some ways this was good, as in

France the people had absolute confidence in a cheque given them by an English officer. Even after the war, when I went with a friend on a walking tour of the former battlefield, and we both looked rather unkempt, I was able to cash a cheque on an English bank in the Banque de France in Béthune.

In other ways this preoccupation with gentility was not so good, and I have never been able to adopt the English attitude to servants. One of the subalterns in the barber's shop also said: "You must never say thank you to a servant." My inner self entirely repudiated this, as I cannot and will not treat another person other than as a fellow human being, unless he is entirely repulsive to me, and even at a formal dinner, when a servant hands me the vegetables, I give a faint grunt of human recognition.

I think it was this difference in attitude to servants (now probably disappeared) that made my parents never quite at home in England. My mother told me that once at Penleigh she found that a newspaper had been taken out before she had read it, and she sent for it. Lady Clifford, an English cousin who was with her said: "Surely you wouldn't read a paper after the servants have had it?" This was very different from Yarra Glen, where one of our local country girls passing along the veranda to bed would call "Good night all" through the window, and we called back cheerfully: "Good night, Maggie."

D. H. Lawrence wrote:

"The Holy Ghost is the deepest part of our consciousness
Wherein we know ourselves for what we are ..."

It is this essential self of another human being which must never be affronted. Even animals have this essential self, and a dog is hurt if someone laughs at him, but not with him.

You may think a man too wicked to live, and kill him if you can; but you do not affront his essential self, and kick him when he is your prisoner.

FORTY TRAINS

AFTER A SHORT LEAVE into which I crammed as many theatres, hot baths, and good meals as possible, I went to Reading to train as an observer, and then to Hythe for a month's course in aerial gunnery. At Hythe we were billeted in the Imperial Hotel. From there, with a young Yorkshireman, I made an excursion to Canterbury. In the evening we were in the cathedral close. The few late leaves on the branches were pale gold. The towers rose up from misty darkness into brilliant moonlight. Here and there light shone through the jewelled windows, and inside the cathedral someone was playing the organ. I was enchanted by the rich Gothic twilight, but the Yorkshireman suddenly burst out in an angry tirade against the evils of ecclesiastical oppression, and said this mystical beauty made him think of dungeons and torture. This was the first indication I had of the difficulty which confronts the man who has been brought up in a traditional culture, but who also has a genuine desire to see the end of social and economic injustice. To the bulk of the "Left" not only cathedrals by moonlight, but even a room furnished in the style in which the gentlemanly "red" or "pink" would feel most at home, is a symbol of oppression.

When we had finished our course at Hythe, we were sent

over to join our squadrons in France. We were deprived of our final leave by the major in charge of the school, as, through some genuine misunderstanding of a notice, we had not attended a lecture. Two or three subalterns made a useless protest against this monstrous piece of military sadism, depriving a young man going to the war of farewell to his family, whom he was likely never to see again.

However, I did manage to get down to Wiltshire to see my brother Penleigh, who was stationed at Sutton Veney with the Australians. In the afternoon we went over to Longleat and sat by the lake. This was within a few miles of his birthplace, and the countryside of which we had heard so much as children. My brother, who was more courageous but less insensitive than I had by then become, was oppressed by the thought of the accumulated pain of the war. There was a weight of sadness on our meeting, especially in these surroundings far from home, and yet for him having associations of childhood, and also because every meeting during the war was likely to be the last.

With three other subalterns who had been with me at Hythe I was posted to a squadron stationed at an aerodrome near Cassel, where Plumer had his headquarters. Our work, if one may use the word to describe these activities, was bombing railway stations and photographing the country behind German lines. In the short days and the bad weather we did only one raid a day. Those who were not on the bomb raid had to go off singly on photography later in the day. This was more dangerous, as a single machine was more likely to be attacked by enemy aircraft. But it was almost worth it to avoid that awful moment before dawn when I was awakened from a dream of schooldays or of home, by an orderly saying: "Mr. Boyd, sir, you're on the bomb raid."

When dressed in our flying suits and sheepskin boots, we waddled across to the mess for a breakfast of boiled eggs. The next ritual for observers was to test our Lewis guns and then rub our faces with stinking whale-oil against frost-bite. We had to be ready in our machines to take off at dawn.

At about nine o'clock on the shortest days, and earlier as the days grew lighter, we used to bomb regularly Roulers, or Courtrai, or Tourcoing. The stretch of battered country behind Ypres became as familiar to me as the morning suburban street to a city clerk. We were supposed to bomb the railway stations but our aim was far from perfect, and we must have done a great deal of damage to Belgian architecture, and must have inevitably murdered many Belgian women and children. One of our observers after the war visited these towns, and in one place the innkeeper told him how the English used to drop bombs every morning at nine o'clock, and how they had at that hour regularly fled to the cellars. He said the damage was dreadful and he was so angry that the ex-observer did not dare to mention that he had been in the Flying Corps, and one of the bombers.

When we came back from our bomb raid we had another and better breakfast, and then went to sleep. In the afternoons we might practise gunnery but we were more likely to go into Cassel, where we had tea at the Hôtel Sauvage; at least, we called it tea, but it was a meal consisting of hot chocolate, soused herring, white wine, pâtisserie, and foie gras.

Before dinner we drank about three pink cocktails each. These were the cocktails *de la maison* and they were very strong. Usually by dinner time we were cheerfully drunk, but we sobered down during dinner, at which we did not drink much, and then after talking for an hour or so in our huts, or dancing in the mess to the gramophone, we went early to bed to be ready for the next morning's bomb raid.

We had very few casualties in the early part of 1918. Now and then there would be a gap at the dinner-table in the evening, but our faint regret for a shattered life did not interfere with the ritual of the three pink cocktails. It would have been impossible to allow it to do so.

The men in the squadron were friendly, interested, and tolerant, and not self-consciously preoccupied with being gentlemen, as were the officers of the regular infantry battalion. They came from every walk of life. I liked them all with the exception of Frankel, a Frenchman from Manchester. He was one of the round-headed type and a sadist. He saw that I was sensitive, and evidently thought he would amuse himself with me. He asked me if I had ever had any unusual sexual experiences. At the time I was emotional and aspiring. I was capable of forming a romantic friendship or of falling idealistically in love with a girl, but was not obsessed with sex. My hatred of Frankel reached the point when I would have been pleased to have shot him. As with Northcliffe, I murdered him in my heart, for which, according to Holy Writ, I shall be judged.

After about four months of more or less routine flying I was given a fortnight's leave. As I wanted to see more of the world, I went for five days to Paris and on to St. Jean-de-Luz. I chose the latter place as I had to give a reason for not spending my leave in England, and Phoebe, an old friend of my mother's, lived there.

I drove into St. Omer with an observer whom we called Bacchus. He drank no more than we did, but he had an air of lazy indulgence about him. He had a mistress in Hazebrouck whom he visited once a week. He was quite young, about nineteen or twenty. He had been to one of the great public schools, and like the Stokes officer in my regiment would also talk appreciatively of boys. We had forty minutes at St. Omer before my train left, and he wanted me to fill in the time by visiting the brothel with him. Just then I was feeling high-minded owing to my tender regard for a young pilot named Everard, so the idea was distasteful to me, and in any case I could not have visited a brothel in the hurried and casual

95

manner in which one drops into a bar for a drink. I wanted sex, but I wanted it with love, and at that time my love could not turn in any possible direction. Bacchus was very disappointed in me. The only men in our mess who showed any regard for chastity were three Roman Catholics, though one of these would commit his sins, and then go and confess in English to a French priest.

Bacchus was killed in the spring, when the sky was more dangerous. He went up on photography, taking off at about ten o'clock. On that morning he was in an extraordinary mood. I had been on an early bomb raid and had nothing to do, so I walked round with him while he was preparing to go up. Unlike his usual self he gave queer and crotchety answers to everything I said. He was carrying a small piece of red bunting about with him. When I asked him what it was for he would not reply. Just as he was climbing into his machine he handed it to me and said: "Here, you can have it if you like." He did not return, being killed, we had reason to believe, by Richthofen, Mrs. D. H. Lawrence's relative.

St. Jean-de-Luz was my first glimpse of southern Europe since I left the cradle. I gaped with delight at the blue fishing boats with their yellow sails, and at the March sunlight on the Pyrenees, though I spent much of the time playing bridge with Phoebe's friends; mostly with some rich Americans who had a beautiful apartment in Louis XIV's palace overlooking the inner harbour, a Bourbon marquise, and a Scottish peer's son with an ageing chorus-girl wife, who flew into a rage if one made the wrong lead. I have from time to time noticed this phenomenon. Women who spend their days and nights playing bridge are almost the stupidist it is possible to meet. They seem incapable of an intelligent comment on any subject. But they play bridge with the brilliant accuracy of a mathematical genius. This has some correspondence with generals and politicians, who know the rules of their own games, but do not relate them to humanity.

Returning, I left civilisation at Boulogne, and went by one of the ramshackle trains to Hazebrouck. In the train was a staff officer who harangued his companion on the subject of chivalry in the Flying Corps. All this nonsense about the gallant German airman would have to go. The only useful Hun was a dead one. I felt an angry repudiation, mixed with a depression I could not then account for, but which I now recognise as the sensation I feel when the voice of authority is the voice of evil.

When I arrived at the squadron I was chaffed about the superlative debaucheries into which I was supposed to have plunged in Paris. I did not deny them, as I would have been far more embarrassed had it been discovered that my leave was innocent.

I returned just before the Germans began the offensive of March 1918. One of our duties on reconnaissance was to count the number of trains we saw moving behind the enemy lines. There had been very few trains lately, never more than two or three. One day when it had been raining heavily from low clouds and there had been no flying, it cleared suddenly at sunset and I was sent up on a last-minute reconnaissance. I counted forty moving trains. When I came back the intelligence officer would not believe me, and he did not forward my report. There is a tendency among the hearty to think that the man with any humane or aesthetic qualities is corrupt and a liar.

By refusing to send this information he may have been responsible for disasters of which it is impossible to estimate the magnitude, disasters affecting the whole course of history. It was obvious that the Germans had been massing troops by night, but on this day taking advantage of the low clouds, and not foreseeing the sudden sunset clearance, they had continued by daylight. We had not seen anything until my evening reconnaissance to indicate their preparations. If the recording officer had forwarded this information, the High

Command might have been prepared to meet the March offensive, when as it was, we nearly lost the war.

With the March retreat our leisurely routine warfare changed. There was no waiting for fine weather. We had to do as many bomb raids a day as we could fit in, mostly on Bapaume, now fifteen miles behind the enemy line. Our planes were intended to be flown at from 15,000 to 19,000 feet, but the low sky was still raining, and we had to fly beneath and through the clouds, within range of machine-gun fire from the ground. We all came back from the first raid, though my machine escaped by a few feet a head-on collision in the mist, and nearly every one had bullet holes through its wings.

On the way back from Bapaume to the aerodrome we passed over the attack on Arras. The crumbling remains of the town were in the middle of a wide semicircle of fire and smoke. I could visualise the details of the hell below me, and thanked God that I had joined the Flying Corps, where, if death came, it was generally sudden. After luncheon on that day a message came through that three pilots and three observers, of whom I was one, were to go at once to army headquarters. When, with about a dozen more subalterns from other squadrons, we arrived at the house on the summit of Cassel Hill, we were ushered upstairs into a room where we found the King of England with his much beribboned staff. We stood in a row against the wall, and after a while King George said to Lord Plumer: "Well I can't see X, and if he says anything you choke him off." He too had the hearty public-school manner. As with the Archbishop of Canterbury, I had expected some noble utterance. He then walked along our line, and our wing commander, who must have been a Pelmanist, presented us in turn, remembering all our names correctly though he had only learnt them himself downstairs a few minutes earlier. The King asked Currie, my pilot, what sort of stuff they had fired at us when we bombed

Bapaume. Currie said: "Everything", and the King laughed. Expecting some noble utterance, I felt a faint internal shock at this laugh. My instinctive belief, though not yet clear in my conscious mind, was that the function of the King was to protect his people from the politicians, and that of the aristocracy to protect them from the bureaucrats. My admiration for Mrs. Allgood was partly due to her vigorous performance of the latter function. But the King laughed at the destruction and death.

I was so anxious to hear what he was saying to Currie that I gave distracted replies to Lord Plumer, who was standing beside me, flinging his eyeglass into the air and catching it, and being extremely amiable. But I told him about the attack on Arras which we had seen an hour or two earlier, and this seemed to be the first he had heard of it.

The King made us a little speech in which he apologised for the uniform of the new Royal Air Force, which the Flying Corps had just become. He said that he had had nothing to do with it, and that he preferred the old Sam Browne belt and shoulder-straps. There was a rumour that the new uniform had been designed by Lily Elsie, the actress.

Here I have some evidence which suggests that the House of Saxe-Coburg-Gotha has an unusual interest in clothes. The first Lord Sysonby in his memoir of three reigns tells how, when he had to go ashore from the Royal Yacht to pay some diplomatic call, he found that his correct uniform for this was slightly shabby, and knowing King Edward VII's particularity about clothes, he was in a dilemma as to whether to wear this, or a smarter but incorrect uniform. He decided to wear the shabby correct one, and to sneak off the yacht by the crew's gangway. Unfortunately he ran into the King and received an angry rebuke for his poor appearance.

On another occasion a peer was invited to dine on the yacht and arrived in a dinner-jacket instead of more formal evening dress. The King was so annoyed that he kept his elderly guest waiting in an anteroom until after midnight, and then pretended that he had forgotten he was there.

King Edward VIII wrote a memoir for a Sunday paper. I looked forward eagerly to this, thinking he would at last give away the secrets of the abdication. The article was nearly all about his influence on fashions, and ended up by saying that as Paris was the Mecca of women's fashions, London was of men's, and praying that on this sartorial empire the sun might never set.

A few years ago Queen Elizabeth II was in Rome, and Hugh McClure Smith, the Australian Ambassador, said that he would like to present me at a reception in the Barbarini Palace. I refused for the genuine reason that I was unwell, and could not stand up for the necessary time. But if I had been fit I doubt if I should have gone, as looking at my darkest suit, which I should have had to wear, I found that the thread binding the buttonholes had faded and was slightly green. Having the above stories of three generations in my mind, I was afraid that the Queen, of the fourth, would notice this, and coldly pass me by.

On Good Friday 1918 our squadron moved to another aerodrome near Hesdin. Before we left Cassel an American squadron came to the aerodrome. We asked two or three of their officers to dinner, at which the band played the American national anthem in honour of our guests. The American squadron commander responded by standing up and saying: "That's the best tune in the world. If anyone says it isn't I'll knock him down."

With the spring the casualties increased. Those on photography suffered most. I was extremely fortunate and did not become involved in any bad aerial combat. I was at that time muddled in my mind about my attitude to the war. I hated the idea of speeding the bullet that would crush a man's bones and pierce his brain and send him to a mangled and hideous death, though hate or fear could make me quite ready to do this. I would gladly have shot Frankel. Once when on photography I suddenly saw nine German planes below us. My pilot climbed away while I emptied two drums of ammunition at them. I did not see whether I hit them. None went down in flames. Thinking dispassionately of those activities I can only regard them as damnable.

The weather now had to be very bad to prevent us from flying, but luckily it was sometimes very bad. We loafed about talking and drinking. Some of us began to drink at eleven in the morning. By the time I arrived back in England I had become so accustomed to consume a quantity of alcohol that I felt the need of it, and if I had not gone to stay with a temperate relative, where I was necessarily cured, I might have become a toper.

One evening we had a fancy dress party. After dinner we drove over to visit another squadron. Three of the prettiest young pilots had dressed as girls. We drank a lot before we left, and when we arrived at the other squadron, their commander and our recording officer had a fight over Winter, the prettiest of the three, and they had to be separated. Winter had taken Everard's place in my regard. Again this attraction, as far as the conscious mind was affected, was entirely innocent. Winter was engaging and cheerfully shameless in manner. He was athletic, lively, and completely heterosexual in his pleasure, in which he was not at all frustrated. He had a liberating effect on my own mind. He returned my affection, but he was shot down in flames shortly after the squadron leader and the recording officer had fought over his beauty. The sense of the colour of life which I caught from him remained strongly with me for two or three years.

THE MASSACRE SUSPENDED

I ARRIVED IN ENGLAND at the beginning of May 1918 and was given three weeks' leave, after which I went back to Reading to begin my training as a pilot. From Reading I went to an aerodrome near Oxford, with an unusually incompetent commanding officer. After the gentlemanly discipline of my regiment, and the easygoing squadron in France, I found this place, where there was no distinction between the mess and the parade ground, and where both were mismanaged, very unpleasant.

I wrote to Mrs. Allgood mentioning, simply as news, this state of affairs. Within three days Sir Godfrey Paine, the Inspector-General of the Air Force, who was a friend of hers, descended on the squadron. The commanding officer was removed but an equally bad one, a man promoted from the ranks of the regular army, was sent in his place.

I went on a three weeks' course of aerial navigation to Worthy Down, near Winchester. Here I met a young man whose amusement was to go along laté at night behind the tents, to talk as if he were drunk, and then to make vomiting noises and to squeeze a wet sponge. Those in the tents who wished to avoid disturbance at once put out their lights. He used to write verses of startling impropriety, but he earnestly assured me that he did not mean what he wrote.

At Worthy Down I saw the promulgation of a court-martial. The victim was some unfortunate young second lieutenant who had disobeyed an order. The whole station was paraded, including the women drivers and clerks. The commanding officer read the sentence of the court and then cut off the young man's rank badges. I think nearly everybody was uncomfortable at this exhibition, and felt it to be rather disgusting. The presence of the women seemed to make it more offensive to good taste, and added a humiliation which the originators of the ceremony could not have foreseen.

At Worthy Down I remember one day a discussion on morals. It was about the time that Pemberton-Billing had stated that there was a list compiled of the "first 47,000" in the land, the bulk of the aristocracy and the higher officials, all of whom were given to unnatural vice. Half the jokes of the year were around this ludicrous case. In the mess a young man who himself was far from innocent, implied that a blameless sexual morality must be a *sine qua non* in a prime minister. I suggested that it was surely more important that he should be able to govern well, and that it was better to be guided to peace and prosperity by a rake, than to be led to chaos by a pure-minded fool. I was viewed suspiciously for giving this valuation, which seems alien to the English mind.

When I left Worthy Down I was a qualified aerial navigation officer. At the aerodrome near Oxford I was learning to fly Camels, single-seater fighters, which I had chosen, as I was not certain that I would be a very good pilot, and did not want to be responsible for an observer's life. Camels were very sensitive machines. It was difficult to get them out of a spin, and there were a good many deaths of men training.

At the beginning of November 1918 I qualified as a pilot. It appeared to me then that only by a miracle would I be alive at Christmas. In France new pilots were being killed at the rate of fifty a day. Most of them were dead before they had even unpacked their luggage. I could fly my machine fairly safely, but I was no good at the "stunts" which were necessary in a fight.

However, on 11th November, when I was sitting in my machine waiting for a mechanic to swing the propeller, a subaltern rushed up to me and said that an armistice was declared. I went over to the mess, changed, and with O'Connel, a young Irish pilot with whom I was friendly, I bicycled to the nearest station to catch a train to London. The church bells were ringing in the village. We sent a telegram to the Savoy to keep us a table for dinner, but half England must have done this. After waiting uselessly for an hour or more, we were picked up by a man from the squadron who took us to dine at his club.

After dinner we went to the Alhambra, where nothing could be heard above the yells of the audience. I saw a brigadier-general dancing with a lance-corporal in the bar. O'Connel asked me to lend him two pounds to go with a prostitute. I begged him not to, as on this night I felt that to do so was a kind of betrayal of that male comradeship which had for me been the redeeming feature of the war. However, he insisted on going, so I lent him the two pounds. As I walked home I found that prostitutes were offering themselves free.

While at the aerodrome near Oxford, my love of the English countryside grew stronger, partly for its own beauty, and partly for its associations of friendship. With O'Connel I used to walk across the fields to tea in a cottage at Islip, a village on the Cher, and we discussed all the things which young men discuss whose essential selves are in harmony. I was at this time full of the poetry of Rupert Brooke, the poet of friendship and the English countryside, the poet of my generation, who expressed the mood of his time, before the sneer came in with Lytton Strachey and the sewer with Freud.

O'Connel was killed about three weeks later, when flying low over Islip.

On the day after the armistice I was sent up on a formation. There were three of us, the leader, myself on the right, and a sergeant-pilot on the left. The leader dived and we followed, but the sergeant-pilot went right over, and crashed in a flat-spin, upside down into the ground. The leader did not see and flew on. It was absolutely his fault as we were told always to turn into a dive on Camels, as this was likely to happen. I landed in a bumpy field beside the sergeant-pilot, who was dead and half-buried. The leader at last found that he was alone, and came back to us. He ticked me off for landing in a bumpy field and went off to fetch an ambulance, leaving me with the body. The country people came round and asked: "Is he dead?" At last the ambulance arrived and I was able to fly home, anxiously watching every wire and strut. I had just received my life back from pawn, and was going to take care of it for a while. The sergeant-pilot's wife was waiting for him on the aerodrome.

A great many civilians were annoyed at the armistice coming so soon. They said that we should have gone on for another three weeks, and have given in Berlin an illustration of Belgium in 1914. As that extra three weeks would almost certainly have finished me off, along with thousands of others, I did not hear this opinion with pleasure.

In some places in France, when our men knew the war was about to end, they fired off their remaining stocks of ammunition into the German lines. I have heard people laugh at this. It was probably not funny where the shells burst.

In 1926, in a pub in Sussex, I heard a woman tell a story of "moppers-up" after a raid. A man called down a German dug-out: "How many of you are down there?" The answer came back, "Seven." The man said: "Well, divide that amongst you", and threw down a Mills bomb. The woman who told this story laughed loudly. The decent Sussex villagers smiled uneasily, and did not meet each other's eyes, knowing that only an enemy of God would laugh at these bestial and bloody tales.

Before Christmas 1918 orders came through for me to go to France as navigation officer at a wing headquarters. Today this seems to me incredible. There is nothing left in my composition to fit me for such a post, even though the wing was already beginning to be demobilised and I had nothing much to do. We had four large Crossley cars attached to wing headquarters, where there were only half a dozen officers, and the padre had a Ford van of his own, so it was easy to get about. The padre was interested in antiquities, and I used to drive round with him. In St. Omer I bought two fine *plaques de cheminée* of the seventeenth and eighteenth centuries, one of which I sold later to the Melbourne Gallery. I also bought a seventeenth century "Holy Family" which I offered to the padre for one of his chapels, but he scorned it. Later it was much admired by Bernard Hall.

The padre used to make me get out of the Ford van to ask the military police the address of the local brothel. He was compiling a report for the Bishop of London or someone, hoping to have them closed. He would not himself ask the military policeman as he thought it would lower the man's respect for the clergy.

The Bishop of London blessed guns, and refused ordinands who would not go first and butcher a few of their German fellow Christians; but he said that he would like to dance round a bonfire of all the contraceptives in the world.

This time at the wing headquarters was the cooling-off of my military life, as my time at the theological college had been the cooling-off of my adolescent aspirations. I had been amazingly fortunate, the wind being tempered to my thin skin throughout. When I heard what happened to bombing pilots in the last war, I thank God I was born into my own generation.

These young men, brought up in decent homes, were sent out to commit atrocities which they themselves repudiated, and which denied every good thought which had ever entered their heads, and every instinct of humanity. Some of them had appalling nightmares and woke up screaming, so that vile psychiatrists were set on to them to recondition them for their devil's work. Air Marshal Lord Portal said that it was almost impossible to get planes to attack military objectives, if Bomber Command knew that somewhere within range was an undefended town full of women and children. In the bombing of Dresden, a peaceful town, full of refugees, but containing not one item of military equipment, they killed 135,000 people in one night. The city was encircled with fire bombs to prevent escape, and then high explosive was dropped in the centre. The animals escaped from the zoo, and ate the dying people. Fathers killed their children to put them out of their agony. All this was done because the British Prime Minister thought it would impress Stalin.

An Air Force chaplain, addressing a group of pilots, told them what splendid work they were doing. They got up and walked out in contempt. In Cambridge during the last war I knew people who called Air Force chaplains "walking blasphemies".

What I should have done if I had been told to carry out these atrocities, I cannot imagine. I hope I would have refused, but I doubt it. I might have gone mad beyond the competence of the psychiatrists to cure, or most probably in misery have shot myself.

After the war, the British Government paid £40,000,000 as compensation for the damage done by our bombers to Krupps, the arms manufacturers, and there was not a murmur of protest from the British people. Their bones had turned to cotton wool. If this money had been given in Christian repentance to Dresden, there would have been a scream of protest, this time from the gutter press.

FRUITS OF VICTORY

JOHN MCDONNELL, who was the European adviser to the Felton Bequest, said to me not long before his death in 1964: "Hope died in 1914." This brought into my conscious mind what my essential self had always known. There were bad things in the world before 1914, but we believed that they were on the way out, and soon the brave new world would come to pass, in which we should all do our part, contributing fine houses, or paintings or learning or whatever useful work was our *métier*.

When I arrived in London from France in March 1919, this hope was as dead as a drowned sparrow. My first symbolic act was to go to the tailor and order civilian clothes, including a new tail coat. My only intention was to enjoy myself. Yet as I have found in life, and tried to show in my novels, good and evil are often tangled together. I had gained freedom but lost the one thing essential to my nature, the company of my own kind, young men engaged in the same activity, with the same interests and the same desires.

As I was so little serious at this time I find it hard to recall much of what I thought or did. Until July I stayed with my Aunt Chomley, and I seem all the time to have been with young people who were dancing, or going to theatres with

Captain and Mrs. Allgood and other friends. I also went down to Dane Court where Mrs. Ramsay took me to dances in the country houses round about.

My brother Merric was in London at this time. Cousin Em took us to luncheon at Hurlingham, of which she was proud of being the first woman member, and for which she often gave me tickets. She was discussing with a general whether it was better to lunch at the Ritz or the Berkeley, when Merric said he thought Lyons was very good.

He went to dine with Mrs. Allgood, and sitting in his Australian private's uniform at her elegant table, he reproved her for speaking bossily to her husband, sitting at the same table but removed from himself by the whole hierarchy of the united services. Having tea at Rumpelmeyer's with an elderly peeress who had been burgled, he said that if he had been the burglar he would have taken her and left the jewellery, at which she was delighted. I trembled in his company.

In London the lady at whose feet I had lain in the Bower Hotel told me that I should marry someone with money, and she gave a party at Claridge's for me to meet an heiress whom she called "Baroness Beetroot", owing to the girl's rather too rosy face. However, although I should have liked to be kept for the rest of my life in the luxury to which I was not accustomed, I could not force any feeling towards her. I told Mrs. Allgood about this, and she said: "Someone has to marry the rich girls, and it's better that it should be someone of our sort."

In July I said good-bye to my English friends, cheerfully because, although it appeared that I was returning to Australia for life, I had a feeling, though no intention, that it would not be for long. I sailed in the *Prinz Hubertus*, a captured German ship, converted to an Australian troopship with half a dozen English officers as passengers. The attitude of the Australians was not very friendly. For the last four years I had lived almost exclusively with English people, and did not now feel more, or even as much at home with my own countrymen. Someone called me a "pommy". This was the first time I had heard this word used to describe an Englishman, though as a child Merric used to call me Pommy because, he said, I was so pompous.

I had been told that returning soldiers were allowed to bring in ten pounds' worth of goods duty free, but when I arrived at Port Melbourne I found that as I was in the English army I had to pay the duty and I had spent all the money I had taken for the voyage. So that what I regarded as my own country repudiated me in the moment of arrival. My father, my brother Penleigh, who had been invalided out, and Helen came to meet me. It was only then that I had any emotion of homecoming, and in that moment I realised what the absence of myself and my brothers at the war must have meant to my father. I was disgusted that about the first thing I had to say to him was to ask for money to pay the customs. It is one of the things which I hate to remember.

On disembarking, a soldier carrying my firebacks fell backwards from the fo'c'sle to the welldeck with the heavy iron weight on top of him. I thought every bone in his body must be broken, but he picked himself up, a little disgruntled, and went on with the job. Someone, when I told her of this, said: "What a good thing they fell on the soldier. They might have been broken." She thought it smart to talk in this way. Women of her kind repel me.

I arrived back in Melbourne to find that Mim had disgraced herself, like myself with the German prisoners, in a way that would have been pleasing to God but was not acceptable to Melbourne matrons, who were afraid of compromising their social position by diverging from the line of the gutter press. She had stated at a public meeting that she would not hesitate to take the hand of a German woman.

A few years after the second war, when the Germans

really had put a hideous blot on the page of history, their president was entertained by the Queen at Buckingham Palace, when she spoke complacently of her German ancestors. Millions are butchered for policies which do not last ten years.

My brother Penleigh was at this time at the height of his success, which was to end so tragically within two years. In his own way, he has since been treated in Australia much as Rupert Brooke in England. He lived at Warrandyte, and his closeness to and love of the natural world he expressed with the lyrical loveliness that is anathema today, but which will return, and quite soon, as it is an eternal part of man's longing. His pictures had the great fault that they were more suitable to hang in a palace than in the lavatory of a lunatic asylum. Worse than this he sold them, and for almost three years was comfortably off. I have not read one article about him in any Australian paper which does not mention this fact with contempt. The one thing that is said in his favour is that if he had lived longer he would have turned to "modern art". I heard his opinion of this in London in 1923. He would have been as likely to turn to it as to eating his dinner in a pigsty.

For the next eighteen months I spent my whole time in idle amusement. I did not want to go on with architecture as the idea of working in an office was oppressive to me, though I still had a passion for buildings. I said that I wanted to grow apples or lemons, and I went about with my father looking for a suitable place, but he very wisely hesitated to buy land for me as he probably realised that I visualised more the life of a country gentleman than that of a hard working fruit-grower.

Apart from being at home, I did not like being in Australia. I was in a muddled condition and behaved very badly to my parents, in not taking on the responsibility of earning my own living. I did not settle down because I was hoping to return to England. I missed above all the comradeship, the great good mixed with the evil of army life. Beyond my relatives and my dancing partners I had few friends in Australia. There was a correspondence in the *Argus*, discussing whether the English army was composed of cowards, which, though absurd, was annoying and made one feel a foreigner. It was unpleasant to live in a country where one was liable to come up against this provincial ill-nature. There is, of course, just as much of it in the English provinces, and I have suffered through being considered an Englishman in Australia and an Australian in England, and the target of the ill-bred of both countries.

My parents and relatives lived in a world of their own. They were easygoing, cared less than nothing for social pretension, and they were consistently witty in a rather *Punch* and Anglican style. I was very happy in that limited world. I liked the intelligent kindness of my home, the interest in anyone's creative activity; I cannot remember ever being bored at home. There was always an audience and criticism, and the willingness to discuss an idea. I had as well a number of friends whom I seldom saw other than in evening dress, between the hours of 10 p.m. and 4 a.m., except for an occasional meeting at an afternoon party or the races. I met them night after night at dances in Toorak, the Mayfair of Melbourne. These parties were very well done, with beautiful flowers, quantities of champagne, and a change of bands half-way through the evening. I accepted all this hospitality as a matter of course, and for fear of being caught by unwanted partners, I would fill up more than half my programme beforehand by telephone.

In 1920 the Prince of Wales came to Melbourne. When he arrived he had already lost the use of his right hand, and shook hands with the huge crowds at two successive Government House balls with his left, helping to reduce it to the same condition. For a whole day he stood on a platform in the Exhibition Building and let the people pass in a steady stream four deep, to have a look at him. I saw him return from this ordeal and sink back exhausted as his car drove into the gates of Government House. At a charity ball in the Melbourne Town Hall, for which apparently an unlimited number of tickets had been sold, he was so jostled that he had to take refuge in the Lord Mayor's private apartments. I was at three or four private dances which he attended. He did not particularly care to dance with the socially elect, and chose those partners who were fair-haired, pretty, and natural in manner. He was the chief topic of conversation while he was in Australia, and there were a great many stories about his playing up behind the scenes. It was all harmless, and seeing that he never once failed in the tremendous ordeal of his public duties he might well have been allowed these pranks. It was said that he went to Miss Walker's house near Sydney, and that he played hide-and-seek round the house with his staff. He was about to empty a bedroom jug of water from the gallery of the hall on to someone below, when Miss Walker appeared and said: "I can't have this." When she saw whom she was addressing she retired in confusion. The prince did the same and hid for half an hour on the back stairs.

One Sunday evening in Melbourne he broke the chauffeur's perambulator while wheeling Lord Louis Mountbatten round the ballroom at Government House. Seeing what he had to endure in public, he might have been excused if he had wrecked the whole establishment.

In spite of the easy life and the fun I was having, I longed to return to England. One day a cousin whom I met in Melbourne told me that half a dozen or so people whom we knew were leaving in April on a one-class boat, and persuaded me to join them. He led me to the shipping office where I paid my deposit, and then I went home and told my parents. I think that they were deeply hurt. They offered mild objections, gave me more money than they could afford, and let me go. In addition to the larger sums they allowed me they gave me undeserved presents on parting. My mother gave me £20 to buy myself a comfortable bed when I arrived in England. When I left I felt miserable and blamed my cousin for persuading me to go. I told my parents that I would be back in two or three years, but I was ashamed to return having achieved nothing, and when at last I was successful my parents had died.

BACK TO EUROPE

ON THE LAST TWO OR THREE DAYS on the ship before our arrival at Tilbury, I began to have qualms as to how I was to live on the small allowance which hitherto had done for clothing and pocket-money. I intended to earn my living by writing, but I had no experience apart from the verses which I had written, and published in Melbourne at my own expense.

H. H. Champion, a publisher in Melbourne, who had been concerned with Bernard Shaw and others in some pre-war political activities which led to disturbances in Trafalgar Square, gave me letters of introduction to several celebrated writers. I sent three of them to Cunninghame Grahame, Galsworthy, and to Bernard Shaw, who, Mr. Champion told me, would fall on the neck of any friend of his. Cunninghame Grahame asked me to dine at his club, Galsworthy asked me to tea, but I only had a curt note from Bernard Shaw's secretary.

Galsworthy's invitation was to his delightful old house in Hampstead. To my surprise I was received in a drawing-room gay with Queen Anne lacquer. I had somehow imagined him in a setting of thick brown carpets, dark mahogany, and book-lined walls. Both Mr. and Mrs. Galsworthy were charming to me. He showed me his old glass, told me that he liked "Reynard the Fox" best of Masefield's poems, and after tea we went into the garden where he threw sticks for the dog. I mentioned Mr. Champion. He hesitated, smiled faintly, and said: "Actually, I don't know Mr. Champion."

The Galsworthys asked me to come again, but I was too like the punctilious marooned Englishman in the *Bab Ballads*.

However, my Uncle Chomley almost immediately gave me a job on his newspaper. He was extraordinarily generous in giving jobs to impecunious relatives and friends. I quite enjoyed this work, and think I did it well. Once when my uncle was away for two or three weeks, I edited the paper myself. Another time, returning from a visit to Oxford, I remember feeling exhilarated to think that I had regular employment. My uncle had been called to the Bar, but did not practise. One day a lady called at his editorial office, and asked to see him. She at once began to tell him of the trouble between herself and her husband, and revealed the more intimate secrets of her married life. When my uncle had a chance to speak, he said: "I'm very sorry, but why exactly are you telling me this?" She replied: "You are a lawyer, aren't you?"

My Uncle Chomley was also interested in economics, and wrote a pamphlet urging that money should be based on the world's goods, and not as at present a separate commodity, able to control and debase production, instead of depending on it. He sent a copy to Kingsley Wood, the then Chancellor of the Exchequer, and went to 11 Downing Street to discuss it. Kingsley Wood's verdict was that as there did not appear to be a flaw in the argument, it must be impracticable.

The flaw in Communism seems evident in the fact that in Russia money is as dominant as in any capitalist country.

While I was in London the owners returned to Dane Court, and the Ramsays bought Lee Priory, near Littlebourne, about four miles from Canterbury. This house was an anchorage to me for the next fifteen years, as was also my Aunt Chomley's house in London. It is hard to imagine what my life would have been without them. In her own house Mrs. Ramsay's creative talents had full scope. Not only was her brother an artist, but her sister Margaret Waterfield was a fine watercolourist. Her nephew Gordon Waterfield is a biographer of distinction.

Mrs. Ramsay applied her artistry to living and to turning the wide spaces of Lee Priory into a delightful home.

It was an interesting house, originally eighteenth century, and parts probably much older. It had been done over by Wyatt in the style of Strawberry Hill, but some of the fine Georgian rooms had been left untouched. Wyatt's rooms had their own fascination. A large Gothic library under the tower had originally housed a private printing press, and Lee Priory editions are still sought by collectors. There was also a charming little white and gold Gothic chapel off Mrs. Ramsay's room.

Mrs. Ramsay often consulted me about furniture and arrangements, and as my taste was much the same as, and in fact influenced by her own, this gave me great pleasure. It is impossible for me to write too appreciatively of Mrs. Ramsay's kindness and hospitality, and of all the work she freely undertook as a responsible country gentlewoman. When I wrote in *A Difficult Young Man* of a character whose "splendid arrangements of flowers reflected the generosity of her own nature" I was thinking of this good friend.

In the autumn of 1922 I went to Italy for the first time since I had slept on the Spanish Steps at five months old. I saw the Tower of Pisa from the train and got out there, though I had intended to go straight on to Florence. When I reached the Campo Santo the sun was setting and glowed on the mellow walls of the lovely group of buildings, the tower, the cathedral, and the baptistry. Beyond their faded golden marble were the evening hills. I had an extraordinary sense of illumination. Their beauty seemed to me to reveal something towards which I had always been groping, and gave me a sense of a homecoming of the spirit. The next day I had the same feeling in Florence. I was like stout Cortez on the peak in Darien.

On my first visit I was too enchanted to be more than dimly aware that there seemed to be a lot of assault and fighting going on in the dark corners of the streets. Political slogans were scrawled on the sun-baked walls. I went to Fiesole, and as I climbed up to the little Franciscan monastery, children ran down the hill and handed me bunches of pink and purple asters. This purely mercenary act seemed to my unsophisticated mind to spring straight from the golden pages of antiquity, and to be linked up with the classic tales of welcome to the stranger. In the monastery the friar who showed me round the church and cloisters, with their illuminated manuscripts and naïve pot-plants, asked me if I would like to stay there and become a monk. I brought a vivid imagination to enhance what already appeared to me entirely delightful, and the prospect of remaining there away from the drabness and undirected effect of my London life seemed to me a prospect of heaven. But as I was not a Roman Catholic and could not speak Italian, it was impossible.

When I was leaving Italy I missed an evening train at Venice which was to take me straight through to Innsbruck, so I went to Verona for the night. From there I went up by daylight through the South Tyrol to Innsbruck. It was autumn and the vines laden with purple grapes were trailing over the silver-green olive-trees. As the train wound its way into the mountains and I saw for the first time the pastoral slopes, dotted with their onion-spired churches, with the forests above them, and then the snow-covered mountains, turning rose and amethyst in the evening light, I was glad that I had missed the night train at Venice. At Steinach I was locked up in an hotel for five hours as I had no Austrian visa on my passport. At an hotel at a junction on the way to Oberammergau the only food I could get was some black bread, and some jam which tasted as if it were made of minced wood. In the train from Munich to Nuremberg I became acquainted with two English people. The young man, to show his contempt for the almost valueless German currency, dropped his smaller coins down the slot where the window opened, adding injury to insult. I lived at the Wurtemburgerhof in Nuremberg for a week for two pounds, including the best wine, and I had a seat at the opera for a halfpenny, as two friends whom I met in Nuremberg thought it lacking in taste to take advantage of the exchange to buy a stall at fourpence, a vulgarity which I would have allowed myself.

Back in London I realised that it was against my nature to live in a city. In the second winter I had bad colds, and the doctor said I would be better out of London, so I went off to Avignon, again "to write". I arrived at night, and recall now the joy with which in the morning I saw the bright February sunlight on the plane-trees.

I was joined by Mrs. G., a Melbourne society woman who was practising minute self-denials to keep an extravagant son at Cambridge. The son came out for the Easter vacation. He wrangled with his mother across me at the dinner-table, and when we were alone together on the top of the Pont du Gard he threatened to throw himself down. The mother, whose self-sacrifice was worthy of a better object, used to relieve her feelings by telling me discreditable tales about my relatives, so I went off alone, walking about Provence, and staying for a fortnight at Cassis with Jean Campbell, whom I shall mention later. I finally arrived at Nice, where the first person I met on coming out of the station was Mrs. G. I wanted to find a quiet inn at some place like Eze where I could settle down to write. Mrs. G. said that she would come and help me look for one, but our excursions generally ended up at Monte Carlo. I spent three months at Nice, wasting my time more or less agreeably in her society, until she went to Rome, where she had a glorious ten years amongst counts and princes. Even if I had found some place where I might settle down quietly, I would have had nothing to write about. I had no clear sense of values by which I might have judged and given significance to what experience I had so far undergone.

At last I decided to return to London. I arrived in England on my thirtieth birthday. I felt that I was middle-aged and had achieved nothing. I had no prospects, and did not know what I wanted, except more money, but I was not prepared to work for this, at least not in a regular job. From one point of view I was a useless waster, but I am not sure that this refusal did not rise from an inherent virtue, from an underlying belief that my body and soul must live and have their being in contact with either the natural or spiritual world, and that they were not merely fodder for the economic mincing machine.

In September I went up to stay with Mrs. Allgood, who had returned to her house in Northumberland. Captain Allgood had died shortly after the end of the war. The Lafones were there and Major Lafone spent the whole fortnight in waders standing in the Tyne and fishing for salmon. There was also a Wykehamist general and his wife. He had to do with the remount department, and I drove about with him looking for horses in much the same way as I had driven about with the wing padre looking for brothels;

or earlier still with my father at Yarra Glen, reading Scott's novels while he talked to the farmers.

Both Major Lafone and the general, whose name I have forgotten, were very nice men, friendly, simple and courteous. It seems inconsistent that I have so often enjoyed the company of soldiers.

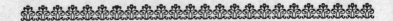

EVANGELICAL COUNSELS

ONE DAY, BACK IN LONDON, I happened to pick up a newspaper in which I read of an experiment that was being made at Batcombe in Dorset to revive the Franciscan Order in the Church of England. Guests were taken at this place, and remembering the delightful little monastery at Fiesole I thought that here was a perfect retreat where I might find myself and write something worth while. I wrote arranging a visit.

This community has since, after reconditioning, become the Society of St. Francis of Assisi, an important body in the Church of England, whose work it would be impertinent for me either to praise or criticise. But at this time it was in a transition stage, having lost its first heroic superior, and not adjusted itself to the new one, so what I write has no bearing on the society today.

The superior, whom I shall call Brother Claude, wearing a mechanic's overall, met me at the station. I asked him if he were the original superior, whom I shall call Brother Ambrose, the one I had read about in the newspaper, and whom I imagined was still in this position. Brother Claude looked annoyed and said: "Oh no, Brother Ambrose is no longer here."

The friary was beautifully situated on the slope of a hill. It consisted of a square farmhouse, which, with a recreation hall and some other buildings, enclosed a square courtyard. Just as we arrived, a man in a brown Franciscan habit came out to ring the Angelus on a bell above the porch. This scene of ancient peace was marred by the contemptuous look on Brother Claude's face. The man in the habit made a bob, crossed himself, and went back into the farmhouse. I asked Brother Claude if he did not wear a habit. He said only in the chapel, and then it was a Protestant compromise, with no cowl. He took me to a pleasant room, scented by the beech-wood fire in the open hearth.

He, said, looking away from me: "You know we expect our guests to help us with the wayfaring brothers."

I had imagined that I would be simply a detached boarder in a picturesque establishment. I replied with a non-committal "Oh." However, "wayfaring brothers" sounded vernal and romantic.

In a few minutes I met them at supper. They were sixteen ordinary tramps and ex-prisoners, picked up by Brother Claude and Brother Ambrose on the roads. I sat opposite a wayfaring brother who had been sentenced for more than one burglary. He had a gentle, intelligent manner, and was the most pleasant of the tramps. As a schoolboy I had had rich and civilised teas with the nuns in Melbourne, and I had stayed with Mrs. G. at a *convent-pension* in Provence, where the food was excellent. The food at this friary was atrocious, and the company did not appear to me either handsome, stimulating, or virtuous, while its cleanliness was in startling contrast with the boiled shirts in the country house where I had been staying till that morning.

Brother Claude was at first anxious about my comfort. For him the new guest was always the important one. Within the next four days he told me the history of the establishment.

Brother Ambrose had attempted to realise the primitive

Franciscan ideal in the modern world. He had undergone a severe training in a religious house, and then had lived for two years on the roads, only his habit and his inner light distinguishing him from the common tramp. He had no possessions and had slept in the casual wards of workhouses, where he had done the necessary labour, breaking stones or whatever it might be, in payment for his lodging. He believed that in the modern world this was the most natural way to emulate St. Francis and the leper. In these places the lice, the smells, and the obscenity were universally prevalent, and it must have needed an heroic effort of will or a miraculous practice of the presence of God for him to retain not only his character, but his sanity. After his two years on the roads, Lord Sandwich gave him the lease of the farm where he tried to found his community. He gathered together about half a dozen postulants and novices. They lived under a strict monastic rule. At intervals they went out to tramp the roads and bring back tramp-brothers, who in the honest work and under the holy influences of the friary might escape degradation. Some of these tramp-brothers were merely unfortunate, but many of them were naturally low, though if they had been born in secure circumstances it is doubtful whether this would have been conspicuous. It is reasonable to assume that where a number of people of low character are gathered together, there will be a vortex of evil, which is perhaps an elaborate way of saying: "Unity is strength." Brother Ambrose had had much experience of an intensive battle against evil and must have grasped this truth. He insisted on his intensive religious exercises to make the power of good stronger than the power of evil in the friary.

However Brother Ambrose had submitted his nature to too high a tension, and he committed what Brother Claude called his "sin", which was no more important than if he had sneezed. He was bullied into making an open confession, not only to the religious brothers, but mischievously and grotesquely to the crowd of low-minded "wayfaring brothers" who must only have thought it a joke. After which he went out like Cain into the wilderness. The man who bullied him into public confession went with him to the train, and told me he wept to see him go. A rule was made that anyone who left the community must never return. The parable of the Prodigal Son was expurgated from their gospel.

After I had been there some time an engaging youth turned up, and I asked him to tea. Brother Claude came in, and immediately and angrily drove him out, to walk back four miles to the station. He then turned to me and said with an expression of horror; "That is the young man with whom Brother Ambrose sinned." I said: "I thought he looked rather nice."

The novices and postulants fell away after the débâcle, with the exception of Brother Hilary, whom I had seen ringing the Angelus.

There was a search round for a new superior. A volunteer came forward in Brother Claude, who till then had been a Low Church Oxford don, with no knowledge of the monastic life, and less liking for its ideals. His aim was to make people kind and Christian and to do good. He hated intellectual exercise, even that which is necessary to allow the mind to wait in tranquillity upon God. He refused a living with an income of £1,000 to come to the friary, and he gave his own small private income to its use. When I first arrived Brother Claude and Brother Hilary were the only religious brothers. Brother Hilary in private life had been a greengrocer, and was now the community cook. He loved the antics and jargon of Catholicism. He prayed with almost erotic ardour, and once when Brother Claude had particularly annoyed him, he ended up by asking the Lord to distinguish between "those who love Thee, and those who pretend to love Thee but are really lying, sneakish, and contemptible". Soon we were joined by Brother Thomas, a retired business man, a bachelor with a taste for mediaevalism which he combined with a benevolent attitude towards the human race. He too was prepared to live in holy poverty as far as it meant giving up his personal property to the common use, but he had no taste for the casual wards of workhouses and confided to me that it would be agreeable if we could have a few dozen of port in the cellar.

The farm bailiff, a very strict Anglo-Catholic, lived with his wife in a nearby cottage. The wife was kindly and tolerant, but the bailiff was in a perpetual simmering passion at Brother Claude's indifference to Catholic niceties and at the slackness of the tramps on the farm.

Brother Hilary, Brother Thomas, and the bailiff had come to the friary, chiefly, I think, to savour the peculiar atmosphere created by formal rituals, the frequent ringing of bells and religious silences, but also because they believed it was a duty to perform some useful social service, and because it was delightful to find these things in such a healthy and charming countryside.

Brother Claude was almost devoid of aesthetic perception. He was ill-at-ease with ceremonies and actively disliked the mystical atmosphere which was the breath of life to the others' nostrils. He was in one sense an escapist. He was like the acrobat who did his tricks before the image of the Virgin. Every Monday he did the washing, including all the tramps' underclothes and socks. This, he explained, was again following the example of St. Francis and the leper, and our Lord washing the disciples' feet. It also saved him from the mental and spiritual effort needed to understand the tramps, and bring about their salvation through their souls. He relied on the mechanical activity of washing their socks to touch their hearts. Brother Claude was continually kicking against the Catholic pricks, and the friary was a centre of discord. He was terrified lest Brother Ambrose might return and oust him, hence the rule against repentant sinners.

This was the nucleus from which was to burgeon a new conception of the spiritual life, clothing the fields of England with the little flowers of St. Francis.

My mother could not bear to see anything badly done. I had inherited from her, and caught from Mrs. Allgood, a sense of personal responsibility and vexation when anything was mismanaged anywhere in the whole British Empire. Miss Emily Hobhouse, whom I met later in Sussex, had this trait in a superlative degree. During the war she went through Switzerland to see that British prisoners in Germany were properly cared for. This brave and humane act raised a storm of fury in the House of Commons. It was against the mood of murder. Then she went to visit a camp of German prisoners in England to see that they were properly cared for. When the sentry said: "You can't come in here, miss," she replied: "Stand aside. I am the daughter of the Archdeacon of Exeter," and he stood aside. When I brought my cadet's uniform home from school my mother said: "This is a monstrous garment to inflict on a boy in this climate," and wrote to the papers and the responsible Minister until they were altered to the soft-necked tunics now worn by the Australian soldier. I itched to interfere in the friary, and soon did so.

As I have said, I had come to the point where my life seemed neither useful nor enjoyable. This was partly brought about by the recrudescence of a love affair with an Australian girl who had been in London that summer, which had come to nothing owing to my own circumstances.

In my first weeks at Batcombe I had a cable telling me of the death of my brother Penleigh in a motor accident. He had always been extraordinarily kind and generous to me, and the closest to me of my relatives. A column of obituary in *The Times* praised not only his work but those qualities which made me feel his loss. I was in the classical condition to renounce the world.

I saw the confused state of the friary, which Brother Claude preferred to call a "home". It had by this time only a freakish resemblance to a regular religious community, and I longed to straighten out the muddle. I was hardly in a Christian mood of self-abnegation, but I was beginning once more to feel that nostalgia for mediaevalism which the monastery at Fiesole or the sound of plainsong could arouse in me. Also, even if I was not capable of acting upon them, I think my mind was sufficiently clear to see the implications of the Christian religion, and what they demanded.

One day I was writing at my window when a young man of about nineteen wheeled a bicycle into the courtyard. He knocked at the door below me, and as everyone was out on the farm I went down to him. He was an Oxford undergraduate, the son of a neighbouring vicar, who had come over to see the friary. I showed him what there was to see, and told him of its activities. He said that he was a member of Toc H and was astonished when I asked: "What is that?" He had a charming and lively manner, and was half-amused at his own eagerness to devote his hopeful youth to the service of God. When he left he said that he would come again in a few days to see Brother Claude and would bring a friend with him.

When they came they were thrilled by Brother Claude's heroism in sleeping in a casual ward, and in washing the tramps' socks. They almost decided then and there that when they left Oxford they would abandon the worldly promise of their lives and join the community. It was a new experience for me, after the disillusioned post-war years, spent among the cynically self-interested, to be with people who were more anxious to give to than to take from their fellow men; and who had so much to give of youth and courage and generous hearts and quick minds. I felt that it was possible that this experiment at Batcombe might really prove, in spite of its discords and absurdities, to be the nucleus of a fresh flowering of spiritual values and disinterested love. So, moved by the desire to interfere, drugged a little by mediaevalism, thinking that as my life was useless I might as well give it to the service of my fellows, and also with a genuine wish to be of use, I decided to throw in my lot with the community. But I was under a disability, as apart from a percentage of corruption in my motives, I believed more in the symbolic than the literal truth of the Catholic religion.

As religion has come into so many of my novels, and as critics have made varying assumptions about my belief, I may as well state what it is I believed then and still believe, that there is "war in heaven"—a constant struggle between the forces of good and of evil. I also believe that an absolute moral law is necessary for the vast bulk of mankind, and that the basic teachings of Christ reveal that law, which could still save the world, now faced with possible annihilation. They are also contained in the religions of the East, and the command: "Do unto others as you would that they should do unto you" is in every great religion of the world. But, as Dr. Arnold Toynbee has said: "Myths are indispensable to man for probing a mystery that is beyond his intellectual horizons." For the Western world the necessary Myth is the story of Jesus Christ and its crystallisation in the Nicene Creed, the factual truth of which is of subsidiary importance to the spiritual truth. To reverse this order, and because of possible errors in the factual truth, give simple people the idea that the spiritual truths have lost their potency, as the modern churchmen are doing, seems to me an act of criminal lunacy. The Church should very slowly and quietly shed some of her doctrinal excrescences, not suddenly spray the whole mystical garden with weed-killer.

The mistake of these people is to imagine that religion is

an intellectual business, which is against the teaching of the Church itself. Christ came to the poor and humble of heart, not to the agile-minded bourgeois. In every collect in the Prayer Book for enlightenment the petition is that the Holy Ghost will speak to our hearts, not to our critical intellects. To try to reduce vast mysteries beyond our comprehension to the limited capacity of our brains is to destroy for us their reality, like trying to reduce the splendour of a great symphony to the capacity of a mouth organ.

Intimations of the Divine Mystery can only be apprehended by the poet and the saint. Most of Christ's teaching is through art, the art of his parables. It is the function of the Church to sort out these truths and present them to the people in a coherent myth, and this it has done through the ages. I believe that this was the attitude of most educated people long before the modern churchmen started blurting out their trivial conceits.

Pope John apparently believed dogmas and practised ceremonies which to the modern churchman would be the grossest superstition, yet he did more than any other man in this century to restore faith in Christian values. During his reign the tension between nations relaxed, and he earned the gratitude of people of every race and belief. He also set an example to all Christian bishops, and if they only had the sense or the spirit to follow it, they would gain immense authority, and people would flock to their churches, even if they stood on their heads and recited their prayers in ancient Greek. It is not superstitions, so-called, that keep people away from church, but the perversion of what everyone recognises as the teachings of Christ, to meet the lowest political expediency. Here is an illustration:

A recent Archbishop of Canterbury went to visit a prison and said to the convicts, in the hearty tones of an old public schoolboy and ex-public schoolmaster: "I sometimes think that if I had taken up your profession I would have cracked a good crib."

Pope John went to visit a prison. A murderer kneeling before him said: "The words of hope that you have uttered, are they valid even for a great sinner like me?" For reply the Pope leant down to the murderer and embraced him.

On another occasion Pope John said: "It is easy to understand how noble is the work of the peasants. They live in the splendid temple of creation. They are in frequent contact with the life of animals, inexhaustible in its teachings, inflexible in its laws, which express without ceasing the providence of God the Creator."

These two paragraphs, illustrating the compassion of Christ, and the wonder of the natural world, are almost enough to indicate what I believe now, and what I believed, but more uncertainly, in the autumn of 1923.

Relevant to this is the attempt to modernise the liturgy, and reduce it to comprehension by the most illiterate minds. Yet villagers fifty years ago, before so much general education, understood clearly their Bibles and Prayer Books.

Eastern peoples believe that the scriptures have a "mantric" quality, that through centuries of use to express the deepest aspirations of the human soul, they acquire a sanctity greater than the actual meaning of the words, in much the same way as a building is said to be sacred, and an object of pilgrimage. There are cadences in the liturgy which have the effect of music in calming the mind, and lifting the heart above the consciousness of time. This valuable asset the modern churchman is prepared to throw down the drain.

The same thing applies to traditional art, the creation of people who believed in the Christian Myth. In their anxiety to be modern, clergy are putting in their churches art which is directly opposed to the spirit of their religion. A modern statue of Christ was put in an East End church. A little girl it, came out and said to her teacher: "Seen Christ? Ain't 'orrible?"

I experienced a contrary effect the other day, when slightly unnerved by crossing one of the most perilous piazzas in Rome, I turned the corner of the Church of S.S. Nereo and Achilleo, and saw its simple classic porch, and felt the peace of eternal proportion.

I have also known, more than once, physical healing by music. The first time was in King's Chapel. I entered with a sore throat and feeling slightly feverish, and certain that I was in for a bout of influenza. I sat back during the anthem, and fell half asleep, but conscious all the time of the music, and responsive to its melody. When the silence brought me back to my surroundings my sore throat and fever had completely gone.

To return to Batcombe, I there awoke to the conviction that if the Church would apply the truths of which it was the guardian, ignoring considerations of prestige, financial security, personal comfort, and doctrinal disagreement, the Kingdom of Heaven might yet arrive on earth.

I wrote out a document which, by its lucid statement of the implications of an acceptance of Christianity, deeply impressed Brother Thomas and the undergraduates. Brother Claude tried to read it but he abandoned the effort at frequent intervals to attend to a smoking chimney.

It was one thing to see clearly what should be done but a different matter to carry it through. Obviously the community could not continue as it was. If so much of the power of evil was to be imported into the place with the more degraded type of tramp, and to be transmuted into good, it seemed only reasonable that the forces of good should have every opportunity to reinforce themselves, which could hardly be achieved by Brother Claude's distaste for religious exercise. He believed that one had only to make a verbal request to God in the same way that one would say: "Pass the butter, please", and if God saw fit he would grant it. But the monk's recital of offices is only a preliminary to induce the state of meditation in which the voice of good is heard, coming from within him or without. It is in the period of silence, after the recital of terce or sext or compline, that he makes his prayers. Even in my short time at Batcombe I knew something of this condition, in which I felt myself tuned in to a universal spirit of good. Rupert Brooke inadvertently described it when he wrote: "This heart, all evil shed away, a pulse in the Eternal Mind." In this condition one sees clearly what should be done, and one has a sense of serene and benevolent power in oneself. I think it is only thus that one can meet evil without infection, and a prayer is only effective according to the degree of this condition in the suppliant.

I went off to London to try to find some support for my ideas of the reconstruction of the community. In London I went down to a kind of Franciscan-Anglican community in the East End, to interview a Father Basil. At one point when I suggested that some Christian precept should be literally obeyed, Father Basil said: "You are not serious." He was very pessimistic and showed us pre-war photographs of his community, when its membership was five times its present strength.

He took us into the chapel where, when he prayed, his voice took on a kind of hypnotic vibration. I felt that he was in close contact with his gods, and that from much discipline and practice he could tune at once and easily into the spiritual force on which he drew.

There was a great deal of talk among these people of the necessity of breaking the individual will. Someone told me that in Father Basil's community a novice might be ordered to spend a morning moving a heap of filth from one place to another, and in the afternoon he would be told to move it back again. This was to teach him not to reason why, and to break his will, leaving him, by the time he had become a complete nit-wit, an instrument for the will of God.

A stupid and cruel means taken to destroy a human will, with whatever aim in view, seems to me devilish, and though by indulging in these practices Father Basil and his brethren may have been able to draw on spiritual forces, it is doubtful whether those forces were entirely beneficent. In a certain number of Catholic churches, both Roman and Anglican, one occasionally senses a black and forbidding power, or at any rate the attempt to achieve it.

While in London I went to see my ex-padre from the wing, who was in charge of an East End parish. Brother Ambrose, who had been in Italy, was now staying with him. Brother Ambrose was quiet and gentle in manner, but did not appear to have his will destroyed. Every morning he stayed in the church from after Mass until one o'clock luncheon, spending four hours in private prayer. He wore a full-skirted Franciscan habit and talked a great deal about suffering. Suffering was the one thing needful, he told me repeatedly. It is true that there can be no progress and no creation without suffering, but I felt that the suffering must not be cultivated. It will come only too surely as a condition of any effort towards the light. It appeared to me that the religious were inclined to pursue suffering for its own sake, and expect the light and the progress to follow, automatically, which unfortunately seldom happened.

While I was there four Eton boys came to stay. One of these, John Erne, was a delightful boy. When the others were talking about the correct sort of waistcoat to wear hunting, he said: "I hate that sort of talk, don't you?" He died of wounds in the second war. His father was killed in the first.

After leaving the mission, I managed to come up for air among my normal associates. Mim was in London from

Vienna, where she had mostly lived since the war, and where later she married Hans Pollak, an Austrian professor.

I told her that I was going to become a friar of sorts. She wisely suggested that I should not tell anyone until I was sure of myself. But I thought that I had burned my boats, and did not like to be secretive.

Mrs. Allgood wrote to me ridiculing the whole idea of monasticism. She said that monks had to shave their heads because of lice. If I had taken the habit I expect she would have sent me lice-proof underclothes, as when I was in France. I do not remember what was the attitude of my Aunt and Uncle Chomley, except that they were kind and cheerful. Both having a Beckett blood, they probably did not expect anyone with this endowment to stick on the bourgeois rails. My mother, although she was hostile to Catholicism, was glad that I was about to work for religion, and sent me more money. I think my father, with his Protestant Ascendancy traditions, must have been upset.

I went down to Lee Priory where Mrs. Ramsay was very pleased at what I was doing, and full of encouragement. Even Mr. Ramsay, though I think he took the "necessary myth" view of religion, was inclined to approve, as he said there was an urgent need of intelligent preachers, which he understood the friars were to become. He had a Scottish taste for a good sermon, and could parody one very amusingly.

When I left Lee Priory, I thought that I had said good-bye forever to the world of boiled shirts and footmen, and I went to stay for a week with the Anglican Benedictine monks at Pershore, where, I thought, I should find the pure vibration of spiritual power, centred in an aesthetic mediaevalism. Actually the monastery was an ugly Victorian house, furnished in frightful taste. The monks, except for the guest-master and the abbot, were not allowed to speak to the guests. The services, which were in Latin and followed the Roman rite, were held not in the abbey church as I had imagined, but in a bedroom badly furnished as a chapel. The guestmaster was a pleasant-mannered, but cynical young man, who spoke of the unredeemed outside world with more contempt than compassion. I asked him about the Roman services.

"We are entitled to the Rite of the Patriarchate, don't you think so?" he asked. He told me that the vicar of St. Mary's, Graham Street, always lent an altar to any of the fathers who were in London, to say the Latin Mass to which they were accustomed. I could not see why they bothered to belong to the Church of England, unless it was for the fun of kicking over the traces.

The food at Pershore was mostly badly-cooked vegetables, and early in the week I had awkward pains in my stomach and had to stay in bed for a few days. This was a further hindrance to any enlightenment I might have gained in the monastery. The undergraduate associates of the Batcombe community, whose number had now increased, said that we should hold a retreat "to discover the will of God" for the direction of our impulse. There was a meeting at Pusey House, Oxford. After long stretches of silent prayer in the chapel, where a reproduction of the miraculous handkerchief of St. Veronica hung over the altar, we adjourned for discussion.

Father Carpenter-Garmer who addressed us said that so much discredit had been brought on monasticism in the English Church by the abortive attempts of inexperienced people to found communities, that he practically urged us to do nothing. The two undergraduates who, when they first came to Batcombe had been public school Protestants, had now turned Anglo-Catholic. One took me to see Father D., a priest who, he said, was living under vows, though not in a community. The most conspicuous feature of Father D.'s dingy little room was a number of gold-topped cider bottles. They could hardly have been champagne. Father D. viewed me with taciturn suspicion, and my visit was neither cordial nor instructive. The undergraduates, however, insisted that Father D. should conduct the retreat, which was held a few weeks later at a very pleasant Georgian house in Buckinghamshire, maintained for this purpose. The half-dozen undergraduates attended and Brother Claude came for a day, bringing an ex-convict from Sing-Sing, one of the worst characters in the community, whose patent hypocrisy had hoodwinked him.

We began the day with Mass at eight o'clock. There was silence till after luncheon and our letters were held back without our knowledge or consent. During the morning Father D. gave addresses which were as relevant to my aspirations as would have been an address on fetish worship in the Belgian Congo. One phrase I remember was, "The kiss from the mouth of Christ." At meal-times someone read from a book of fantastic mediaeval nonsense. At the end of the retreat one undergraduate said: "Well, if that is Christianity, I'm not a Christian."

I heard afterwards that Father D. and one or two young Anglo-Catholics he brought with him deliberately set out to side-track the movement, such as it was, into a dead end. They were afraid that I was going to start some spectacular Protestant order that would bring discredit on the religious orders in the English Church. Protestantism was their bogy. I was concerned with neither Catholicism nor Protestantism. On the whole I disliked Protestantism more because of its more negative attitude. The Catholic emphasis is on the Incarnation, the God in man, and the divine endorsement of human activity, while the Protestant emphasis is on salvation through denial of life's goodness. Apart from my percentage of unworthy motives, what I was aiming at was a literal application of the essential doctrines of Christianity in everyday life, that people should be in such a state that the cream handed them in a silver jug would stick in their gullets if they knew that it was skimmed from the milk of the children of the poor. I wanted a revolution in each individual which was to begin in the members of the community. They were to live in the state to which I have already referred, in contact with the force of good. It did not seem to matter whether they tapped this source of strength through a High Mass, or in a barn, or through some private method of their own. But it appeared to me that only this individual revolution could save Europe from its easy chute to Avernus, whither it had already begun to slide.

Beginning to feel that I had little affinity with organised religion, I returned to Batcombe. I found Brother Claude, Brother Hilary, and the bailiff still at loggerheads. Brother Hilary was more peevish than usual and looked ill, but he could not go for a holiday as there was no one else who could cook. I had grilled chops and made omelettes in my flat in London, so with that rash interference of which I was still uncured, I went to Brother Claude and offered to do the cooking for the sixteen tramps, if Brother Hilary were sent on a fortnight's holiday. Brother Claude called Brother Hilary and said that I would do the cooking, and that I would go into the kitchen for a few days and "sit at his feet".

Brother Hilary said indignantly: "There'll be no sitting down in my kitchen."

I turned out to be a much better cook than Brother Hilary, though I could not make gravy. For a fortnight, with the help of a kitchen boy, I cooked for the sixteen tramps.

The Bishop of Salisbury, Dr. Donaldson, came to visit us. I had already met him when he was on a visit to the Ramsays. Someone said that if one threw a raw egg into the air, and let it fall on a lawn, it would not break. We amused ourselves by trying this, and only the bishop's broke.

He had driven forty miles through pouring rain to Batcombe and arrived in an unamiable humour. A good deal depended on our gaining the bishop's approval, but, as soon as he arrived, Brother Claude greeted him by recalling the incident of the broken egg, which I had told him, not dreaming that he would repeat it. The bishop was rather bothered by having this nondescript community in his diocese, and he was cold and hungry from his drive. This greeting did not improve his mood, nor did the appalling luncheon which followed. I was no longer cook and Brother Claude would not allow Brother Hilary to make any improvement in the menu. He said: "I want the bishop to take part in our everyday life as we live it", so he put his lordship at the foot of a bare trestle table, between myself and an ex-burglar, and gave him a plate of curried tinned salmon drenched in vinegar.

After luncheon there was a confirmation in the farmhouse parlour which was converted into a poor and colourless chapel. Brother Claude, as a sop to the bailiff, had asked the bishop to bring his cope and mitre. When he came, a fretful mountain of cloth of gold, into the drab little room, he must have been on the verge of exasperation, but he gave a truly sympathetic address to the tramps, in which he said: "There is not one of us who, if all his thoughts and actions were exposed, would not wish to sink through the ground in shame."

He withheld his endorsement of the community. Lord Sandwich, our landlord, also came to visit us. I cannot remember that Brother Claude paid much attention to him either, except to introduce him to the tramps as "Brother Sandwich". I had a long talk with him at tea in the bailiff's house. All I remember of it was his asking me what my parents thought of what I was doing. I was surprised at the idea that a man of thirty should be subject to his parents to this extent. I said they had no objections. He replied that they were very lenient.

In the spring the tramp-brothers became restive. They

complained that the community was too Catholic. Brother Thomas at meal-times read aloud an account of the childish religious vapours of the Curé d'Ars, and some incident of a statue of the Virgin in a cherry-tree particularly offended the more Protestant susceptibilities. The tramp-brethren were on the whole as amoral a collection of crooks as it was possible to find outside a jail, and it was ludicrous to allow their criticism of the religious side of the community, especially before they had shown any signs of regeneration. Also the community had been founded by a Catholic as a Catholic institution, and it was silly impudence for men who received its benefits to object to its essential nature. If at the time I had made any statement as forcible as this, my Christian charity would have been estimated at zero.

I must qualify the above remark about regeneration. One of the tramps, who had been the most sly and evil, and whose every remark had some disgusting implication, did, for two or three weeks after his confirmation, appear to have suffered an inner revolution. His eyes became straight and happy and the tone of his conversation changed. But after a month he returned to his old self, having no help or stimulus to hold him on the new path. My faith was subsiding rapidly. One of the undergraduates asked me why I did not go out on the roads. To do this without a sense of useless degradation I should have had to be filled with the love of God, or be charged with the vibration of good, whichever one chooses to call it. But there was nothing in the community now to fill one with disinterested love. It was more provocative of detached amusement. It was, of course, my duty not to give way to this amusement, to try more urgently than ever to draw on the force of good, and persevere in my original intention to lead a life of evangelical virtue. But I had not sufficient strength of character to do this, certainly not un-aided, and in an atmosphere which I increasingly realised was foreign to my nature. The most positive thing I had brought to the community was a quick and critical mind, which now remained high and dry.

Spiritual exhaustion and poor diet produced a boil on my leg. The bailiff's wife very kindly asked me to stay in her cottage, where she surrounded me with comfort. Good food, attention, and a comfortable bed completed my apostasy. When I could walk with comfort I went to stay with my Aunt Chomley, where I confirmed my decision not to return to the community. The world seemed once more full of light and colour and the possibility of fun. I felt that I had risen from the dead.

I wrote to the bailiff's wife, thanking her for her kindness, telling her I would not return, and asking her to forward a suitcase which I had left behind. She replied, ticking me off for not writing to Brother Claude. I had not written because I could not do so sincerely without churning up reams of argument in which I was no longer interested. However, I sent him a short, polite note to which he replied very kindly, and sent me a paper-covered copy of Studdert Kennedy's verses.

I went down to Lee Priory, where Mrs. Ramsay said that Archbishop Davidson had told her: "The whole thing was ruined by a few spikes." A spike is ecclesiastical slang for an extreme Anglo-Catholic.

Lord Sandwich wrote asking me to stay at Hinchingbrooke. Although I would have liked to see that famous house, I was afraid that he might want to make some further suggestion about Batcombe, so I did not go. In 1946 I saw Hinchingbrooke for half a crown.

The undergraduate with whom I was most friendly joined the reconstituted community. About a quarter of a century since I had last seen him, while crossing Regent Street we met on an island. I said: "Hallo F." and we began our conversation much where we had left it off. In the second war he helped the injured and carried the Blessed Sacrament to the dying, himself protected in miraculous escapes. He now cares for lepers in Africa.

Worldly people are inclined to speak slightingly of these activities. What have they done better?

IDYLL IN POVERTY

SINCE THE WAR I had been like someone steadily climbing out along a branch, away from the main trunk, and now at last I had crashed through the twigs. I did not fully realise the seriousness of my position, that at thirty-one years of age I had no means of earning my living, but I must have appeared more unstable than water to my relatives and friends, though none of them made me aware of it.

My parents, their goodness failing never, wrote that if I would like to come home they would pay my fare. Throughout their lives they had this sense of stewardship, using what they had, apportioning it justly for the benefit of others. I find it hard to believe that people who have lived in this way have no greater spiritual destiny than those who have used their assets for purely selfish ends, or even in doing evil.

I did not accept their offer as I did not want to be condemned by the whole clan as a complete waster. Again I said that I was going to write, and this time I did. I wrote a novel and published it under a pseudonym. It was a mixture of my Batcombe preoccupations, still unresolved, and a sort of hectic levity, the result of finding myself free in the world again, and these did not blend well.

The undergraduates practised their precepts and read it

143

without resentment. One of them came with me for a holiday in Brittany. My other friends were quite kind and amused about it. I have not read it for forty years, and wish it could be forgotten.

My Aunt Chomley had a seaside house on the Sussex coast, and she very kindly allowed me to live there when they were not using it and even when they were. I went there in 1925 and at first my chief and almost only friend was Dick Hoskins, the grocer's boy. It seems to be my life-style to accompany others on their lawful errands, driving with my father to discuss the crops; with the padre to look for brothels; with the Wykehamist general to look for horses; and now with Dick to deliver groceries. I used to go out in the morning on my bicycle and meet him at a gap in a hedge, and ride with him on his rounds to the outlying cottages of his customers. The fields bordered the sea, and these morning rides were happy and tranquil. I felt that I had entered a remote and freer world, where artificial barriers between human beings were unknown. He was sixteen and close to nature. He would stop by the way to look at a yellow-hammer's nest, or some detail of hedgerow life. Sometimes on his afternoon off we went fishing together. His birthday was within a day of my own, and in spite of the difference in our ages and between our lives hitherto, our essential selves were in harmony. He called me Sarcophagus, probably because it was the only classical word he knew, and though ignorant of what it meant, he thought it suited my wider culture. He remained my good friend until I went back to live in London seven or more years later. Before then he became engaged to my aunt's housemaid, and often they came to see me in the evening, and we played cards, and with these simple happy young people I was contented.

In the first months of the second war Dick was killed in a collision in the blackout. He died uncorrupted by hatred and murder, and was spared, perhaps, unspeakable injuries to body and soul.

When I began with *Scandal of Spring* to write under my own name, someone said to me that the book had a "vernal" quality which was not in my earlier work. This was true and was due to my friendship with Dick. Dallas Kenmare, in a unique chapter called "The Unknown Eros" in her book *The Nature of Genius* shows a profound understanding of this kind of poetic inspiration which has nothing to do with "inversion".

Here I might say something about friendship and love for boys, which also comes into my novels. Young people, boys and girls, are the most beautiful of all the creation that we know. They show the perfection of the human body before it is disfigured by the burdens and diseases of life, and their eyes have the liveliness and candour of those whose responses are still instinctive and true.

Since the industrial revolution it has been said that good looks are wasted in a boy. It was certainly not said in any previous civilisation, and they are not wasted in any of God's creatures, a horse, a dog, a tiger, or a flight of cockatoos, let alone a human being, who is the image of God, in which the Greek and the Christian Myths are agreed.

> "He prayeth well, who loveth well
> Both man and bird and beast."

Thomas Traherne has written how a man whose faculties are controlled by his Holy Ghost will see the world: "Young men were glittering and sparkling angels, and maids strange seraphic pieces of life and beauty. Boys and girls, tumbling in the street and playing, were moving jewels."

Wordsworth wrote:

> "Shades of the prison house begin to close
> Upon the growing Boy,

But he beholds the light and whence it flows,
　　He sees it in his joy.
The Youth, who daily farther from the east
　　Must travel, still is Nature's priest,
　　And by the vision splendid
　　Is on his way attended."

And so the greatest poets, sages and artists, Socrates, Shakespeare, Michelangelo and Christ Himself, have loved these creatures from whose eyes the vision of delight has not yet faded. They are capable of generosities which the cautious man would regard as madness, but they are steadily inculcated by their teachers and parents with ideas of self-interest, violence and social superiority. The hatreds of dead generations and the obstinate vanities of their rulers are fastened on to them to be expiated with their blood. Even if they survive, their bright spirits fade into the light of common day.

Soon the invasion of the coasts of England from within came to this peaceful place. One day, while seated with my cousins at luncheon, we saw with horror a disused railway carriage trundled into the village, and dumped in a field a few hundred yards away, where it was converted into a bungalow. Others followed, villas were built, and a new population arrived, but I did not have much contact with them until the 'thirties.

In the 'twenties I spent my winters in Sussex, writing novels, and in the summers I went to France and once again to Italy. These novels were still fortunately under a pseudonym, but recently (when it was reprinted in Melbourne) I acknowledged the third.

My next books were refused, not only because Constables had lost on the earlier novels, but because there was something wrong with the books themselves. Away from London I was out of touch with the exact, sharp rhythm of the thought and idiom of the moment, and my writing had not the virtue which is above fashion, and makes it irrelevant. I said to Jean Campbell: "The only important thing is to be adjusted to one's environment." She replied: "Indeed it isn't. The only important thing is to be adjusted to oneself." This showed that even though an agnostic, she recognised the existence of her Holy Ghost, and had realised a truth towards which I was only groping, that when we feel mentally ill-at-ease, it means that we are sinning against our essential selves. This is all we know and all we need to know. The Kingdom of Heaven is within us.

Fundamentally I accepted Matthew Arnold's distinction between the Barbarian, the Philistine, and the Elect, between Hebraic "Fire and Strength" and Hellenic "Sweetness and Light". I was all for sweetness and light, but did not know where it lay, nor how much strength it was necessary to have in reserve to prevent it from being simply silly. Shortly after I went to Sussex, Hugh Fausset built a house in the neighbourhood and came to live there. He was almost the first person I had met who had any first-hand awareness of values as distinct from conventions, and he was able to indicate to me the direction in which self-adjustment might be achieved. He was one of the major influences of my life, and comes into my story at this point.

At Cassis in 1926 I first touched the fringe of the Bloomsbury constellation, and at the same time received the first dazzling impact of Mediterranean life. On the first morning when I went down to the sea, the golden brown bathers to me were sparkling angels and strange seraphic pieces of life. The young men wore the briefest slips, instead of the stuffy costumes of my youth. It was the first time I had seen this, and I felt that I had walked into the Parthenon frieze. When I bathed, the water was so clear that looking down my feet seemed to be encased in glass.

The sense of physical liberation was exhilarating beyond

147

description, and was accompanied by the mental liberation of the Bloomsbury conversation on the beach. Among these people I remember Frank Birch, a Fellow of Kings, and his wife, Roland Penrose the painter, and Ivy Elstob. We often lunched or dined together in restaurants overlooking the port or in hotel gardens and I remember Roland Penrose, sitting opposite me on one of these occasions, exclaiming at intervals: "Why, you're just like the 'nineties."

I had already stayed at Cassis in 1923, when in flight from Avignon, Mim, as I have mentioned, had given me an introduction to Jean Campbell, who was living with Peter Teed, a retired Anglo-Indian colonel. They had bought Fontcreuse, a seventeenth century château or manor-house, with some acres of vineyard, to which they added during the years, and produced very good white wine, for which Peter received a decoration. For a time Duncan Grant and Vanessa Bell rented the top floor, and later had a smaller secondary house among the olive groves. At that time Fontcreuse was a Mecca to which my thoughts often turned during the long English winter; and not only mine, but those of many others I knew. On this my second visit to Cassis, Jean and Peter gave a dinner party under the mulberry-trees on the terrace, which I have described in *Lucinda Brayford*—the great bowls of fruit, the wine cooling in the wooden tubs, the good Provençal food, the warm night air, and the author of *The Monkey Wife* singing a strange sad ballad of the woes of a cabin boy.

During the 'twenties I was very poor, yet it seems to me now that I had more delightful pleasure during that period than later when I had much more money. The world was not disfigured, and the worth-while things cost little. And though hope had died in 1914, it was the wider hope. Our personal hopes still remained, and did not give way to anxiety till the 'thirties.

Jean and Peter, in spite of their irregular relationship,

which they made no effort to conceal, were probably the most respectable couple in Cassis. Jean with Scottish integrity refused to change her name. They were, sometimes *malgré eux*, wonderfully hospitable. They grew their wine, partly because it was a noble occupation, but also to make a living. But they poured a high proportion of it down the throats of their friends, and of friends of friends who found Fontcreuse a pleasant afternoon's walk from Cassis.

Once during the second war, I thought I saw Jean in Trinity Street, Cambridge, and felt tremendous excitement and joy, thinking she had miraculously escaped; but it was only someone very like her. Incidents like this reveal our true feelings towards our friends.

After a month at Cassis, I began to feel ill-at-ease in the Bloomsbury ethos, though the Birches with whom I spent most of my time were delightful companions, highly intelligent and often very amusing. But there were others who seemed to talk in a moral vacuum. A thing was either pleasing or displeasing to their sensibilities, and nothing else mattered. The necessary Myth itself was only decorative, or ugly in parts, or amusing.

Leonard Woolf was probably the impresario of Bloomsbury and the *New Statesman* its Bible. He tells in his memoirs how when he was up at Cambridge, he took an undergraduate to see some of the early Bloomsbury nucleus, and how this young man would not go again, saying: "Those people are bad." The reason they were bad is found in the *New Statesman* itself. During the 'thirties when Europe was foundering under Nazi collisions, and *The Times* filled one with disgust, more than once I turned to the *New Statesman* for sanity and truth, and found it, but only in negative criticism. After two or three weeks I could not stand its sterile attitude and gave it up. For forty years or more, like the modern churchmen, it has been trying to create a brave new world by using only weed-killer. And for all this time in the column "This England" it has been sneering at its own country. These absurdities and evils are often entertaining, but considering the title of the column they are deathly; and for all that period, they have coloured the attitude of every young would-be intellectual who had not the background to resist their poison. Not only the absurd and the evil happen, but if they were to print a column of good deeds every week to hearten people to do likewise, it would be insipid on the vitiated palates of their readers. Not long ago, a thief, chased by the police, saw a boy drowning, and jumped in to save him, though it meant certain capture. This also happened in England, but if the *New Statesman* readers found such a thing in its columns they would think the editor had gone off his head; though that thief certainly, in the language of the Myth, will be with Christ in Paradise.

Leonard Woolf also said in his memoirs that no man recovers from the psychic trauma of birth. Half an hour after reading this I went out for a walk, and passed a field where some young Italians, shouting, tumbling, laughing, yelling, running, were playing football. They seemed to have recovered perfectly from the psychic trauma of birth.

The real trouble with the intellectuals is that they are cowards in the face of the good. They dare not look in its direction, but find their justification in cerebration undirected by their fading Holy Ghosts, the divorce of science from conscience, which Rabelais said would bring the doom of mankind. Cowardice in the face of evil can be forgiven, for evil, if one is not braced to meet it, is terrifying. But the cowards in the face of good are the damned.

W. J. Turner, the poet, said to me that the *New Statesman* people had "nothing below the neck". They have, but it is not in the region of the heart.

From Cassis I went on to Italy, and stayed for some weeks at Fiesole, where I began to write *The Montforts*. It was based on the history of my mother's family over the last five generations. It was widely read in Australia, and awarded the first gold medal of the Australian Literature Society; but when in 1960 I read it through to trim it before reprinting, I felt as if I were trying to eat a dry blanket. Constables published these three books, giving me far better terms than I can get now for a mature work. But I am dealing with purely "literary" matters in a separate chapter.

While I was at Fiesole, suddenly one afternoon all the bells started to ring. An attempt had been made on the life of Mussolini. Next day posters appeared everywhere with pictures of the heroic Duce, with a plaster on his nose.

I returned to Sussex for the winter, and continued writing *The Montforts*. Miss Emily Hobhouse in the last months of her life had taken a cottage nearby, and I used to go in sometimes to play halma with her. She had all the Tory instincts in everything outside politics. She disapproved of labour-saving devices as they tended to make the servants idle. But she was notorious in both the Boer War and the 1914 war for her humanitarian efforts. She had the instincts of the squire's or clergyman's daughter, and applied them to the world instead of to her parish. A frontier sentry to her was as insignificant and impudent as a village woman who would not let her pass into her kitchen to see if it was clean.

After she returned from her attempt to inquire into the wicked conditions in the women's concentration camp in South Africa, she was almost completely ostracised, and had to take refuge at Talloires on Lake Annecy. When she made her scandalous effort to alleviate the condition of British prisoners in Germany, travelling there through Switzerland at the height of the war, she was equally reviled.

In the cottage in Sussex she was suffocating herself with three oil stoves. She said: "I need the climate of Egypt" which made me feel I needed the climate of Finland.

She was writing her memoirs which she was very anxious to get done, but she complained that though before she rose

151

in the morning her brain worked quickly and clearly, as soon as she was up she could only write with difficulty. I said: "Then why don't you write in bed?" She was shocked at such a sluggish suggestion, and continued to prefer the appearance of industry to actual production. Her memoirs were finished by a friend, who apparently liked to think of her as possessed of a Quakerish mildness. In reality she was much more of a noble rebel.

I went to France every year up till 1930, and looking back in spite of my vicissitudes, the suns of the 'twenties appear brighter than any that followed.

THE UPPER MIDDLE CLASS

In 1928 I rented a picturesque cottage in a large garden, about a mile inland from the coast. It was pleasant in the summer, and had flagstone floors in the dining-room and the passage. I went to France in the summer, so I was mostly there in the winter, shivering over the fire. Hugh Fausset's house, originally in open fields, was being surrounded by bungaloid growths. He fled to rural Essex, and kindly lent me his Sussex house until he sold it. When this happened I moved two miles westward along the coast, to a village on Chichester harbour, where I rented an eighteenth century cottage.

Here the invasion was socially superior. Most of the people, apart from the indigenous villagers, were like Mrs. Carruthers on the ship, of "the upper middle class". One difference between these people and those I had known hitherto, was their questioning attitude to a new acquaintance. Everyone is inclined to assume that others are like himself. For example, a penniless young man was taken to call on a woman who owned a fine estate. Looking out of her drawing-room windows she said to him: "I advise you always to plant oak-trees in your park." When I was feeling snobbish, I separated those who assumed that I owned a park with oak-trees from those who questioned me about my status symbols.

As I was very poor during this time, these were probably inadequate. Once, crossing a field, I passed a woman I had met at a cocktail party, and took off my hat. She asked haughtily: "Do I know you?" Another woman gave me an earnest lecture on the importance of having money to deserve the respect of one's fellows. One young man told me that I had "the face of a mediaeval peasant". He meant this description to be offensive but it gave me great satisfaction, as it seemed charged with poetry. The mediaeval peasant was close to the natural world and heaven was only a few hundred yards above his head. Another young man asked me to what class I belonged, to which I could only reply: "God knows" as, apart from Dick, there was hardly anyone I knew in the place who I felt was of the same species. They spoke contemptuously of "the lower orders".

What I write of the "upper middle class" is prejudiced and also inaccurate, partly due to the above examples. Potentially good and bad people are born in equal proportions in all classes, but their class develops their virtues or failings in its own particular colours, and to me failings with an upper middle class tint are exceptionally disagreeable.

It is odd that in these democratic days class is more emphasised than at any other time. In reviews and biographies the word comes in on every other page. As I have said, I never heard it in my youth. There were gentle-people and others, and the difference between them was not abitrary but based on different idioms and interests. Among good people they could respect each other, and live on terms of friendship.

John McDonnell once said to me: "The English are the rudest people on earth." As he had wide experience in his search for pictures for the Melbourne Gallery, he could speak with some authority. This is not true of simple people and villagers, satisfied with the ancient dignity of their occupations, but I think it is true of large numbers of "the upper middle class", and even of those above them.

Maud McCarthy, a cousin of my mother's, became a nurse, and had the highest administrative position in the 1914 war, for which she was given the G.B.E. A general said to her: "It's not very nice for our ladies if you nurses are to be given titles."

Judge Chomley was one of the representatives of Australia at the Coronation of George V. Being a widower, he took his eldest daughter with him. A few days before the event she was at a women's luncheon at which she sat next to a duke's daughter, who asked her from where she was going to see the coronation. She said: "In the abbey." The duke's daughter turned on her with the fury of a fishwife, saying there was not enough room "for our people, and you colonials come over etc . . ."

I could give many instances of this sort of thing, some even more incredible, but unfortunately true.

I was more conscious of this English rudeness when I was in Sussex. The explanation may be that then I was poor, which makes it even worse. However to me it was part of the malaise of the 'thirties, as its exponents were those who I believe were, and are, most responsible for the disasters which have come upon us. The "upper middle class" Tories, who felt that their social position, such as it was, depended on giving blind support to anything their Government chose to do, put the Prime Minister as a "father-figure" in the place of God.

Cyril Connolly described the 'thirties as "a dirty, dishonest decade" and the extent to which this was true, is due to these people. It is not entirely true, as half the population of England was striving against the gadarene slide.

Throughout this decade in the mining districts of Wales and elsewhere, hundreds of thousands were living without hope, their youth rotting away in idleness and semi-starvation. Some came up to London and with almost Oriental passivity, lay down in the streets, only asking for work. They would have been justified in smashing every window in Bond Street. In spite of the noble restraint of their protest I heard an "upper middle class" young man from a good public school arriving at a South Kensington cocktail party, exclaim: "I'd like to run over the brutes."

Lloyd George, perhaps remembering his promise of a "land fit for heroes" suggested that the Government should spend £200,000,000 in providing useful work to prevent the decay of young lives. The Government said they could not afford it. Later, after three years of war, the City of London alone provided three-quarters of this sum in one week, to pay for the war. They gave for death what they could not afford for life.

It was because of this abandonment of its young manhood that Hitler said that England could never fight again, and it was a major direct cause of the war. This was told me by an ex-Nazi.

Most of my friends have been public schoolboys, but not of the above kind. Their good qualities are their own, not a veneer of synthetic gentility. I believe that the influence of the public schools has been mostly harmful. They are Fascist in their philosophy. Dr. Arnold's remedy for the appalling social injustice of his time was to "flog the rioters and fling their leaders over the Tarpeian Rock". To set larger boys to beating smaller boys for such trivialities as forgetting a cricket score, not only confuses the boy's sense of justice, but inculcates perversions for which later the same people who sent him to the school send him to prison.

Also a large number of my friends have been those who are described as "upper middle class" but they are not conscious of the fact. It is those who are consciously so, to whom I refer when I write of this class. Their defects have affected the whole country. They have created an artificial caste, based on money, and the caste mark is conformity. The caste marks of the aristocracy were individual taste and independent judgment; and blood was more than money.

For me, the personal symbol of our ruin is the Etonian business man. This is arbitrary and may be quite unjust, but I shall give some of the *obiter dicta* of one or two of these, partially to justify my selection.

One objected to the cost of the milk given to small school-children. I said: "It is nothing to what they spend on armaments." He replied: "But those are necessary." To the big business Tory death comes before everything, except his own pocket.

Another business man Etonian said to me that if a thing was sufficiently rewarded in cash you simply had to do it.

Another business man Etonian said that they ought to pay more to Ministers of the Crown, as it was not worth while going into politics for such poor rewards.

When I spoke of the crime of burning wheat a business man Etonian said: "They have to keep their prices up." Thirty pieces of silver are more valuable than the Body of Christ. Without the Myth they cannot distinguish their crimes.

After the second war I was dining with a business man Etonian, a lord-lieutenant, who was also an ex-M.P., and a friend of the Prime Minister's. An undergraduate was there who related how at Oxford, a number of "viscounts" (apparently a generic term for rich hooligans) had smashed all the windows in the new building at Magdalen. The lord-lieutenant said heartily: "I'm all for that, aren't you?" This was at a time when there was a desperate shortage of housing, and builders would have to be taken from useful work to repair the damage.

A high-ranking diplomat to whom I spoke of the danger to the world's population from lack of food said: "There's plenty of food. Plenty of food in America. A few niggers might die."

The likelihood of hearing this sort of thing has made me reluctant, much as I liked grand houses and nice food, to go into "good" society.

All the same I have liked personally the men who said these things, which makes them more dangerous.

I have come rather far from the few "upper middle class" families in the Sussex village, but I am putting in the dark background of the "dirty dishonest decade". Here is one more instance which illustrates the change of temper. I was walking into Kensington Gardens where, on the gravel near the palace, I saw a dog yapping at the heels of a restive horse, with which the rider was having difficulty. The only person near was a middle-aged woman whom I asked if she owned the dog. When she said she did I said: "Will you please call it away from that horse?" I told this to a friend who replied: "That wasn't very well-bred of you."

I was astonished. One was to risk a man's being injured or killed rather than be so ill-bred as to tell a silly woman to control her dog. It was not the attitude of my fox-hunting grandparents, who at least had the virtues of their kind, and would not fuss about ill-breeding on such an occasion.

The same friend said that we could not expect Chamberlain to stand up to Hitler as he was a "Christian and a gentleman". I had been brought up to believe that Christians and gentlemen stood up pretty forcibly to dishonest blackguards, and spat their pips into the middle of the table if necessary.

This was the first indication I had of the mealy-mouthedness which was coming over the English people, covering every sign of treachery and corruption. The success of Mr. Churchill was probably because he broke through it and said frankly: "We'll make them bleed and burn." This was supposed to be due to his aristocratic eighteenth century ancestors, but really came from his Chicago grandfather.

Once in the 'thirties, when I was at Lee Priory and criticised some Government action, Mr. Ramsay said with half-amused tolerance: "You've been talking to some of these mischievous writer-chaps." I put this into the mouth of Lord Crittenden in *Lucinda*. I am prejudiced in favour of the old families as their emphasis is not on money, and they have been nicer to me personally. But this remark shows the one weakness of these good, sane, honourable people. They would not dream, for example, of allowing a perpetual cancer of unemployment in their own villages; though this is part of the big business Tory's policy, *pour encourager les autres*. Yet they attributed their own decency to the big business Tory, because he had acquired at Eton the same surface as themselves. The public schools had destroyed them.

There may be inconsistencies in what I have written, but one has conflicting impressions. If I were entirely consistent I should be like a machine and dead.

ROGER

IT IS HARDLY FAIR to fasten all the last chapter on to a Sussex village, where I spent some delightful summers bathing and sailing in an old tarred fishing boat called *Fly* which I had bought for a few pounds; and where as time went on, I made some good life-long friends.

Bernard and Noël Adeney bought a house in the village, and came there for the holidays with their children, Richard, now the flautist, and Charlotte. Bernard was a foundation member of the London Group and they were undoubtedly "Bloomsbury". From them I learned the best interpretation of this word, which was a dependence on one's own personal sensibility. In people like themselves with a solid basis of culture and fine creative gifts, this resulted in beautiful sensitive work, particularly evident in Noël's still-life paintings. They brought a sudden patch of life and colour into my life, also they taught me to look for the essential value behind any words or painting and to abhor anything slick.

In addition to her strong artistic sense, Noël was one of the best literary critics, at any rate of fiction, that I have ever known; which was because for positive criticism one must have a touch of genius, which responds to that of the writer or painter.

Under Noël's unconscious influence I began a novel which I was determined should be free from any slickness or false value. Every word was to have quality and meaning. It was called *Scandal of Spring* and to my delight Richard Church accepted it for Dents, and I had crawled back once more on to the literary map.

Other friends I made there were Dagnall Ells and his family. He was a member of Lloyds, but was rather a rebel against the City Tories, and preferred the artistic and theatrical worlds. Someone told me that he saw me walking across a field, and that he said: "I think I could talk to that chap." We met, and he did, and I hope he will continue doing so for years ahead.

In 1933 I moved to London, but though I regarded the Sussex coast as an unfortunate region, I still went there in the summer, instead of to France as in the 'twenties, because I had there these friends. Also, every two years Miss Alice Creswick, an Australian lady in her eighties, used to come over to visit a married niece. She always brought with her an entourage of young great-nieces, which made her household very lively and entertaining, and I generally stayed there. She took them on holiday trips, up mountains in Norway, or up the Amazon, which astounded the sedentary vicar, who was half her age. I had too other friends with whom I went sailing and bathing. One of these was a schoolboy called Roger.

If I tell his brief story it may explain more why I think bitterly of those who made "the dirty dishonest decade", and with *attendrissement* of those who redeemed it.

I had met him once or twice while he was still at Stowe, but our first conversation was after he had left. At one point he said: "We are extraordinarily alike in some ways." I was naturally surprised, as I had no idea what he was like, though he had read my novels and may have had a fair idea of my character. I was affected by his direct, unsuspicious friendliness, and was sufficiently senile to be flattered at receiving it from someone so young.

After he had left Stowe, where he had associated mostly with the sons of the rich, he went into a firm of road engineers, where one of the directors was his uncle. He was to begin at the bottom and work his way up to a position of responsibility. Here he associated with labourers and working men. As might have been foreseen, this violent contrast of association had a disturbing effect on a boy whose nature was essentially generous.

Once when I was ill and could not keep an engagement, the next morning a box of grapes arrived at my flat, sent by Roger and his sister. A woman whom he had met a few times and with whom he had had some friendly chaff was leaving for Australia. He sent her an amusing telegram of farewell to the boat. He was friendly to old people, treating them not as mummies but as people of like passions with himself, and was alert to help them. He loved to enjoy himself and could only do this by making enjoyment as universal as possible. If he came to see me in London and if he thought that I wanted flowers, he would bring me flowers, careless of misunderstanding. No one was less effeminate.

Here I recall another incident. Aubrey Waterfield's second son, who was called but not christened Johnnie, came one day to see me in London, just as some rather loud, overbearing people had left. He brought a bunch of daffodils into the quiet grey room. That is the whole incident. Yet it restored my tranquillity, and seemed to belong to the eternal pattern of civilisation, so that it remains in my mind to this day. Johnnie's was yet another of the young deaths which punctuate my story, and I record this to his memory.

Roger could not understand why one or two unemployed young men in the neighbourhood did not attempt something adventurous. "I would if I were free," he said, "but I can't leave my job because of Mum. But they could clear out to South America or Kenya or anywhere."

He shared fully the conditions of the working man's life and he thought them intolerable. He did not mind the hard work, but he felt it unjust that the working man enjoyed so small a proportion of the fruit of his labour, and that insecurity should be added to hardship. He liked the essential patient decency of the working man, and he liked pubs. He said: "I find a lot of ready-made mates there."

In 1935 I again took a cottage in Sussex for six months. Roger was then at Littlehampton, tending furnaces on night shift. He came over to spend a short week-end. He arrived looking like an exhausted tramp and spent all Saturday afternoon asleep. On Sunday morning he asked me to criticise his verses which he had posted on ahead. They were full of an intense love for the natural world, particularly for our salt-marsh and harbour, and of indignation at man-made suffering.

One sunny afternoon three or four of us who had sailing dinghies set out in a small fleet for a picnic. Roger came with me in *Fly*. First we went down to Hayling and then back to Pilsey Island, a deserted horseshoe of reeds and shingle, where we had tea. It was very hot and Roger lay in his bathing trunks on the bleached floor-boards while I steered through the drowsy afternoon.

"I love *Fly*," he said. "She has the real quality of a boat. She's like all boats that have ever been."

He said: "Shall we get a boat and go round the world in it? One about forty foot." He enlarged on the possibility of this—on the type of boat and the countries we would visit.

"We should have to have a girl on board," he said. He grinned and added: "a black woman". This was not only a Gauguin touch to give picturesqueness to the conception, but a repudiation of the bourgeois design of life into which he was to be fitted.

"I don't want to live in the suburbs on a thousand a year," he repeated many times.

Later in the year there was a period in which he seemed not only reconciled to his lot, but pleased with the progress he was making in the firm. When I met him he would describe it at length. He looked forward with satisfaction to his thousand a year, equal then to four or more thousand now, at thirty, and seemed to have not only the prospects but the instincts of a successful business man. I thought: "Well, that's a good thing for his relatives", but I was secretly regretful that ardent idealism could so seldom survive the age of nineteen.

Then in London in the autumn he brought me a long poem describing a night shift in a factory. It was vivid and moving, and was far too sympathetic to be written by a successful business man. He brought too a number of small lyrics, which had the effect which would be produced if one were suddenly to be handed a bunch of primroses in a winter street.

During the year or so following, Roger became increasingly "Left" and finally declared himself a Communist. He was furious that the Government would do nothing to protect British ships taking food to Spain. He was angry, not only because he was "Left", but because he had a sense of national dishonour. Probably he had learned at Stowe, as I had learnt years earlier in Australia, about the little *Revenge* that ran undaunted down the long sea lane of Spanish ships. It was bewildering to anyone who had been brought up to believe that Tennyson's ballad represented the British attitude to the seas, to find the whole British Navy standing by, while a few pirates destroyed the ships which were taking food to a starving people, and a people who were doing what, we were told at school, was the noblest activity of man, fighting against odds for the liberty which they had been denied through centuries of atrocious oppression.

164

One evening I went to dine with Roger at his home. As the evening wore on and Roger was chipped about his Communism, he became furiously doctrinaire, and would listen to nothing but pure Marxism. His views repelled me as much as the determined self-interest of the rich. When I left, with a return of his usual friendliness, he came down to the door. I had a vague impression that there was a kind of urgency in his manner, as he opened the door of the car in which someone was giving me a lift home, and there was something in his mood comparable to that of Bacchus on the morning he was killed. As soon as I got home I went to bed and fell into an almost unbroken sleep of thirty-six hours. It was the week-end when Hitler marched into Austria. Once or twice on Sunday I woke to hear the newsboys shouting, but I was too exhausted to move, even to ring up someone to ask what had happened. Below the window I heard two men talking about war. It was as if I had responded to the forces of both good and evil, and that warring inside me they had destroyed my vitality.

On Tuesday morning I had a letter from Roger. He had left for Spain. His address was given care of the International Brigade in Litchfield Street. He wrote:

"Please don't think I've done this from any sort of heroic motive. I can guess what war is like and that's enough for me. I imagine the worst and then, perhaps, it won't be too bad. If I believe and I live, I must live my belief. My only qualms are re Mum."

He said that he was not even sure that he was a Communist, but he was sure that there were forces moving towards light and freedom and decent conditions for all men, and that those forces were being opposed in Spain by Franco. He felt the shame of an Englishman whose Government would not protect the ships which were taking food to starving women and children. The only way in which he felt he could live his belief and rid himself of this shame, and breathe again untainted air, was by going to fight. I rang up an "intellectual" friend to tell her that Roger had gone. She said: "Isn't that rather silly?"

About a week later I went down to Sussex to stay with Miss Creswick. I was greeted by a woman whom Roger had thought to be one of his friends, with: "Isn't Roger a little swine?" One or two others who had been most closely associated with him took up the same attitude.

The number of topics which made any social gathering difficult was increasing. The Tory members of Parliament inadvertently cheered when news came through of the bombing of a British ship. The attitude of some of the people I knew suggested that the ancient sages had lived, that Christ had been crucified, that the martyrs had endured their torments, that the great heroes had struggled towards freedom, and that the whole world had groaned and travailed in tribulation until now, to enable upper middle class women to play bridge and golf, and that anything likely to impede this agreeable routine was "anti-God" and "Red".

One day a neighbour came over to tea. He was a distinguished soldier with a string of decorations. He was quiet and courteous and had always seemed to me the ideal English officer. Someone asked: "Where's that nice boy—the one with the boat?" I braced myself to remain polite and said; "Roger? He's fighting in Spain." When I said it was for the Government, the distinguished soldier sat up with a start. His face went mean and narrow. He appeared almost to squint.

"For the Government?" he exclaimed. "He deserves to be shot."

I met another soldier who had known Roger. He, too, had a distinguished record. He had lost an eye in some war, and spent his time sailing on the harbour. He said:

"I don't know about all this Communism. I don't understand it, but I admire young Roger for going to fight for what he believes in. He's a fine boy. I hope he's getting on all right."

About this time I had a letter from Roger. He wrote:

"It was grand to get the fags. We smoke them till they burn our lips and share them round. Let Mum know I'm O.K. I never know what I said last but it's much the same, bombing, strafing, marching, digging, and running. Man to man we could drive these wops to Rome, but they shell our positions until we have to break, and then come over. The I.B. only goes back when the flank breaks and we are ordered back. Every one of us would fight to the last and go down with clenched fists. I've seen that. Oh, what the hell!

"There are thousands of foreign and Spanish volunteers here in the hills who simply can't fight for lack of arms. Thank God, this sort of country is easier to defend than attack.

"I felt so useless at home with the whole world threatened by this inhuman brutality and me just talking.

"Please go on writing. I don't mind what sort of twaddle you say, I love so much to hear from you, and please put a sheet of paper and an envelope in so that I can reply. I have seen quite big envelopes come in but not parcels. I hope I get the rest of my mail. Surely—and—and—* have written to me? I haven't heard a word. The sun is just setting so I can't see much more. There is a big steep ridge of rock about 3,000 feet high, two kilometres across the valley, all the face bright red in the late sunshine, as far as I can see north and south. There is so much beauty here I can't help being happy, beauty of soul and spirit as well as of scenery.

> "Good luck and God bless. Love.
>
> Roger."

This was the last I heard from the little swine who deserved to be shot, and who got his deserts.

* Three friends who had no good word to say for him.

A month or two later I was handed a poem he had written before he left. He describes how in his sleep he heard an exquisite song that was

> "Like the swift sunlit stream
> That pierced the dark forest,
> Or a rocket of fire
> That furrowed the night."

As he went about his work,

> "All through the hot day
> It hid in my brain
> Like a lizard in grass
> Or the breeze in gold grain."

The poem ends with the recapturing of the song the following night, but then he knew that it was only a song in his sleep.

CHAPTER XIX

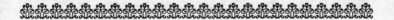

BRIGHT INTERLUDES

THOUGH THROUGHOUT THIS PERIOD there was growing apprehension, some good things happened to me personally.

When I first moved to London I had three rooms in a small Georgian house near Baker Street. One afternoon in the mid-'thirties I was walking along Holland Street at the foot of Camden Hill. I had just been reading a book by Maurice Baring in which a young man had some wooden panelled rooms near Versailles, and was thinking: "I wish I could have some panelled rooms near an historic palace." At that moment I looked up and saw in a glass case outside a newsagent's an advertisement for a flat to let. I went in and asked where it was. The woman in charge said "Here" and led me up a Queen Anne staircase to the top floor, which consisted of three panelled rooms. In the largest, the sun streamed through three windows which looked over to the roof of St. Mary Abbot's church. The back room, panelled at an earlier time but also painted white, looked on to a plane-tree. In three minutes I could walk past Kensington Palace into the gardens. In this charming place I lived through the final squalors of the decade.

During this time I published about five books which were well received, though I do not like any of them very much, because I did not know the sort of people I was writing about. I knew the outward circumstances of their lives, but not the previous conditions which had produced their outward circumstances.

The "vernal" quality of *Scandal of Spring*, captured from my association with Dick, a completely integrated person, rooted in the life of the country where he, and probably his ancestors since Saxon times, had lived, was dissipated by my contact with the "invaders".

I do not repudiate the novels I wrote in this decade, except perhaps *The Picnic* in which my faults at that time are most evident. None of the people belong anywhere, and this not-belonging has not been realised and made a theme of the book. I have not read any of these books for twenty or more years. I have even lost my copies of them, but I saw *The Picnic* in a friend's house last summer and read a few pages with discomfort.

The last of my novels before the second war was free of this not-belonging, as it did not try to belong. In 1938 Daryl and Joan Lindsay were in London. One day, when she was lunching with me in Holland Street Joan said: "It's no good writing today a novel assuming that society is stable. You must either deal with the mess we are in, or else write of something quite fantastic, say, a lot of nuns wrecked on a desert island and call it *Nuns in Jeopardy*." I said: "Very well, I will" and I did. A reviewer said that it was marred by an uneasy air of symbolism. It was not marred by it. The whole book was a symbol of the transmutation of the human soul, told in physical terms. All true art must be symbolic of something more. Otherwise it is just photography. In other words, all good art is religious.

These novels brought me in a little money, and with some reviewing, mostly in the *Times Literary Supplement*, I managed to keep alive, and even persuaded my parents to stop my allowance, though still an occasional cheque arrived.

My mother died in 1936. Her youth had held exceptional promise. She had much talent, good looks, a lively wit, and was the child of rich parents. But after the crash of the land boom, at the time of my birth, I do not think that she ever lived under a clear sky. Two of her sons were killed in accidents. She was always anxious lest the temperament of another should bring disaster; and my erratic existence on the other side of the world, writing books which she could not have liked, must have saddened her. My sister told me that after her death it was found that nearly every counterfoil in the stubs of her cheque-books was for people in need. This does not seem to me an unusual pattern. I have known too many people of my own generation, whose equally bright promise has been clouded by sorrow and misfortune.

I was now anxious about my father. Helen my sister had married Neven Read, a naval commander, and though she asked him to live with them, it would have meant leaving his surviving friends and the region he knew, and living in the various capitals where her husband had appointments. I was worried at the thought of my father's loneliness, but I also had a more unworthy anxiety. Recently a relative of Cousin Maud McCarthy's, whom I have mentioned, had lost his wife after fifty years of happy life together. Everyone was very sorry for him, and a daughter leaving for the East, said to Cousin Maud: "Do look after poor father, and cheer him up." However almost immediately he picked up a housekeeper in a train in Scotland and married her. I was afraid that my father might do the same sort of thing, and that I would lose all hope of escape from my poverty.

Among the brightest interludes during the dark decade were my visits to Hugh Fausset and his family at Widdington in Essex. Here I found the recognitions of my pre-Sussex life, together with a deeper wisdom. What the Adeneys gave me aesthetically, Hugh gave me intellectually. When I was stumbling to give expression to an idea he took it and

171

clarified it in a few words. It was as if someone took a badly hanging garment and pulled it straight. He had a clearer view of the malaise of the decade than anyone I knew, as he understood the nature of the moral and spiritual forces which were breeding the dirt and dishonesty. In conversation he often expressed this with a lively and sometimes ribald wit, and often I said: "I wish you would write that." But he was concerned with more enduring values and wrote for people on a different level.

I generally visited him for a week once or twice in the summer, and I remember peaceful walks by the fields and hedgerows, lively games of tennis with his children, tea on the lawn under the trees which surrounded his beautiful garden where it seemed warm days would never cease, and in the evening those illuminating conversations.

The Faussets were vegetarians, and Marjory, a poetess, had a genius for arranging delicious and poetic meals, which, the essence of a good cuisine, brought the feeling of the natural world to the dinner-table.

This diet had as good an effect on me physically as the intellectual (though this is too narrow a word for it) atmosphere had on my mind. I returned to London from Widdington, restored in body and soul. On these visits Hugh generally drove me over to Cambridge, and this lovely town for me became a sort of City of God.

THE MORGANATIC LIE

THE ABDICATION OF EDWARD VIII is now past history, but it was the most dishonest of all the treacheries of the 'thirties. It aroused such passionate loyalties and repudiations in myself that I cannot write the story of my life without some reference to it. I did not fully understand the nature of my feelings, and what puzzles as well as hurts us makes us twice as angry.

One reason for my indignation was my increased understanding of how the older men had butchered my generation, of which Edward VIII was the symbol. Their attack on him was a further attack on all of us, their victims. I remembered the feeling of hope when I first saw him as King on the screen of a cinema.

Another feeling, and a true one, was that he was eager for social justice.

Another reason was that I am essentially conservative. As my father observed when I was seven, I was born that way. I believe in pruning unhealthy growths on the social order, but not in major operations, which always have created more suffering than they have relieved. I also had a possibly irrational belief in the Divine Right of the legitimate king. My juvenile Jacobitism had switched over to King Edward.

CHAPTER XX

But the chief cause of my anger was my hatred of blatant impudent dishonesty, and of the hypocritical mob yelling abuse at one good man.

King Edward went down to Wales. He refused to pass along the beflagged streets, and insisted on seeing what was behind them. He saw the horrible poverty, and the young men rotting in idleness. It is said that he wept. He certainly said: "Something must be done." That was the real cause of the abdication. He had outraged the city gents by suggesting that the flesh and blood of his people were more important than money. The next day a South African journalist had the effrontery to attack him in *The Times*, though he was fulfilling his proper lawful function, that of protecting his people. It was not till three weeks later that Mrs. Simpson was used in the attack.

When the King saw that an ordinary marriage was impossible, he asked for a morganatic one. Mr. Baldwin said that there was no such thing in England, and that a woman must take her husband's rank. He said forcibly in the House of Commons: "She would be Queen."

Six months later when the Duke of Windsor married Mrs. Simpson, George VI issued Letters Patent to say that she was not to take her husband's rank of Royal Highness, and the marriage was morganatic after all. The abdication was based on an admitted lie. Either the Duchess of Windsor is "Her Royal Highness" or Edward VIII is still King. They cannot have it both ways.

The incredible vindictive meanness towards the ex-king displayed by the Government, and by the Royal Family itself, but probably at ministerial dictation, is one of the dirtiest manifestations of the dishonest decade. Its absurdity was illustrated over twenty years later, when a man with one wife and two ex-wives still living, sat opposite the queen in Westminster Abbey, and appeared with the Royal Family in the balcony of Buckingham Palace while the Duke of Windsor was still in exile.

But almost immediately this absurdity was revealed when at the coronation of George VI the Abbey was filled with peers and members of parliament who were themselves divorced, while one of the most disreputable performed hereditary functions around the altar and the throne.

A pitiful sequel to all this took place only a week ago, as I write. It took over a quarter of a century of exile, old age, and a serious illness to evoke one feeble gesture of kindness towards the cheated King. The Queen went to see him in hospital, without demanding the absence of his wife. Seeing that the Morganatic Lie had not been withdrawn, the duke showed amazing charity in consenting to this visit.

Shortly before the coronation of George VI I went to see Cousin Maud McCarthy. With her was another relative, a peeress, with whom she was discussing the robes they would wear in the abbey. In the middle of their loyal talk this lady turned to me and said: "Of course we don't really feel he's the King."

The Harrovian business man had destroyed the mystique of the monarchy, as twenty years on an Etonian business man was to destroy the mystique of the aristocracy, by allowing peers to renounce their titles. If they do this they should also be compelled to renounce the estates that go with them. The Duke of Windsor was not allowed to keep Buckingham Palace.

So the "Conservative" Government has destroyed the traditional order, the paternal monarchy and the responsible aristocracy. At the abdication they gave birth to the horrible amorphous "Establishment" which, if it can be defined, is anything that pays. The Duchess of Windsor in a recent interview said that it was a powerful force, but indefinable. She ought to know, as her husband is its pre-eminent victim.

The substitution of this indefinable force for the order I

respected gave me a distrust of politicians from which I have not yet been able to free myself. However, as my feelings now are less heated, I shall end this chapter on a lighter note.

Long afterwards Lady Kinnaird told me that at the coronation of George VI, when the peers were released from the elaborate ceremonies, they made for the buffet where refreshments were provided. Lord Luke of Pavenham fell over in the rush, but the hungry peers just gathered up their robes and jumped over his prostrate body. Lady Kinnaird, more humane, knelt and gave him a pill she had brought in case she felt faint. This knocked him out completely. The next morning when she rang up to ask how he was, she was severely scolded by his wife for her interference.

Another recollection of this time, though unconnected with the abdication, has, I think, a kind of atmospheric relation to it.

Cousin Maud asked me to luncheon to meet Mrs. C. B. Fry and Sir Walter Allen. I doubted that I would be of much use in conversations about cricket, but she said they would not talk cricket all the time. However it was an ingredient of every topic.

Sir Walter told how he had gone to see Lord Knutsford, to ask if a patient in whom he was interested might stay in hospital longer than the regulations allowed. Lord Knutsford regretted that it was impossible, but thought a moment and then asked: "Aren't you the father of the captain of the English Eleven?" Learning that this was so, he said: "Oh, then that will be quite all right."

Sir Walter told this anecdote with ironical amusement, but Mrs. Fry, with shining eyes exclaimed: "Isn't cricket wonderful?"

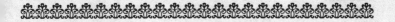

EUROPEAN SUNSET—THE DIRTY
DECADE DIES

IN THE MIDDLE 'FIFTIES Hertha Biheller, an Austrian friend, married Arthur Hay of Park, in the male line Chieftain of that clan, but owing to the Scottish law of female succession he had been separated from his family titles except a baronetcy. The most important had gone to the son of that Boyd who had lost his own, together with his head, after the 'Forty-five. Aware of Scottish tenacity I thought that Arthur might view me with misgiving as one of the usurping clan; but when Hertha brought him to see me, and he noticed some seventeenth century prints of "The Old Pretender" as Prince of Wales on my walls, we became good friends.

Arthur was imbued with Scottish history, and illuminated for me the more remote parts of the backcloth of my childhood. When we visited together the sad little Muti Palace, in the Piazza S.S. Dodici Apostoli, the home of the exiled Stewarts, he said with wistful irony: "All because Bruce murdered Red Comyn at the altar of Dumfries"—so putting the curse on the Stewart dynasty.

In the summer of 1937 the Hays were going to Austria, but Hertha wanted to go on ahead, and she asked me to accompany her. She justified to her mother the propriety of

177

this journey by my extremely tenuous connection with her husband.

A few days before we left, my agent rang up saying that the managers of the Arts Theatre wanted to do a play which I had written, but they would not be in London until early the following week. I said that I was just leaving for Austria. The agent said: "I strongly advise you to wait to see them." Hertha said she would drive on and wait for me in Cologne. I went to see the Arts Theatre people in a house in Golden Square which had belonged to my great-great-grandfather, the ninth William, and thought mistakenly that this was a good omen. They said they would do the play but wanted me to make some alterations, to be done by the end of August, a job which restricted my holiday. When I brought it back I heard nothing from them till Christmas, when they said they could not do it, I was told owing to lack of money. After further similar vicissitudes, my agent, who had advised me to write it, said: "Why don't you turn it into a novel?" I did this and when it was published, five different reviewers in leading London newspapers said what a marvellous play this novel would make. This sort of thing has been frequent in my literary life.

We drove from Cologne to Vienna through an almost unbroken avenue of fruit-trees, and past the fairy-tale Southern Bavarian towns with their friendly people. Owing to my initial delay, and Hertha's having an appointment with her corset-maker in Vienna for three o'clock on Friday, this journey was hurried, and my appreciations keen but sketchy.

As we crossed the frontier into Austria, and Hertha approached her native mountains, her heart became lighter and she exclaimed: "See how well and happy the people look. It is because they are all in love before they are eighteen."

On the outskirts of Schladming, when we were travelling south from Vienna, we came upon a boy with a suitcase. He

178

was waiting on a wooden bench underneath a pear-tree, which was covered with small green fruit. He was Wucki, Hertha's son by her former marriage, whom we were to pick up and take to his grandparents at Velden. He wore white stockings and a Tyrolese hat with a jaunty feather.

We arrived at Velden in the late afternoon. The waters of the lake were a cobalt blue, and the whole place had a kind of Riviera gaiety only fresher and cleaner. There was an ecstatic family reunion among my friends, with much kissing of hands and faces.

It is difficult to evoke the quality of a holiday, but the week at Velden remained long fixed in my mind. We bathed in the lake, and lay about in the sun with the lovely Carinthian mountains in the background. The conversation was a mixture of French and Viennese German. Wucki fell lightly and amusingly in love with Maria, a girl of the party, one of those golden-skinned, blue-eyed creatures that appear impossible on tourist posters. He had charming manners and something of Roger's eagerness to help people and to create a general atmosphere of pleasure. They all had that mixture of courtesy and genuine friendliness which is too rare in England.

Hertha's stepfather was General Vaugoin, who had been War Minister in the Dollfus Government, and before that, Chancellor of Austria. He arrived from a fishing expedition bringing delicious trout, which we had for dinner at a table under trees by the lakeside. There was such an atmosphere of pleasure and family happiness and security that it was difficult to realise the threat under which they were all living. Yet within a year the general was in a concentration camp, where he received injuries to body and soul, from which he soon died.

The Duke and Duchess of Windsor were staying nearby, and inevitably came up for discussion. When I said that whether one approved of the marriage or not it was against all precedent to turn the King of England off the throne on account of a woman, Frau Vaugoin agreed, though she was a devout Catholic and observed all the feasts and fasts of the Church.

General Vaugoin had been staying with the Abbot of Melk, who told him that after he had shown the duke and duchess round the abbey, he had received a letter of abuse from an Englishman. President Miklas had told him that if it was known that the duke was going to be in a certain place, the English people avoided it, though this may have been in consideration of the duke's feelings. I heard two English people talking loudly and slightingly of the duke to two others across the tables of the Mosslacher Café. I turned and let them have it, with even more ill-breeding than when I had tried to save the horseman in Kensington Gardens. They looked startled, as they were "upper middle class" people, who thought they were doing the right thing.

In a leading article in *The Times* it was written that the way the English people had conducted the abdication was the admiration of the whole world. In my experience it had earned them the contempt of the whole world, and the only foreigner I met who approved, was a neurotic French Protestant woman at Cassis, who screamed all through dinner: "Paris vaut une messe", giving her opportunist Henri IV as a precedent.

Hertha told me that when General Vaugoin was in office he had lived over the ministry. The Nazis had made a plot, of which her parents knew, to blow it up, but they would not leave and live elsewhere as they were the bait which they hoped would catch the plotters, as it did. On another occasion when her father had been going on a journey, but was delayed in setting out, the train by which he had intended to travel was wrecked.

When we left, Frau Vaugoin was in tears. Living so dangerously she felt she might never see her daughter again, and that this might be their last family holiday. That night we drove to Heiligenblut.

Wucki was very depressed at leaving Maria, but he ate an enormous quantity of dumplings, each of which had a whole apricot in the middle.

I said: "Quand on est jeune on vit pour l'amour. Quand on est vieux on vit pour l'estomac. Mais vous vivez pour l'amour et pour l'estomac, tous les deux."

He looked at me doubtfully. Then he leant across, touched my face and said: "Schön."

These trivial semi-idiotic conversations and slight gestures of friendship are so much a part of the ordinary happiness of life, that some of them should be recorded.

The next day he sent Maria a postcard from the hut outside the tunnel on the Gross Glockner pass. He wrote: "Dear Maria, I could not sleep last night for thinking of you. We had the most beautiful sausages to eat up here."

The day after that, we left Wucki to join some friends. He looked like someone who had all the good things of life before him, yet the shades of the prison house were beginning to close around him, as they were round every boy of his age in Europe.

Roger, if he had lived longer, and Wucki might have been trying to kill each other; yet if they had met in ordinary life they would certainly have been friends. At Christmas 1914 the English and the German soldiers met in war, and still became friends.

Happily Wucki came safely through the evil years, and is now married and "the stern father of three children", as Hertha described him in a recent letter.

Hertha drove on to Salzburg, and I took the train to Steinach to meet Mim, who shortly after the first war had married Hans Pollak, a Viennese professor. Daryl and Joan Lindsay were also there. With Mim and Hans I made excursions up the mountains, where they pointed out even higher peaks they had climbed in previous years. Daryl was more inclined to stroll off down a side street to look at a baroque shrine. In one church an arch cupid, holding his finger to his lips, was perched on a pink and blue confessional box, which should have had a notice "Peccadilloes only".

In Ireland, a priest belonging to a religious order who hated hearing confessions was obliged to do so owing to the crowd of penitents before some great feast. Coming into the church, and dismayed at the queue awaiting him, he shouted angrily: "All those not in mortal sin go home." So perhaps graded confessionals would save trouble.

Mim and Hans were happy among their beautiful mountains, and for the time being seemed to have resigned themselves to the terrible menace under which they lived. Hans was a Jew, and his face clouded if anyone mentioned the Nazis. I asked her why they did not leave Austria, as she had money of her own. She said that it was her husband's home. He would have no work elsewhere, and in seven years he would have a pension. She recognised that she was unduly optimistic in thinking that Hitler would keep out of Austria for seven years.

She told me that roughly one side of the road that runs through Steinach was Nazi, the other anti-Nazi. On Sunday the whole village, people of every age and sex, turned out to Mass. I asked her how they could be Nazi if they were so Catholic. The countryside was littered with Materln, the small wayside shrines, and the hotel corridors were like those in a monastery with their madonnas and huge crucifixes. She said that it was part of the agreement between Schussnigg and Hitler that the Nazis' anti-Christian activity should not be reported in Austrian newspapers. Here was another example of the insanity of the decade, giving up part of one's defences to placate an enemy, to hear of which hurts one's brain.

Hans's sisters were staying at the hotel. They were widely

read and travelled, and had charming and distinguished manners. One of them was delicate and could not walk far. They were in Vienna through the Nazi pogrom.

On Sunday evenings the village band played in Steinach. The same man had conducted it for a great many years, since well before the war. On the Sunday before I left he gave his last performance. Mim and Hans came to see me off. As the train drew out of the station, opposite the hotel where I had been locked up in 1922, they called: "Come back next year."

In Cologne while waiting for the Ostend train I went to the cathedral where, between two pale candle flames, a priest was saying Mass at the nave altar. Some fair-haired German hikers were waiting with serious faces to look round the cathedral. As I turned to go I saw them passing through the wrought-iron gates to where, behind the sanctuary, the early sun streamed through the high eastern windows. They were like young gods in the morning of the world, passing into their heaven, but it was only a Valhalla of skulls.

General Vaugoin, who could have saved himself when Hitler marched into Austria, scorned to do so and was sent to Dachau. Frau Vaugoin's house was ransacked by the Nazis. Cultivated Jews and their womenfolk were compelled to scrub out the crosses painted on the pavements, a strange confusion of ideas, and to clean out filthy lavatories. Mim and Hans at last escaped, when she had given up her entire private fortune. They managed to bring Hans's books as far as Hamburg, where they were held. Mim, when they arrived in London, rang up her cousin Archie Weigall, a Conservative member of parliament, to ask if he could help her in this. He replied:

"Come to luncheon on Friday. Ribbentrop's coming and I'm sure he'll do what he can. He's a very nice chap."

This illustrated the attitude of the Tory members at that

time. He could not realise that Hans would rather have lunched with the devil himself than with Ribbentrop.

At last Mim and Hans arrived in Sydney, having miraculously escaped death and worse, but having suffered great losses, and endured torments of anxiety which they still felt for their friends in Vienna. Also they had left their mountains to which it seemed they could never return. On arrival Mim rang up a family friend who had often stayed at St. Margaret's. This friend said: "Oh Mim, how are you? We're having a dreadful time, moving into another flat in the same building. I shan't possibly be able to see you for three weeks."

Probably lack of imagination is the real curse of humanity. It enables people to acquiesce in evils they cannot visualise, and propagandists to use phrases which make the worst devilries sound innocuous. They write of "plastering an area"—language which could be used to describe a minor piece of interior decoration, but does not convey the reality of men killing their mangled children; thousands roasted to death; and the wounded eaten by animals from the zoo.

About this time B. H. Liddell Hart, *The Times* military correspondent, wrote an article in Vernon Bartlett's *World Review*, in which he suggested, as far as I remember, the forming of a new party, of which one of the aims was to inspire a sense of manhood and hope, and virtue in its ancient meaning into the youth of the country, who had been left to rot for ten years. At this time at least half the population of England was bitterly opposed to the government's policies. The overwhelming victory in a by-election of Vernon Bartlett himself, proved it.

I wrote to Liddell Hart that if he were to form a nucleus of this new party, and then ask everyone in the country to pay a shilling and join it, he would be amply supplied with the necessary funds. A month or so afterwards he wrote asking me to attend a meeting in a private room at the Caxton

Hall, to consider this idea. He had invited about forty people, mostly well known as against the Government. Among them were Lady Violet Bonham-Carter, Low the cartoonist, and the Duchess of Atholl, who was against the Government's Spanish policy. He had asked an M.P., later a Cabinet Minister, and still prominent in politics, to take the chair.

These people were gathered in the private room when more and more began to arrive, and finally it was necessary to move down into the hall itself. Here under the guidance of the M.P. it developed into nothing but a demand for rearmament. I saw Liddell Hart sitting away from it all, and went over to him, saying that this was hardly the spirit of his article. He replied with utter contemptuous disgust: "He has broken every promise he ever made to me."

"He" was the M.P. who, presumably to gain publicity for himself, had given away the whole show of the "secret" meeting to the evening papers. These are the sort of people who have been governing us for the past forty years, and this man will probably again be in the Cabinet.

We had now had Abyssinia, Hitler in the Rhineland, Spain, the abdication, the Anschluss, the young men rotting in idleness. There was only the shame of Munich to come.

It may seem inconsistent to write the "shame" of Munich, when I am opposed to the butchery of any human beings for political reason, but no one is entirely consistent, not until death. Certainly I was not patriotic in the nationalistic sense, regarding patriotism of that kind simply as the snobbery of the mob. But I was patriotic in that I wished my country to be a land of justice, human wellbeing, and creative achievement. I also thought that as an Englishman or Australian, I belonged to an honourable human group, as in a smaller way I belonged to an honourable family. I did not believe it possible that the British Government, having assumed a moral responsibility towards the Czechs, could abandon their country to dismemberment and their people to an alien tyranny. I found it was possible, and I felt as one might feel who had reason to believe that his parents were good people, and then found his mother cheating a servant of her wages, or his father running away from a lane where a child was being murdered.

After Munich the dirty, dishonest decade was practically finished, to be followed by one containing greater crimes against humanity than the world had ever known, but which the dirt and dishonesty had produced.

I shall leave the final comment on this period to an old man in Hampshire. A friend who was visiting there told me that he met his host's retired butler in the village, and asked him what he thought of the general situation. The man replied, referring to a leading Cabinet Minister: "When I was a young footman I held Mr. — as a baby in my arms; and by God I wish I'd dropped him."

MY OWN VINE AND MY OWN FIG-TREE

Soon after war was declared my father died, and in this last act again came to my rescue, as I did not see how I was going to earn my living. I could have obtained war work, and been patriotic in a safe job, but this time I was not going to gag myself in a ministry or in a military post.

I wrote to *The Times* urging that throughout the war the Government should stick to its declared aims, and not vary them according to the amount of success achieved. I had a furious letter from a clergyman at this suggestion of any rational objective. Chamberlain, declaring war, had spoken of the German people "with whom we have no quarrel". He had reason for this, as when he arrived in Bonn to meet Hitler, he was wildly cheered by the people who thought he was bringing peace, while Hitler was ignored on his balcony, and flounced angrily indoors. Vernon Bartlett had asked a bank clerk in Munich if he thought there would be war, and the young man burst into tears. A few months later Churchill spoke of "the dull brutish mass of the German people" whom he intended to make "bleed and burn" adding "if they don't like it, let them go out into the fields and watch the home fires burning".

There is somewhere in the Bible a passage: "When that

187

time shall come, flee to the mountains, the hour of your redemption is nigh." The time had come. The evil which had clouded the 'thirties had burst into a storm. My redemption had come not on a mountain, but in a small berth in the capitalist ship, just as it was beginning to sink.

The money left me by my father and by my mother, the latter now released to my use, enabled me to buy a small property at Little Eversden, seven miles from Cambridge. Of this village A. C. Benson wrote: "I think life should be lived more in such places. I was very happy there for an hour, in its quiet lanes and orchard ends." My purchase was of an orchard, a meadow bounded by a stream, a field, nine acres in all, a row of barns, and a thatched cottage of six rooms, on the windows of which French prisoners during the Napoleonic wars had scratched loving epigrams about the farmer's daughters. Here I intended to grow food, which was of use to my fellow humans and harmed nobody. But I wanted to do it in as civilised a fashion as possible. I built on a spacious drawing-room of classical proportions, the walls divided by pilasters and the ceiling curved.

In spite of the fact that as a result of the last decade I had now more or less repudiated the social order, I immediately, with antique furniture and a few inherited pictures, set about furnishing this place as much like a gentleman's country house as possible, which shows that I had not *au fond* repudiated them at all. I must have succeeded to some extent as a village woman coming into my newly built room, looked about her and said: "Dear old place, isn't it?"

The fact that without any twinge of conscience I could set out at the beginning of a war to secure myself elegant surroundings, is due to my upbringing among people who, as I have said, had by-passed the industrial revolution, and the post-Arnold, basically Fascist English public schools. My parents had built a new house during the 1914 war, and it never occurred to them that normal activities should be suspended. An extreme old Tory said to me: "In a civilised period the non-military population should not know there's a war on." Lady Gough had been amused at the idea that "in a nice house" like her own, there should be any wartime restriction. Captain Allgood had protested when Mrs. Allgood had made some economical rearrangement of their dining-room.

Mrs. Allgood became ill early in the war. When she knew that she was going to die she went off alone, to Cornwall I think, so as to give no trouble to her friends. Had she also no greater spiritual destiny than the whining self-indulgent?

One of the themes of my books is the interweaving of good and evil in our lives. So often a good thing comes to us through a bad one. For example, I should never have gone to Dane Court if I had not become ill at Crowborough; though I absolutely repudiate the idea that evil is sent by God to chasten us. It all comes from the devil. Christ did not go about inflicting diseases on people to chasten them; He came to give them life more abundantly, with good wine at marriage feasts, adorned by the lilies of the field, and the presence of children, the jewels tumbling in the street.

This is one of the themes of *Lucinda Brayford*. Her misfortunes are inseparable from the exceptional good fortune of her circumstances. The good and evil are interwoven through the greater part of her life.

So it may not be as strange as it seems that, though I loathe war, both wars have brought me great benefits. The first gave me an immense widening of my horizons; many lifelong friends; the comradeship of men of my own age; and a healthy life, as long as one was not killed.

The second war sent me to Plumstead, my house at Little Eversden, and the vicinity of Cambridge, the town where, ever since I had driven there one summer day with Hugh Fausset, I had wanted to live. It was also within easy reach of Hugh, and at a time when I needed the reassurance of his philosophy. My own house gave me perfect satisfaction. It combined the ancient peace of an old cottage with the gratification of my own architectural impulses. I planted box hedges in addition to those already there, and roses, tobacco and night-scented stock in the flower beds outside the drawing-room windows.

A neighbour called one summer evening, when the scent of these flowers floated through the open windows and a Mozart sonata was coming from the wireless. The next morning I met her and she said: "How peaceful and charming it was in your lovely room last evening, with the music and the scent of flowers." But she had talked steadily the whole time about bus timetables. This was another of those trivial incidents which make up so much of life.

In my first autumn when I spread out the kindly fruits of the earth, apples and pears, walnuts and tomatoes in the thatched barn, I felt that at last I had arrived where I longed to be, growing my own food and with my feet on my own land.

Also I felt here, as I did not in Sussex, that I had some ties with the place where I lived. My Kirby ancestors were East Anglians, and their portraits by Gainsborough were in the Fitzwilliam Museum. A large Dutch flower painting over my fireplace, after a hundred years in Australia, had returned to East Anglia. My mother's brothers and my father's cousins had been up at the university, and it had formed part of the backcloth of my childhood.

In a pleasant cottage nearby were two women friends Miss Barraud and Miss Haines, generally called John and Bunty, who before the war had felt the need of contact with the natural world, after the excessive cerebration of Bloomsbury. During the war they worked on the land, and John published a book of her experiences. They were helpful and neighbourly and provided me with a wider range of conversation than I could find elsewhere in the village.

My housekeeper Mrs. Jakins was a splendid type of country woman, ready to tackle any job, with a complete knowledge and love of all country activities, generously stocking my garden from her own. She also had the dignity of people of her kind, who because they respect themselves, show respect to others.

Some Italian prisoners were encamped near the village. In their first year Mrs. Jakins said that she would not go to the village dance if they were invited. A year later she said that she would not go if they were *not* invited.

Sometimes Hertha came down to stay, and made damson wine, which I was very pleased to have two years later.

I now began to turn the field into a market garden and had to help me, first a young man who was waiting to be called up, and when he left, a conscientious objector who was studying law, and was an interesting as well as useful companion.

Another lasting and valued friend I made at this time was Elliott Howes, the son of an artist who had, against his own inclination, become a bank manager. Ten years before he retired he bought some acres of land at Barton, and planted them with trees. On his retirement he employed a master builder, and with himself as architect built a group of five small flats, in the tradition of almshouses, round a flagged and flowered courtyard. The gardens were laid out with orchard walks and clipped hedges, and the whole place had the classical charm of a French *pavillon*. In every way his life was and is creative, and he gave immense pleasure to his friends, all the greater for its natural simplicity.

The fall of France gave me the same feeling that travellers must have when their ship begins to heel over, probably because I could imagine what it would have been like if it had happened when I was in the trenches. A general's wife said to me: "Imagine our being kicked out of France for only 30,000 men"—the number killed or taken prisoner. If she had been one of the 30,000 she might not have thought the number so small.

Some time after the fall of France Madeline Keyes came down to luncheon. She told me that her brother Roger had been liaison officer between the British and King Leopold of the Belgians. When the latter saw that his defeat was certain he sent at once for Keyes and told him, but said that he would go on fighting for a week to enable the British to get away from Dunkirk. He made this tremendous sacrifice on our behalf, as undoubtedly he could have got better terms by immediate surrender. Yet Churchill in Parliament, to mitigate the defeat, said that King Leopold had let us down. Roger Keyes, who was then in the Commons, went up to him and in a few terse naval words gave him an estimate of his character, and left the House. Churchill called after him: "Whatever you say to me, I shall always love you, Roger."

I began to revert to my old belief that kings were preferable to politicians. The Emperor Charles had offered a generous peace in 1916. King Alfonso had suggested a United Europe about the same time. Both had been rebuffed by Lloyd George. King Edward VIII tried to save his subjects from destitution and was tipped off the throne by Baldwin. King Leopold had been loyal to his allies to the last gasp, and won the gratitude just described.

In 1942 a man from some ministry called to look at my market garden and said it was not big enough. It covered an acre but I intended to take in the whole field. I told him this, but he would not allow me to employ any help. At the same time the basic petrol ration was withdrawn, which deprived me of means of transport for my produce.

I could have applied for a special allowance, but before this a friend, who was a pilot in the Air Force, had come to see me. He had been escorting convoys, and was horrified at the cost in human life of bringing petrol to England. He could have drawn a big ration for his leave, but he would not use any, as to him a pint of petrol was a pint of blood.

A magistrate in the county, who was particularly savage in his treatment of conscientious objectors, was found to have his wine cellars stored with illicit petrol, and himself went to prison. However my friend's revelations also deterred me from asking for a special allowance. So I went up to the post office and began filling in the form obligatory on laying up a motor car. I had to give the details three times on the same piece of paper. Exasperated I said to the storekeeper: "I don't suppose you want to buy a car?" He said: "Well, I do as a matter of fact" and he came down to look at it. He said: "What d'you want for it, forty pounds?"

As the Adeneys had just sold their perfectly good Hillman for one pound and said they were lucky to get it, a grin of satisfaction spread over my non-poker face, which he saw and said: "Say thirty-five" which I did.

After the war a secondhand car like mine cost £300, and fifteen years later I saw it still buzzing merrily about the streets of Cambridge.

Having sold the motor, I shut up Plumstead and rented two rooms on the top floor of 1 Jesus Lane, Cambridge, a little Georgian house overlooking Sidney Sussex gardens. I secured this, as a bomb falling four doors away had frightened out the previous tenant. Someone else's evil had brought me good.

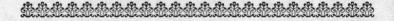

DEVILS AND ANGELS

I HAD HAD TWO YEARS of good physical life. Now began my good life of the heart and mind. One of the greatest benefits of my life, one that helped me to keep the balance of sanity, was that during the war I was able to attend, every evening in term, the services in King's Chapel. Whatever horrors were happening across the sea, whatever betrayals in our own country, here I could restore myself with the reassurance that man's true function was to employ his creative spirit, and that all that was happening outside was a horrible lacuna in human existence.

Evensong was sung at half-past five, just as the darkness was closing in, by probably the finest church choir in England. Few came to listen, often not more than half a dozen people, and generally the same people. The men and boys took an absorbed care in their singing, creating beauty for its own sake, which in the Myth is creating it for the glory of God. But I think they were also grateful to the few faithful who came to hear them, and this made a kind of charity between all who were there. The splendid glass had been removed, and the windows were filled with some black composition. Beneath the remote dim vaulting of the roof the choir was a pool of candlelight, and one felt as the early Christians might, in some centre of peace, secluded from the evil pagan world. The dean at that time was Graham Campbell, and one felt that his goodness of spirit contributed to the influence of these services.

But these beautiful psalms and anthems were sung by human beings, not disembodied spirits. The young boys although they took the greatest pride in their noble work, were still young boys. Sometimes they were amused. Once one looked up smiling and our eyes met. From then on we were conscious of each other's presence, and though this feeling of charity united all who were there, its focus for me was this boy. I had no physical feeling for him, but his beauty, and that of the music, and of the soaring chapel were fused into one quality, and when he was not present that quality was less.

One evening a psalm ended with the words: "This God is our God for ever and ever: He shall be our guide unto death." In that moment I once more accepted fully all the values of life revealed by Christ. It was not an act of the mind but of the heart. I did not know or care or think whether the Myth was factually authentic, but I knew that it was eternally true on a different plane, and that life without it was deathly.

I used this sense of peace and blessing between myself and the chorister in *Lucinda Brayford*, developing it beyond its actuality. Critics of poetic discernment gave this part of the book the highest praise, but it provoked the inevitable jeers from the oafs. It was not thought to be wholesome. A man in whom the sensitive spirit has been killed is about as wholesome as an infected tooth in which the dentist has to destroy the nerve.

Later this chorister and myself became friends in the light of common day. During the summer holidays we met in London, where Alan Lennox-Boyd entertained us, with a memorable bottle of wine, at luncheon in the House of

Commons, after which we heard a speech by Churchill, an anti-climax to Byrd and Palestrina.

I soon had many friends among the undergraduates and younger dons. There was a restaurant called "The Peacock", run by Hungarian refugees, where one could get a buffet lunch or supper, and this became a sort of club. It was in the small garden square opposite Trinity gateway, and only about three minutes' walk from my rooms. To be able daily to have one's meals at a place where one could be certain of lively and intelligent conversation was surely one of the greatest privileges one could have. One day I felt, coming away, that every corner of my brain had been exercised, and this gave me a sense of almost physical satisfaction.

In the 'thirties I had gone Left against my essential instincts. My mother had called herself a Socialist. She merely meant that she wanted a more even distribution of wealth, and the abolition of the poverty which had so horrified her in some of the cottages in Wiltshire. She would have been bewildered by the doctrinaire Socialists of today, who are more concerned with ideas than human beings. My Leftism was of the same nature as hers, and brought about by the failure of those who should have used their traditional power to affirm traditional values; but who instead had succumbed to financial interests.

In Cambridge I found tradition everywhere, in buildings, in customs and in thought. Even in the middle of a war, in spite of 18B and "alarm and despondency", men still could speak the thing they would.

Madeline Keyes's story of the King of the Belgians had helped to restore my faith in the old order, and I was verging back to the Right before I came to Jesus Lane.

At the beginning of the *Cardboard Crown* I gave a half-serious definition of the division between Right and Left, using the heraldic term "pale" for the dividing line. Roughly those on the Right were all people connected with the land, who were occupied in creative work, artists, musicians, craftsmen, clergymen, soldiers and sailors, in fact all those whose primary concern was with their occupation, not with the money it brought in. On the Left of the pale were all those whose primary concern was with money, and thought that living matter was something they could control like a machine, without reference to the vengeance of God, which in the language of the Myth awaits those who do not consider the ultimate effect of their actions.

Among those who helped me to restore my essential self was Alistair Crombie, then a Fellow of Jesus, now a Fellow of All Souls. He was a scientist but also an Aristotelian. One of his aims was to heal the divorce between science and religion, which Rabelais had prophesied would bring the doom of mankind. He was an Australian, and at that time an Anglo-Catholic, so we had other things in common besides an awareness of the virtue in the inheritance of the Western world. He took me to a lecture on the Natural Law and the Moral Law, given by some Dominicans, and this brought into my conscious mind what I had always instinctively believed, that the latter was only the former in a different key. If D. H. Lawrence could have heard this lecture he would not have written anything so crude as *Lady Chatterley's Lover*.

Another friend was the poet Walter Roberts of Clare, whose dramatic personality added colour to the Cambridge scene, and whose appreciation of its traditions enhanced my own. I was at his marriage in the County Hall. I had never been to a civil marriage before, and it seemed like a cross between a church service and buying a dog licence. When the clerk combining a priest's function with his own, said: "Wilt thou, Walter etc." Walter interrupted, asking with a certain hauteur: "Is it necessary to use the second person singular?"

I also met there for the first time George Kinnaird, though in the early 'twenties I had been to his grandparents' house,

Chatham House in St. James's Square, now the home of the Institute of Foreign Affairs. His cheerful direct manner, and conviction that life was meant to be enjoyed, were a refreshing break in the slightly enclosed atmosphere of the academic world, much as I enjoyed it.

Here is a slight guarantee of my accuracy. Once I described Mrs. Allgood to George, without mentioning her name. He said: "I knew a woman exactly like that, a Mrs. Allgood."

I wish that I could put into words the richness my life acquired from these and many other friendships, the many lively meals together, the music shared, the swimming at Sheeps Green and the walks through the lovely courts and gardens of Cambridge. The ever-present awareness that it might all be shattered in a night gave our companionship a deeper bond, and made it as Walter wrote, "a hasty garland gathered from despair". He also wrote me a poem on my fiftieth birthday, which began:

> "You have conquered, O pale Geminian
> As you yellowly slide towards death."

At Plumstead I had begun to write *Lucinda Brayford*, and now for the first time being free of the necessity to earn immediate money, I resolved to write only what I felt, and to do it as well and thoroughly as in me lay. One summer morning in 1944 George came into Sidney Sussex gardens, where I was sitting writing under a mulberry-tree, and exclaimed: "I never saw anything less like the second front."

This brings me to another side of the picture. All through the war I was fighting a rearguard action either on my own behalf, or when I could, rather like an ant trying to stop a runaway steamroller, on behalf of others.

In 1942 a journalist called Cummings wrote in the *News Chronicle*, advocating the opening of a second front: "We can now afford to lose half a million men." I wrote to him saying that in the 1914 war I had often been surprised at the alacrity with which politicians and journalists were prepared to kill thousands of young men, but then at least it was presumed to be for the benefit of our own country, not of Russia. He answered saying my remarks belonged to the street corner. I replied that I was glad of this as it showed that some sense was beginning to dawn among the people. If this man's agitation had gathered strength and forced the Government to act in that year, it would have been an irreparable disaster, and brought mourning to half a million English homes; yet the author of this would have borne no responsibility, and would have gone scot free.

A few years ago I was invited to dine with some top journalists in a Roman restaurant. One told how in 1940 he and others of his kind had sat in the National Liberal Club, deciding whether the war should be continued. He then sent a young waiter out for a cigar. In ten minutes another waiter brought a cigar, but said the youth who had been sent out had been run over in the Corso and was seriously injured. The journalist's wife gave a little laugh and said: "Well, you've got your cigar. That's the main thing." The pitiful fool evidently thought that she was behaving like a Marie Antoinette-type aristocrat. I have met a surprising number of upper middle class women who thought that brutal utterance made them grand, instead of merely repulsive. It is only chivalry that makes people grand.

During my Cambridge period, at intervals I stayed at Plumstead. During one of these visits shortly before Christmas, a petition was drawn up by Dr. Underhill, Bishop of Bath and Wells, Lord Ponsonby and other people of high character and position, to end by mutual agreement the night bombing of cities, which had now become senseless massacres. I put one of the printed forms of this petition on the village notice board, and one on my gate, saying it could be signed at my house. The notices were torn off at night. I put up another on my gate, which suffered the same fate. I then put up another inscribed: "The object of this petition is to stop the murder of women and children. Will those who think this aim undesirable, please come in and explain why, instead of tearing this notice off under cover of darkness?" No one came, and a farmer's wife in the village said: "It is a pity Mr. Boyd put up those notices. It quite spoiled the Christmas spirit." Incidentally the rector was furious with me.

Nothing angered the clergy more than pacifism, except the consistent few who were themselves pacifist. A conscientious objector was sent to prison, where the chaplain asked him in an unjudging manner what he was in for. If the boy had said: "I brained my grandmother to get £10 from under her mattress, and then went out and raped and strangled a school mistress in a wood" the chaplain would doubtless have said: "Ah well, we are only human. You must try to do better in future." But when he said he was a pacifist, Christ's priest shouted: "You filthy scum, you ought to be shot."

While in Cambridge I attended the meetings of the Peace Pledge Union and the Fellowship of Reconciliation in the Quaker Meeting House. I was not an absolute pacifist, but this was the only way I could help to check the insane ambitions and will to destroy of those in charge of our country. Lord Wavell, when ordered to make some useless theatrical manoeuvre, sent a telegram to Churchill: "A big butcher's bill is not necessarily the sign of a successful general."

The Duke of Bedford, the most prominent pacifist, and fulfilling, like Lord Lansdowne before him, the true function of the aristocrat, that of protecting the people from unscrupulous politicians, wrote an article explaining his position. He said that obviously if he were Prime Minister, he could not immediately throw up the sponge, but he would do everything he could to bring the war to an early conclusion, by propaganda, by restraint of butchery, and by helping the great number of Germans who detested Hitler to get rid of him themselves.

The Bishop of Chichester, Dr. Bell, was in Sweden during the war, and there met the German generals who were organising the plot against Hitler. They asked him to go back and persuade our Government to repeat publicly their original war aims and announce that they would stop the war if the Germans got rid of the Nazis and evacuated the occupied countries. The bishop conveyed their message to Eden who said it would be risky. Churchill scribbled on the memorandum: "Most encouraging" and a few weeks later demanded unconditional surrender, so putting every German in despair behind Hitler. The result of this was the prolonging of the war for another year or more, the slaughter of hundreds of thousands, the destroying of every traditional virtue, and of the European social structure, with the Russians menacing Western Europe from within. I adhered to the views of the Duke of Bedford, and was prepared to do my best in my position of ant before the steamroller. In self-justification I quote this excerpt from *The Times* leading article at the time of Churchill's death:

"Whatever risks were needlessly taken, whether victory could have been achieved at less cost in blood and treasure, if a different kind of victory, leaving a better world order than we now enjoy, might by other means than Churchill's have been won—these are questions that cannot yet be finally answered." In fact, a good many have already been answered in the revelations of generals and others in the daily press.

All the same, in spite of my qualified pacifism, I had the greatest admiration for those young people in whom it was complete, and who said in effect: "Murder is murder, and no political expediency can make it anything else." They were keeping alive the value of the human individual, and to me they were the salt of the earth. To obey the Holy

Ghost within you, in face of the hostility of your family, your friends and your country besotted with war, was the bravest thing a man could do. I had not the courage to do it in 1914, and I could only make up for that by befriending those who did it now.

Again I have to make qualifications. Among those I met in the Quaker Meeting House were a few intellectual Leftists. Their pacifism was more the result of ideological commitment, or whatever jargon they used, than of belief in the essential value of the human body and soul. Stalin's liquidations of a million peasants did not trouble them.

Kingsley Martin came to address the Union. He seemed to me sterile, negative and fretful. A little later a naval captain also addressed the Union. He said: "You say this is a war for Christianity, yet you use the most abominable means to prosecute it." One felt that the whole hall, filled with some of the best and most intelligent young men in England, endorsed his statement.

A cousin, the last à Beckett of the English branch, and a retired colonel, came to stay with me at Plumstead. He too felt as the naval captain in the Union. There was a filthy propaganda film, in which men of his type, at first protesting, were gradually brought to admit that we must roast women and children to death in the cause of civilisation. All this gave a further impetus to my movement to the Right of the Pale.

Someone told me of the horrors of the bombing of Hamburg, the corpses hanging from the telegraph wires, the women driven mad, shrieking in the streets. My informant said we were going to reproduce these scenes in Berlin and in all the cities of Germany.

Again the ant in the path of the steamroller, I wrote to the Archbishop of Canterbury, William Temple, asking him to warn the Government that if they used these means of warfare, he would withdraw the Church's support for the war.

He replied that he supposed I was a pacifist, which I should know he thought quite wrong, and that when the war was over we "must find some way of showing justice and mercy" but in the meantime "the one wrong thing was to fight the war ineffectually".

This was a typical "Establishment" reply. One did not consider basic values, only group labels. I was a pacifist, that ruled me out. The staggering thing was that they had no idea of how they were going to drag out justice and mercy from their welter of destruction when it was over. No responsible man creates a chaos greater than his capacity to restore order. Yet this is what they were all doing, and only a few responsible generals like Lord Wavell were trying not to do.

I replied to the archbishop that I had not written as a pacifist, but only to ask him not to descend below the standard of Christian chivalry. This must have touched some chord in his casuistic brain, silent since he was Nature's priest, if he ever was. He replied at length, writing with a fountain pen in a train, and saying that the Church and State were the same people acting in different capacities. I might have replied that the Holy Family flying into Egypt, all there was of the Church at that time, and Herod who was trying to slaughter them, were the same people acting in different capacities. However I wrote that this made the witness of the martyrs meaningless, as they could have thrown their incense to Caesar in their capacity as citizens, for the sake of national unity. I had referred him to the Gospels, but in reply to this he referred me to Dr. Niebuhr of New York, who apparently had formed his mind. I still have his letters, stored away somewhere in Melbourne or Cambridge.

It is a coincidence that when the archbishop appointed a

day of prayer for the war, with special epistles and gospels, they chose the Sunday on which the proper liturgical gospel was that of the rendering to Caesar of the things that are Caesar's, so that in this year its message was suppressed.

It is only fair to mention one thing in the archbishop's favour. In the report on the bombing of Dresden, published a year or two ago in English newspapers, in which the responsibility for this is placed on Churchill alone, who thought it would impress Stalin, it is also admitted that Archibald Sinclair, now Lord Thurso, concealed from the archbishops the nature of the bombing. In one of Dr. Temple's three letters to me he stated: "The Air Minister assures me that only military objectives are aimed at." The posters however boasted of the plastering of residential areas.

It may be objected that I am supposed to be writing an autobiography, not a political commentary, but these high matters affected my whole attitude to life, so they are relevant. They are part of my human evidence.

I was also during this period trying to save myself from the steamroller. I was just within the age at which men had to register for national service, which I did at the Cambridge Labour Exchange. As I said that I had a market garden, but they had taken away my labour, they ordered me to report every day in Cambridge at 7.30 a.m. as a farm labourer. I was still at Plumstead but had sold the motor. When I protested that I should be allowed a few weeks to find suitable work, the privilege allowed to conscientious object-ors, the clerk having become overnight a national service officer, with extraordinary powers over human lives, replied: "That's the fault of democracy. If it weren't for democracy, we'd soon have 'em roped in."

At this the spirit of Mrs. Allgood descended on me, and I told him that he was illiterate and incompetent and that I would get him dismissed. I had no idea of how I was to accomplish this, but the man looked slightly unnerved, and now, not unnaturally, had his knife into me. A year of wrangling passed. I made appeals to a board of Cambridge citizens, who said they had to get labour to run their businesses. I saw girls and women come weeping out of their rooms, having been ordered away from their homes. At last it looked as if I would be forced into some impossible menial job. I said to the clerk: "Surely there is a list of the work I would be allowed to do." He said: "It's a secret government document. You find a job and I'll tell you whether you can take it." A friend advised me to go off to a school near Bristol where there was a job going, and where I should be under another Labour Exchange. I did this, but I wrote to Lord Bruce, the Australian High Commissioner, asking him to intervene on my behalf. I also wrote to Maie Casey, whose husband was then Governor of Bengal. I did not like to ask for help from a woman, but I said I would be grateful if she would jog Bruce into action. She very kindly replied that she would do so, and reminded me that twenty years earlier she had painted a portrait of me called "Murderer Resting", as for some reason I was sitting in an armchair holding a hatchet. When I returned to Australia she gave me this portrait.

The school near Bristol was owned and run by a pacifist lady with Quaker associations. It was in a large and ancient country house, something like a castle, commanding magnificent views. My work seemed to be mostly taking small boys to the Bristol zoo, and playing "Up Jenkins" with them in the evening. Once I took three or four to Tintern Abbey, and nearly drowned one in the Severn on the way back. It was March, so we had to go into a field, take off his clothes, and cover him with straw from a stack, so that he would not get pneumonia. I was still inclined to use military language, and kept saying that various cabinet ministers should be shot, for which I was reproved by the headmistress.

After a month I judged it safe to return to Cambridge. I

think the headmistress, though perfectly courteous, was glad to be rid of me, but my charges gave me an affectionate farewell.

Meanwhile Lord Bruce had put my case before the Director of Manpower, who sent to Cambridge for my dossier. In a funk they sent back a made-up story, which the Director sent to Bruce, from whose secretary I had a cold note informing me of my black record.

I wrote back equally coldly stating the facts, and saying: "You may care to put this before the Director of Manpower to justify your intervention." I did not expect him to, but he did. A few weeks later I went into a bar, and asking the barman for some beer, found I was addressing the "national service officer", who had been transferred to this more useful occupation. I heard no more from the Labour Exchange and was free to continue my Cambridge life and *Lucinda Brayford*. This book earned a considerable sum of dollars at a time when Britain badly needed them, so I was of more service writing it than scrubbing a hospital floor. I discovered that a great number of people in Cambridge were delighted at the sacking of my persecutor, who had been drunk with self-importance.

After the war an "upper middle class" woman trying to make me sound a respectable member of the Establishment, asked me: "What was the name of that school where you did your national service?"

At the beginning of the war there were posters all over the country: "Freedom is in peril, defend it with all your might." When the Labour Exchanges got into their stride these notices disappeared, and it would have been creating alarm and despondency to display one. The only attempt of which I know to protect a citizen, apart from Lord Bruce's, was that of the Bishop of S. Alban's when a woman in his diocese was ordered into a factory where they made rubber contraceptives. This and the Bishop of London's expressed wish to dance round a burning pyre of these things, justifies the writer in a recent book of Roman Catholic essays who said: "If contraceptives, instead of an atom bomb, had been dropped on Hiroshima, there would have been a scream of protest from the Vatican."

After the war a man in the Midlands was directed to leave his home and take work in another part of the country, which he refused to do. He was arrested and sentenced to prison. On receiving his sentence, he raised his hand, and cried logically: "Heil Hitler."

THE TENSION EASES

SOME UNDERGRADUATES OF KING'S founded a literary society. Every week some more or less well-known person was invited to give them a talk on a celebrated novelist. I was invited to these meetings, which I much enjoyed. Among those who spoke I only remember Arthur Koestler and Enid Starkie, who seemed to judge the merits of living French authors by their attitude during the German occupation. She also said that Anatole France was "out for good".

Arthur Koestler said that figuratively the novelist should sit at an open window with his feet in a basin of hot water, and look not only into the garden below, but to the factory chimneys beyond. He must take in everything. This idea, that the artist must not be selective, strikes at the very roots of art, and seems to me like so many modern pontifical utterances, sheer rot.

Another maxim of this kind is that "the artist must express the spirit of his age". This simply means that he must express someone else's spirit, instead of his own. On the contrary he must express the Holy Ghost within himself, and if what he expresses is good and true, and has something of the eternal, it will contribute to the spirit of his age.

Most of the greatest art was achieved in Europe in periods

of appalling social evil. The artist's function is to reveal the true and the beautiful, and to increase man's understanding, which, as Blake says, admits him to Heaven. To ignore this is to confuse the function of the artist with that of the politician.

John Hayward attended these meetings, and I walked away from the Koestler lecture beside his chair. He said: "I asked him a question, but he only gave me a Central European sneer." John Hayward was very entertaining, but I have a grudge against him, as any occasional penetrating criticism, or vivid image from myself, was in the minutes attributed to him owing to his more dominating personality. At the end of an evening he left the impression that he had made all the *bons mots*.

After the war he shared a flat in Chelsea with T. S. Eliot. From there he paid a visit to Graham Greene. At bedtime he needed the services of a valet, and Greene himself performing them, said: "You are being put to bed by the greatest living novelist." John Hayward replied: "As I am put to bed every night by the greatest living poet, I am not impressed."

Robert Nichols, poet of the 1914 war, also attended these meetings, but having lived in a valley in Provence between the wars, he had not lost the idiom and attitude of the 1914 subaltern. Leaving one night, after a talk on Proust or Ronald Firbank, he said to the rather precious company: "Cheerio chaps! Had a champion evening."

Another society whose meetings I attended was one which had a lecture every term on some ecclesiological subject. Once D. L. Murray, the editor of the *Times Literary Supplement*, came up and gave them a learned address. He risked his life to do this, as he lived south of London, where the bombing had begun again, and he had to pass through it coming and going. The dons were very polite and appreciative introducing him and thanking him for his talk, but apart from this they completely ignored him.

Although only a guest myself, I tried to make up for this, and had a lively and interesting talk with him. I also had a slightly corrupt motive in my kindness, as I thought that if he remembered me, my next book might receive careful attention, but when it came out he had resigned. A few years ago this good, learned, and talented man took his own life, in despair at the condition of the world. All his values appeared, outside of himself, to have collapsed.

The world was now approaching this condition, as the war was drawing to its disastrous close. The Russians were streaming over the Oder into Western Europe, and Eisenhower was ordered to halt his advance to let them first into Berlin. I had the same sensations as at Munich and at the fall of France. On the counter of my bank was a money-box for subscriptions to a monument to Roosevelt. I could barely restrain myself from flinging it through the plate glass window.

In a newspaper, when our Pyrrhic victory was achieved, appeared a cartoon of a soldier struggling out of a trench with the wreath of victory, and saying, as he handed it to a politician: "Here, don't lose it this time." It had already been lost in advance at Yalta, and the recompense for all the blood, tears, toil and sweat was a situation as perilous as that of 1939.

Berlin was divided between the four allies, but surrounded by Russian-occupied territory. A child of ten, faced with such an arrangement, would have said: "There's no way in for me." But this deduction was beyond the reasoning faculties of the great statesmen who were guiding the destinies of nations. Archbishop Temple had died before this happened, and so was spared the necessity of finding some way of showing justice and mercy. In Eastern Germany this task was left to Stalin.

During that last terrible fortnight, when a second generation was being betrayed, and its stupendous sacrifice deprived of meaning, I was back at Plumstead, writing the final chapters of *Lucinda*. If that chapter is full of bitterness, this is the reason for it. And yet the last scene, where Lucinda after all her loss and grief can still believe that the future will be better for mankind, shows that I did not despair. I doubt if I could write with such simple faith today.

My passionate Cambridge life had ended. During those years I was more alive than at any time since my adolescence. I had friendships of the heart and mind. I was full of hatred for the evil in mankind, and of love for the good, and these two passions were resolved in illuminated moments in King's. My book *Lucinda*, whatever its faults, is, I am certain, my best book, as it reflects the heightened condition of my life as I wrote it.

I finished it four years after I began, on the day the war ended. The way it had ended, together with this last effort, reduced me to complete exhaustion of spirit. I went to bed and lay supine for three days. The last time I had fallen into this condition was the night I parted from Roger, when Hitler was marching into Austria.

Now the dread of the 'thirties had become the reality of the 'forties, and had passed, leaving new evils.

Wilfred Owen, changing the Myth to match our conditions, tells how the angel called to Abraham out of Heaven:

> " 'Offer the Ram of Pride, instead of him.'
> But the old man would not so, and slew his son,
> And half the seed of Europe, one by one."

RECOGNITION

Soon after the war ended I took other rooms in Cambridge in the house of a Roman Catholic priest, an Etonian, a convert and an Oratorian. He was Father, later Monsignor Humphrey Johnson, and was reported to be very rich. I imagined that I would be entering a house of renascence luxury, with gilded baroque thrones, crimson brocade, glimpses of champagne bottles, and a faint smell of incense and good cigars. Instead it was all brown linoleum and photographs in Oxford frames.

Father Johnson's fortune had been made by his father from barbed wire, and he had a corresponding mentality, in that he took extreme precautions against burglary. Though far from ill-natured, he was delighted when the next-door neighbour's bicycle was stolen from his basement, as it justified his attitude.

Once I went on a bicycling holiday in Norfolk, and lost the Yale key of the front door in some muddy lane, a hundred miles away. On my return I said: "I'm awfully sorry, Father, but I've lost the front door key somewhere in Norfolk." He went pale, pondered a while, and then said to calm my perturbation, which he imagined equal to his own:

"Well, I don't suppose that whoever finds it, will actually know that it belongs to this house."

He was a considerable anthropologist. The vicar of an important church in Cambridge, a pleasant and courteous man, often called to ask him for information on the subject. The housekeeper inexplicably said: "Why does he keep coming here? Is he being converted? We don't want people of that sort in the Church."

Father Johnson also had a better understanding of Europe than most members of parliament and saw beyond the Government's *ad hoc* policies.

Alan Shadwick who had been working on the land, became one of Father Johnson's tenants, and we often had our evening meal together, gossiping cheerfully and discussing life and liturgy. He later became assistant editor of the *Church Times*, and a companion of my travels. The pattern of my Cambridge life was much the same, but more *andante*. It had pleasures but not joys, and they were not against a background of pity and terror. Life was no longer Walter's "hasty garland".

One of my friends, Quinton Geering of Jesus, recently graduated, became engaged, and was married at the County Hall. I was standing beside Jill, his bride, when the clerk came round asking for details of her parentage, including her father's occupation. She turned to me and asked: "What is Daddy?"

I said: "I don't know. He's a land-owner, I suppose." The clerk said: "Poof! Anyone can be that." I said: "Well he's a country squire." He had never heard of this species. Remembering the legal term for a man who lived on his revenues, I said: "Well, he's a gentleman." This word brought an even more contemptuous reception. Then Jill said with relief: "Oh, once he sat on a Forestry Commission during the war." So her father was entered as "Forestry Commissioner".

This indicates the change that was coming over England,

that country squires who had played the major part in its history, the knights of the Middle Ages, the parliamentarians of later times, were an unknown species to a man sufficiently educated to conduct marriage ceremonies.

Relevant to this is the fact that Hertha had received a notice from the Labour Exchange addressed "Mrs." I said that she should send it back and tell them to address her properly, and that her title was not a trimming she had stuck on herself. It came from the Crown and these people were the servants of the Crown and must acknowledge it. This may sound absurd fussy snobbery, but it was nothing to do with snobbery. It was due to my awareness that the bureaucracy was deliberately blotting out all social patterns that preserved individual identity.

One sunny morning I met Quinton on the steps of the University Library, and he said: "We've nowhere to live." I said: "You can come to Plumstead if you like." So they did, and livened the place up delightfully for about a year. Christopher, their son and my godson, was within a few hours of being born there. After this they took a cottage of their own.

About this time Dents accepted *Lucinda Brayford*. I had an enthusiastic letter of appreciation from Richard Church, who invited me to luncheon at the Athenaeum. There I met Professor Andrade who had just returned from Russia. He said that the Russian women had no milk for their children, but that the Communist ruling class had food of superlative luxury. It seems obvious that revolution never relieves misery, but increases it. As soon as men achieve power they become personally ambitious, and the people of the world are pawns in their rotten game.

Here this Italian story may be relevant. When Italy was founded, the Italians said to God: "Please give us a fertile country." God said "Certainly" and there it was. The Italians then said: "Please give us beautiful women." God said "Certainly" and there they were. The Italians said: "Oh, how marvellous! Thank you very much indeed." They then said: "Please give us a good government." God looked very worried, and said regretfully: "It is not possible." History and the present condition of humanity, living in dread of extinction, confirm that this is true, not only of Italy, but of every country in the world.

If a prime minister or foreign secretary had normal moral intelligence, he would consider his own advantage and importance as nothing, when faced with the appalling international problem of today. When he arrived at one of these conferences to decide our fates, instead of attending banquets, he would retire early to his room, and read some book of wisdom, knowing that if he could solve this problem, his supreme achievement would be all the reward he would ask, and in the language of the Myth he would offer it to God. But they prefer their photographs in the newspapers.

A month after I had lunched with Richard Church I had a letter from Dents, saying they would not publish *Lucinda* after all. Seeing that it ridiculed savagely the Establishment, the great war leaders, the bishops, the business men, in fact everything except the landed gentry, the creative artist and the Christian religion, all in decline at the moment, I was not surprised. Noël Adeney said that the real reason they refused it was because one character chose his servants for their beauty instead of their domestic efficiency.

Richard Church was very angry at this *volte-face* and recommended the book to Dennis Cohen of the Cresset Press, to whom he advised me to send it. Cohen did not care for it much and asked the opinion of John Hayward, who told him that he would be mad not to take it. I went to see Hayward in his rooms at Merton Hall, the Rothschilds' house in Cambridge, and together we arrived at the title.

John Hayward was also English adviser to Scribners of New York. In this year he recommended to them both

Lucinda and *Animal Farm*, which they refused. When published in America both these books were Literary Guild choices, which meant an immediate huge profit for the publisher. This gave him a grim negative satisfaction.

In the year *Lucinda* was published a leading newspaper instituted a prize for the best book of the year. The committee appointed by the ennobled proprietor chose *Lucinda*. He rejected their choice and appointed another committee, which also chose my book. He arbitrarily picked the winner himself. His refusal was not surprising as the villain of the book was an ennobled newspaper proprietor who had begun his career by selling dirty postcards. A Canadian whom I knew in the Air Force told me that once he had gone to Lord Beaverbrook for a job, having left his employment as waiter on a train because he was expected to sell dirty postcards. Lord Beaverbrook said: "I would have done it." So I thought my fictional portrait of one of his kind fair enough.

I was not sorry at this refusal, as I would have felt humiliated at receiving, amid much publicity, a cheque from a man whose species was anathema to me, and it saved me from the odium of declining it.

I still had my rooms at Father Johnson's house in St. Peter's Terrace, so I let Plumstead to another young couple, a research fellow and his wife. I kept the drawing-room, which could be entered separately, so that I could go out and do a day's gardening occasionally.

Once when I was leaving to return to Cambridge my tenants said: "Won't you stay to tea? We have a friend coming." The friend turned out to be Bertrand Russell, and I had an hour or two of the best conversation I have ever heard. In spite of his views its matter was traditional. He told me that his grandfather had dined with Prince Charles Edward's widow, which put him into my backcloth. He played with the ideas of the Myth, and said that though angels were of higher order than we, so also were the devils, like wicked dukes.

He said that his younger son Conrad began to take part in philosophical discussions about as soon as he left the cradle. But once, when he was about two, some French people came to luncheon, and the conversation was in their language. He looked bewildered for a moment and then burst into screams of rage.

Bertrand Russell also said that he hated the Roman Catholic Church, and when I took an argument, quite logically, beyond the material world, his eyes clouded. He acknowledged the validity of the logic, but it led into a region he had forsworn. It seems incredible that this man who already was whitehaired, and who had in addition to his unique intellectual qualities a deep concern for the happiness and the survival of humanity, should fifteen years later, because of this concern, have spent a week in prison.

After a few weeks I was again at Plumstead, when my tenants said: "Bertrand Russell is coming. Won't you stay to tea?" I said I jolly well would.

This time another guest was there, a woman who talked the whole time of complaints of the spine, while the best talker I had met, numbed by the mechanical rattle of her words, sat silent in the corner. If any of these monologists should read this page, I beg them to consider that after the first five minutes they have emptied their brains, and that after that their noise is simply that of a motor engine, left on by accident in the garage, and pulling nothing.

Once Bertrand Russell crossed the room and spoke to me at a meeting in Cambridge. Our conversation was just becoming interesting, when a woman, who did not even know him, thrust herself between us and said: "Oh, Lord Russell, I feel I must speak to you." With the self-protecting technique of the famous he drifted away, leaving me with the lady. I only once heard his voice again, and that was from the wireless.

My tenants, although their minds were highly civilised, domestically were the advance guard of the beatniks. Their children were not house-trained, and tore the wallpaper from the bedroom walls. The wife had advanced ideas about the pernicious effect of the chemicals in soap, and would not allow it to be used in the house, which every time I went there, appeared to be in a further state of decay. I said that I wanted it back by Christmas, and the wife went weeping to a neighbour saying what a heartless brute I was. When they did leave, it cost me more to restore it than the amount they had paid for their eight months' rent.

When I pointed this out to my tenant, he replied that everything wore out, and one would not expect a house to be exempt from this universal law. The part of the house they had occupied had stood for four hundred years. Surely it was over-accelerating the natural process to wreck it in eight months. But this corresponds with the ideas of the intellectual delinquents of today. Our spiritual home, built over two thousand years with marble from Athens and rock from Galilee, they are trying to wreck in a generation.

I thought Mrs. Jakins would never return to me, and tentatively I asked her to come and look at the house. Her eyes gleamed at the challenge of a sixteenth of an inch of black grease covering the kitchen floor, and she attacked it with gusto.

My release from the tenants was brought about by the illness of Lady Russell, who had to go to a nursing home, and they went to look after her husband. Again my good came through someone else's evil. During this time I was listening to a "Brains Trust" programme on the wireless, when a question was asked as to where old people should live. I heard Bertrand Russell's precise voice become wistful and say: "I think old people should live in hotels."

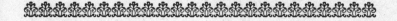

THE REMOTE BACKCLOTH

BY 1946 I HAD NOT BEEN OUT OF ENGLAND for eight years. The Continent was still difficult, so I decided to make an excursion into the backcloth and went to Ireland. I had luncheon on the train to Holyhead. Shortly after this meal, on the steamer, as the sea looked rough, I thought I would have a cup of tea before sailing, and asked a steward to bring it. He did so, and put down beside it a grilled steak, as much as my whole week's meat ration for the last six years. This was like the olive twig in the beak of the returning dove, indicating that a world of plenty still existed.

At dinner in the hotel in Dublin, I foolishly ate the first two courses of soup and fish, and by then my dwindled war-time stomach was full. I had to sit gazing impotently at turkeys, sirloins of beef, ice puddings, and every kind of rich food, like a eunuch in a harem.

My map showed a railway line to Killala, but when at the station I asked for a ticket to the home of my fathers, I was told that the line had been pulled up, which put it all further into the backcloth. So I took a ticket to Castlebar, where also some of the family had lived. There were several tombstones with our name, and eulogies of the departed. Of William, the doctor whom I have mentioned, it was said that among other merits he was "generous without improvidence", a virtue I wish I had inherited.

A quarter of a mile out of the town was the house where he had lived, not much bigger than a farmhouse, but built in the style of a palace, with the lower floor a semi-basement, to allow branching steps to the *piano nobile*. It must have seemed pretentious two hundred years ago, but as so often happens, the pretentiousness of another century is delightful in our own. There was a loch below the house in which was a "Boyd Island". The place was now a farm, and I talked to the owner while he was milking his cows. I thought that it might be nice to live here, but there was a lunatic asylum at the gate, which was only about a hundred yards from the house.

My family had left these parts a century earlier, yet in the few days I was there, I was asked twice to tea in a pleasant country house, once to tea with the vicar, while a local land-owner, a distant kinsman, who met me outside the church, asked me to dine.

He was an Etonian brigadier, and like Father Johnson, far on the other side of the pale from the public school stockbroker. He had lost much of his property after "the troubles" but was determined not to give in. He had glasshouses from which he hoped to keep the place going, and he still kept his own pack of hounds. He was an interesting talker and I admired very much the fight he was putting up.

During the evening he mentioned that one of his relatives, a peer in the same county, had gone to England to offer his services to the War Office, which had not accepted them. He had then returned and spent the war years on his estate. For this my host would no longer meet him. Being sharply reminded that my "subversive" views are apt to cause social inconvenience, I thought: "Oh Lord, what have I let myself in for now?" My host said: "You don't agree with me?" But he discussed the point in a perfectly friendly manner.

Not long after this I was dining with George in London. His parents, Lord and Lady Kinnaird were there, and also his brother-in-law Hugh Gough, now Archbishop of Sydney. After dinner I testified against the Church's endorsement of night bombing, and again my attitude was accepted without offence. Hugh Gough said that when the "Christian Commandos" conducted their mission in London, the first question they were asked in every pub, mostly by ex-soldiers, was: "Why did the Church support the war?" He admitted that it was difficult to answer. A friend came up to Cambridge in a railway carriage where there were six soldiers, who were laughing disgustedly at the Church's attitude to the war. It is now reported, twenty-one years later, that the Bishop of Portsmouth intends to dedicate the new nave of his cathedral to "D Day". This seems as appropriate as naming a battleship "St. Theresa of the Little Flower".

Hugh Fausset at the outbreak of war was visiting a rich businessman. In the evening, while his host was in the garden, he was giving to his wife and sons a dispassionate analysis of the causes of the war, which involved some criticism of Mr. Baldwin. His host who had been lurking outside the windows, came storming into the room, saying he would not have his sons corrupted.

These three stories are examples of what has formed my prejudices. But I must admit that there is evidence from the opposite direction. An earl's son, hearing that a Labour M.P. was being entertained to luncheon in his club, went round and kicked him down the steps. "Aristocrats" of this kind, the same sort who smash college windows, should be sent to clean out the pigsties, if they are capable of doing it without injuring the pigs.

I heard nothing more of the brigadier after this evening as his guest, until a few months ago, nineteen years later, when I met some Irish people at a party in Rome. I said I had been to County Mayo, and they asked me if I knew this man. I said that he was about the only person in Ireland I did know. I was sorry to be told that an increase in rates had finally defeated him, and that he had retired to England.

On the way to Killala I stopped at a vicarage to ask if I might see the church. The door was opened by a hall boy in white livery, but rather grubby. I was shown into an eerie drawing-room, like a Rackham illustration for a fairy tale. The vicar came in, wearing conventional black clerical attire, but with white tennis shoes and a dark unshaven chin. This was the sort of thing I expected to find in Ireland, but met it nowhere else. Here too I was invited to tea.

When I arrived at Killala I went to the deanery, to ask if I might see the registers. Dean Ashton asked me where I was staying. When I said in an hotel, he said: "You must stay here." I had arrived in County Mayo quite unknown, I had been there six days, and now had received the same number of invitations.

It may have been this that gave me a feeling of belonging to this neighbourhood, and it may have had nothing to do with my blood; but I certainly had the feeling, and even one of familiarity in the countryside.

I went to see Crosspatrick House. The dean advised me not to call there, as the owner was ill, so I walked up the drive and looked at it from a hundred yards away. It was a small eighteenth century manor-house, and again I thought it would be a nice place to live, but here there was a cemetery at the gates. In it was a curious statue of a man who looked like a sailor, which the dean said had something to do with our family.

He and Mrs. Ashton were extremely kind, bringing out old maps and telling me all they could about the neighbourhood. One of my father's great-grandmothers had been a Knox of Castlereagh, and the dean told me that when he first saw me standing in the hall, he thought I was a Knox. This family had diminished during the last half-century, and as each one died, they merely took out the body and locked the bedroom door. When the final tidying up came, wardrobes were discovered to be full of dusty uniforms of the 'seventies, and mildewed ball-dresses of the 'eighties, and chests of drawers packed with shirts and underpants of the 'nineties.

The dean's story of these kinsmen weakened my desire to live in County Mayo, not because of their bad housekeeping, but because he also told me that they had a rent-roll of £18,000 a year, skimmed off the Irish peasants. A Protestant minority, they occupied the old churches of this Catholic country, and I had the feeling that we had never had any right to be there. At least the Knoxes appear to have spent their money in Ireland, unlike the fourth Earl of Bristol, who had himself consecrated Bishop of Derry, with a revenue of £20,000 a year, and then went off to Naples where he spent it in debauchery. The "Bristol" hotels on the Continent are named after this right reverend roué.

From Killala I went to Westport, where the sudden access of plentiful calories at last took effect, and I fell into a coma which lasted thirty-six hours, but fortunately recovered just in time to catch the train back to Dublin, and the boat to England.

In the winter of 1946-7 I began to pine for the sun, and wrote to the P. and O. Company to put my name on the list for a passage to Australia. It was then necessary to do this a year in advance. Robert Lindsay, in whom the family artistry was confined to appreciation and discriminating taste, wrote advising me to weigh well all the advantages and otherwise of a return. I replied that if I did feel cut off from former friends and interests I had only to think of a thatched cottage in midwinter, with icicles a foot long hanging from the eaves, and I would be perfectly contented.

During the summer I forgot about my application, and in the autumn went down to see Jean and Peter at Fontcreuse, where they had returned from partial captivity in the

Ardêche, though Jean had spent a week in a concentration camp. Fontcreuse had been the headquarters of the Gestapo, who had pulled down some old tapestries, but had improved the plumbing.

The scarcity and price of food were great. A poor meal in a wayside restaurant cost £2 a head, equal to about £6 today. I had a ration card from the local authority, and although Peter and Jean were hospitable to the limits of their resources, I have never been so hungry in my life, and for that fortnight I used to go into the orchard and pick up almonds.

When Hitler moved into Southern France, they stayed up all night burying wine in the garden, and planting onions over it. On their return this wine was in perfect condition, but they gave it to American soldiers in gratitude for their liberation.

In the next winter the twelve-inch icicles really were hanging from the thatch eaves, and I wrote again to the P. and O. for a berth.

An additional motive for my wanting to go to Australia was that any improvements I made at Plumstead were only for myself. I would rather have spent my energy on planting trees and selecting furniture that could go on to a nephew.

This became a possibility when I heard that my cousin, the thirteenth William, might lease or sell me the Grange, my mother's childhood home, which I have mentioned earlier. He lived in Melbourne, and owing to a disastrous will, could not maintain two houses. An uncle, becoming confused in his mind in his last fortnight on earth, went to a lawyer (not his own, who refused his instructions) and made a will leaving his large inherited fortune to charities which he picked at random out of the telephone book, and for which the generic term is "Cats' Homes". This necessitated selling valuable, jointly held city property, which dealt a shattering blow to the family fortunes.

My cousin contested this will, which was deplored by

genteel and parsimonious relatives who were not affected by it. They had the same sense of propriety as the friend who thought it was better to let a man break his neck than to tell someone to whom one had not been introduced to control her dog. My cousin lost the case, but the sympathies of the judge were clearly shown when he ordered the defendants to pay the costs.

My neighbour Mrs. Vere Webster, who had written an amusing children's tale called *Spindle Spider* and who is a talented painter, had a son, Colin, who had been invalided out of the navy after an attack of rheumatic fever. The doctor said that he should be in a warm climate, and it was arranged that he should accompany me to Australia. This was fortunate as he lost all trace of his illness, and at thirty was playing Rugby football.

In the spring of 1948 Alan Shadwick, Colin and myself went for a holiday in the Touraine. This was the first of a number of delightful holidays I spent with Alan on the Continent. It was also the first time that Colin had been in France, and our trip was full of amusement and interest. On a holiday with Alan always one or two phrases provided a motif. The only one I remember on this occasion was when, after drinking rather much Vouvray at luncheon, we climbed on a hot afternoon up the staircase at Chambord, and he described our condition as "château bottled".

My last months at Plumstead were taken up with preparations for departure. Only two pictures remain vividly in my mind from this period. One is of a concert in King's Hall, when the choir sang Purcell's *Dido and Aeneas*. In the interval, accompanied by the pleasant babel of cultivated voices, floating on the evening air, there was supper on the lawn.

The other was of a truculent young "Leftist" passing the chapel and saying to his companion: "They ought to pull these places down and build factories."

AI NOSTRI MONTI

I ARRIVED IN MELBOURNE in the third week of August. It is a curious fact of my life that most of my major changes have occurred within a few days of the twenty-fifth of this month. I feel that I ought to describe my sensations on returning to the country of my youth after twenty-seven years' absence, but I cannot remember what they were. I was full of curiosity and perhaps a little bewildered by meeting suddenly so many relatives, some of whom I had never seen before, while I had met others in Europe since I left.

My first impression was one of great vitality in the people, and a general feeling of optimism and appetite for life. After eight years of rationing both of food and clothes, the well-covered bones and bodies and the animated eyes of the people made a vivid impact.

We went to the theatre, and everyone was in evening clothes, some of the men in white ties and tails, which I had not seen for nearly a decade.

My cousin Brenda Gurner drove me out to see Aunt Lily, and on the way we passed below Como, the large mansion of the Armytage family. I asked: "What has happened to Como? Is it flats or something?" Brenda said: "Oh no. The Armytages are still there." These were three ladies I had

226

known when I was ten, and had played in their orange groves. I had thought that they were then old ladies, and I had the same feeling as if she had said: "King William IV is still on the throne." When I met the Misses Armytage I found that they were only about the same age as myself. The distances seemed longer than I remembered, so I had to make readjustments of proportion in space as well as time.

On my first evening I dined with William, whom I had never seen before, but whom I recognised as an à Beckett when I saw him in Collins Street on the way to the hotel. He warned me that the Grange was in a shocking condition, and that he would not be offended if I refused to consider it as a possible house.

The next day Colin and I went up to look at it. William had not exaggerated. While he had been at the war the place had been "looked after" by a caretaker, who one imagined must have encouraged the processes of ruin. There were men working on it, but even so I judged the restoration to be beyond my capacity. However, Colin was enthusiastic about it, and I felt that with such keen moral support all things would be possible. I first bought a life tenancy, and then a year or two later, finding I was pouring so much money into the place, I asked to be allowed to buy the freehold. We waited for the furniture to arrive from England before moving in.

When it arrived I was informed that I must report at the Customs Office at 9.30 on a Thursday morning, which I did. I was told at Australia House, before I left England, that any furniture over a hundred years old was admitted duty free, and a friend had a letter stating the same thing in writing. Nearly everything I brought was over a hundred years old, and had the seal of the Antique Dealers' Association. At the Customs Office I was told I must pay £600. I quoted my informant at Australia House. The Customs man said: "That's right, there's no duty, but there's primage and sales tax." The man then turned to the clerk from the shipping office and like a sadistic schoolmaster, bullied him for forty minutes about a mistake of twopence, which he affected to find in his statement. After this he turned again to me and said: "You may go, Mr. Boyd." This performance so angered me that I found it hard not to say: "You can go to hell, and I shall go back to England."

However, instead of cutting off my nose in this fashion, I apologised to the shipping clerk for being the occasion of his disgusting experience, and wrote to Chifley who was then both Prime Minister and Minister of Customs. He replied that he could not alter the regulations because Australia House had made a mistake, but he let me off £250 on three family portraits which I was not at liberty to sell, and on a valuable painting which had already been in Australia.

Here was an evil of the deified state. If one had a written guarantee from a business firm, they would have to stand by it. My stay in Australia was punctuated by one or two such disagreeable incidents. Another was when I called at the goods platform of Dandenong station to collect the wine, and asked: "Are there any boxes here for me?" The clerk said there were not. I called again three days later and received the same answer. I was puzzled as I knew they had been sent. Turning to leave I saw them, with "Boyd, Dandenong" painted in large black letters. I said: "There they are."

The man replied: "Those aren't boxes, those are cases. They were here when you came before." If I had reported this, and the authorities had taken any action, there might have been a railway strike paralysing the country for three months. So, as with the Customs man, I could only, in the language of the Myth, offer it up as a mortification.

On the other hand, at the passenger platform the clerks and porters were helpful and friendly, and would keep the train waiting a minute if one was delayed at the booking office.

Also if the government officials were insolent, the burglars in Melbourne were extremely considerate. A friend, whom I shall call Mrs. Dolby, had her flat burgled. The two young men who carried out this operation thought it judicious to gag her, which they did with a shirt, but one of them reassured her saying: "It's all right, Mrs. Dolby. It's a clean shirt." They did not repudiate their common humanity, as is usual in England today, where a helpless old man or woman, having been robbed, is usually gratuitously beaten up or killed.

Though Australia was originally settled by convicts, its criminal record lags behind that of European countries. At Yarra Glen, the nearest policeman was eight miles away at Lilydale, with two townships in between, and I do not remember hearing of a local crime in all the time we lived there. I have recently learnt that 50,000 convicts were sent to Australia during the seventy years of transportation, which ended a century ago, while vast numbers of immigrants have followed since. During those same years 2,000,000 people were sentenced for crime and imprisoned in England. So unless an Englishman can identify all his thirty-two great-great-great-grandparents, he is more likely than an Australian to have convict blood. Not that it matters.

We moved into the Grange the day before the furniture arrived. There were only our beds brought from Melbourne and a few pieces of furniture surviving from my uncle's time. The electric light had not been connected, and as holding lighted candles stuck in bottles, we walked up the cold stone passage to bed, suddenly there was an appalling noise in the roof. We thought the place was haunted; but it was only possums, which had become protected, and I heard were destroying gardens and fruit-trees, even in the suburbs of Melbourne. I illegally shot two or three, once when a justice of the peace, who had stolen my fencing posts, was walking through the stable yard. I suppose it is now safe to admit this offence, and that I am unlikely to be extradited from Italy to answer for it.

The next eight months I spent largely in manual labour, and in coping with builders, decorators and bureaucrats. Before moving in I had been to see my brother Merric and his family. I imagined that by now his children would have had enough of the precarious life of the artist, and would probably have gone into the city to work their way up into some noxious position of plutocratic power. I half hoped that they had. However, I found to my delight that they were seething with creative imagination. Arthur's work particularly impressed me, because it had what, in reference to the liturgy, I have called a "mantric" quality. It was the work of someone with age-long secretions in his blood. This is the difference between genius and talent, as the words themselves convey.

The Grange, although not a big house, was too big for me, even though I had had to pull down three rooms of which the woodwork was infested with white ants, and the cottage for the servants had been removed. However I found that by closing a door and filling up another bathroom I could turn it into two flats, one for myself and one which would house a young couple. I commissioned Arthur to paint murals round the room I was converting to my own dining-room. After eight months the house was habitable by normal standards, and I gave an afternoon party to warm the place up after its ten deserted years, and also to show off Arthur's murals.

This party taught me not to worry. A hundred people had accepted invitations, and they were all coming by road. I had been too busy to realign the months against the seasons, and although I knew intellectually that May was the equivalent of November in England, my poetic imagination could not divorce the sound of the word from visions of apple blossom, young lovers and green lawns.

The day before the party it began to rain, and I imagined

about fifty motors sinking into the mud of the paddock to be used as a car park. I was in despair, but then reasoned with myself, thinking that though it would be ghastly at the time, trying to extract fifty expensive motor cars from the mud while their bedizened owners stood watching from a leaky veranda, afterwards it would be very funny, and that I should look on the bright side—the amusement I would have recounting it.

However the rain ceased, and the party was a great success. Miss Kathleen Abbott, the friend and former governess to my uncle's family, gave me gallant support, finding caterers, florists and Italian waiters, while my aunt, widow of the twelfth William, sent up beautiful damask tablecloths, formerly at Penleigh and Wilton, to put on the trestle tables.

This party, largely a reunion of the "Old Brigade", is mentioned in *The Cardboard Crown*, including the incident when one old cousin said of another: "I hadn't seen Edie for sixty years. We had quite a lot to talk about."

My three years in Australia were spent almost entirely at the Grange, with short visits to Melbourne, where I stayed either at the Melbourne Club or the Windsor Hotel. I also frequently went down for the day. A critic wrote that I had little knowledge of Australia, and that my social range was limited. Though grotesquely untrue of my life in general, it was true of these three years, so it is difficult for me to write as much as I should of what I regard as my own country during this time.

The Caseys lived five miles away at Berwick. During a three months' strike, when there were no Sunday trains, they very kindly offered to drive Colin, after his week-ends at the Grange, back to Melbourne, where he had a job. I used to drive him over to Edrington every Sunday night after dinner, and for half an hour had lively and interesting conversations before they set out.

Once Casey said that I should go about Australia and

write of the great ventures and advances that were being made throughout the country. I replied that it was not my line, that what I did perhaps was of little political value, recording the existence of a vanishing social group, but I had to stick to it. Maie Casey said, herself putting into a chiselled sentence one of the basic principles of my life: "You can't expect a chisel to do the work of a circular saw."

So apart from a brief visit to Sydney, all I can write about Australia in these three years is of social contacts in Melbourne. With Colin, I drove to Sydney along the Prince's Highway, which, from its name, I thought would be as smooth as Bond Street; but parts of the road were corrugated, and one came upon warning notices, first: "Four miles of curves" then seven, then twelve miles of road winding through hills, with blind corners every few hundred yards. The country we traversed, beginning with the Gippsland lakes, was as beautiful as any I have ever seen. Once something happened to the motor, where the road passed through a vast area of "bush", giant forest trees and undergrowth. The silence had an extraordinary positive quality, and made vivid the tales of the terror of people lost in this density, who one felt, must either go mad or have a vision.

George Kinnaird had told me that I should look up a woman whom he had known in England, and who was perhaps the most prominent "society hostess" in Melbourne. My cousin Mary Clegg, now back in Australia, told her about me and I was invited to call on the following Thursday. On the way I looked in to see my Aunt Lily Gurner, then nearly ninety, who was going out for a drive and offered to drop me at the house of this lady, whom she knew, but had not seen for some time.

I thought that we would sit by the fire cosily chatting about George, but I found I had arrived at a charity reception, mostly of women. When I was announced, and spoke of George, my hostess said: "Oh dear Geordie, but I thought he was killed at Dunkirk." Trying another tack, I mentioned my aunt, Mrs. Gurner. She said: "Yes, I did miss her when she died." I thought of saying: "She has just left me at your door. You might catch her if you run."

I was introduced to another "leader of society" at some function where my nephew Robin was present, and who had also been introduced to her. I was expecting a few gracious words, but she said haughtily: "This is the second person called Boyd who has been introduced to me this evening." I thought, too late as usual, of a number of possible retorts. I might have said: "I knew your nephew. He used to boast how rich his father was." I told Eileen Chomley this, and her comment was: "She would only have said reverently: 'Yes he was very rich.'"

A little later I was at a dinner party at the house of Tristan Buesst, a patron of the arts, whose wife was a niece of the painter Rupert Bunny. A woman there said to me: "Why do you make us all so common?" I looked round the room full of agreeable cultivated people, and for the moment could think of no reply. The answer should have been that I do not. English reviewers have expressed surprise that I make Australians so civilised. Actually I have drawn far more deplorable English characters than Australians, but I draw my chief characters as people, not as nationals. It is true of course, that those like the two ladies I have mentioned make more impact on one's mind than the normally pleasant and polite, and it is fun to describe them. I do not give the above two as typical examples of women in the Melbourne social world. They are only a sparse sprinkling, and are rather a joke in their own groups.

The English, on the other hand, are inclined to judge people of another country by their worst specimens. This is noticeable and irritating here in Rome.

It seems to me that, in strange contrast with its valued democracy, there is an undercurrent of Fascist feeling in

Australia. In 1950 there was, and still may be, a secret association prepared to take action if things went too far to the Left. A man who belonged to it told me that if there was any trouble they were ready to "rope in every shade of pink", which meant anyone with the mildest ideas of social justice, including probably myself. When the Government introduced the Communist Party Dissolution Act which if it had been passed would have legalised intolerable suppressions of individual rights, the referendum was only defeated by a narrow majority. Also the Act would have been superfluous, as there was already ample legislation to deal with people who openly declared themselves the enemies of the State.

This Fascism even tinges social occasions. I read an account of a dinner party at Government House, Canberra. The etiquette sounded as elaborate as that of Versailles under Louis XIV. The women had to make about half-a-dozen curtsies before they escaped. I went to a ball in Melbourne which the State Governor attended. Before he arrived the floor was cleared and the drums rolled. He then entered and marched, followed by his staff and hosts, in solemn procession to a dais. It only needed a few ecclesiastical properties to make it like a funeral cortège. At dances in my youth, when the Governor appeared, he would stand beaming with the happy red face of an English country gentleman, while the band played a few bars of "God Save the King", and then shake hands amiably with his friends.

The Fascism shows itself more seriously in any people employed by the State, as ʳ v experience with the Customs revealed.

In an Australian newspaper it was recently stated that there is a group of Fascists in Sydney University. When so many of their kin have died fighting Fascism, they might as well call themselves by a name which I hesitate to write. In England there are even people who, after Auschwitz and Buchenwald, can call themselves Nazis.

At one dinner party in Melbourne I sat next to the wife of a Federal Minister, who said to me: "I do admire your brilliant family." I made modest deprecating noises, but she added: "And do you do anything?" A woman across the table said that she liked my pottery. (Nephew Guy Boyd's.)

Robert Morley was at this party, and dominated the dinner-table in a way that reminded me of John Hayward, a sort of blend of Dr. Johnson and Oscar Wilde. When we went into the drawing-room, no one else spoke, but he was very entertaining. When shortly before leaving, I tried to make an observation, he said to me: "Be quiet. You've been talking all the evening."

One day while lunching at the Melbourne Club, at a table with three or four men whom I did not know, I expressed the opinion that while it might be necessary, conscription destroyed the intelligence, self-respect and moral integrity of those who were subjected to it. I did not know until six months later that I had given great offence, or that in Melbourne one's respectability depended on one's enthusiasm for war and all military activities. Seeing that the major achievement of the war had been to establish the Communists with a stranglehold on Eastern Europe, this was strange. Brenda, sitting in the Alexandra Club, the feminine opposite number of the Melbourne, heard a woman behind her say: "Martin Boyd is just a Communist". My objection to conscription was extremely conservative, because it lumped in all the chisels with the circular saws, and took young men of finer talents away from their education at the most critical age.

Among certain types anything with which they are unfamiliar must be Communist. If I had said: "Napoleon was a usurping butcher, and the execution of Louis XVI a tragic crime", they would equally have judged me to be a Communist, as I had spoken against a famous general, and one

235

who is the hero of their type. On the other hand I heard a good deal of sense from older members of the club.

One evening I was dining with a man of my own age, then nearly sixty, and a retired judge of eighty who said: "Don't you boys wait for me." He slept with his windows barred, and a revolver by his bed, as he was afraid of the ghosts of the men he had sentenced to death.

There was a story that one of the oldest members went up to the reading-room one day after luncheon, and slept with a newspaper over his face. It was not until three days later that he was found to be dead. This was told me by a young member of the club, but I do not believe it.

When the Archbishop of Canterbury, Dr. Fisher, came to Australia, he was entertained at dinner by the club. He expressed astonishment that it was "an almost Athenaeum". I had had an acrimonious correspondence with him about his alleged Erastianism, and wondered if my name would recall it when I was presented to him. But he did not wince, and later he patted me convivially on the shoulder. It seems odd that I should have had contact with so many Archbishops of Canterbury. I had had a luncheon and a private blessing from one, a polemical correspondence with another, a correspondence with and a pat on the shoulder from another; and I was yet to be swept into the gutter from the narrow footpath of Jesus Lane, Cambridge by a fourth, though I had twice been introduced to him; but as doctors say of an unsuccessful vaccination, neither of these introductions had "taken".

I seem to be recording only slightly bizarre social occasions, but there were many others where in delightful surroundings I met my friends of thirty years ago. Particularly I remember Toorak House, the home of the Spowers family, where I had danced in my youth, and which, sixty years before that, had been Government House when my grandfather was Military Secretary. Daryl and Joan Lindsay lived twenty miles away at Mulberry Hill, their really beautiful home near Frankston. Over massive clipped hedges, they looked down to Port Phillip Bay. The house was perfect in every detail, and yet with an atmosphere of great domestic ease and comfort. They had achieved what I was trying to effect at the Grange.

I attended three or four literary gatherings in Melbourne. It seemed to me that the younger "intellectuals" thought it necessary to be Communists, and to adopt the sterile theories of logical positivism.

At one of these gatherings a woman said to me: "You have said everything you have to say in *Lucinda Brayford*. What more can you write?" This struck me as a true and highly intelligent remark, and I am sorry that I cannot recall the name of its author. But it did not disturb me, as my mind was full of the operations at the Grange. Yet it was there that I found the impetus and material for my future novels. The first chapter of *The Cardboard Crown*, in which I discover my grandmother's diaries for most of her married life, is as much fact as fiction.

For three years my life and interests were centred in this house and its surroundings, though this made my existence rather solitary. Apart from the Caseys, only one local family called. The house was comfortable and rather interesting, with paintings, furniture and tapestries of the seventeenth and eighteenth centuries, and my food and wine were good, but except to large parties it was difficult to get anyone to come to eat it. I remember with gratitude one afternoon when, having tea with my dog, I heard the silvery tones of Mrs. G. from whom I had fled at Avignon, calling in the hall: "Anyone at home?"

One woman drove a friend up, and went on to lunch by herself in the Berwick inn, refusing even to set foot in the house. This suggests that I must have a repellent personality, but I have not noticed its anti-magnetic effect elsewhere. They may have thought I was a Communist, as I believed in aristocratic government and the Divine Right of Kings.

In my grandmother's diaries I read of constant social activity in the neighbourhood, where people met at the tennis courts in Berwick, or played whist in the evening in each other's houses. But this was sixty years earlier, before the motor car, and country people had to create their own social life, and with it better friendships and a sense of community.

There were however two young people to whom apparently I was not anti-magnetic, and one of them was straight out of my backcloth. They were Patrick and Rosemary Ryan. He was a nephew of Maie Casey's, and Edrington, their place near Berwick, had been left jointly to her and her brother Rupert Ryan, a member of the Federal Parliament. Patrick's mother was Lady Rosemary Hay, a direct descendant of the last beheaded Boyd, whose son had changed his name to Hay, on inheriting his mother's title and estates. Patrick's uncle Gilbert had resumed the name of Boyd on coming into a barony of Kilmarnock, given as a sop to the family by George IV who liked to appease the Stuarts. Even Queen Victoria had an inferiority complex about them. Later I met Kilmarnock in London. For me he was the embodiment of eight hundred years of history. He lent me a slightly macabre but highly entertaining novel about a haunted room in Scotland, written by his father. I tried to get it republished, but it was not in the mood of the moment.

Patrick and Rosemary brought some more lively hours into my *andante* existence. He informed me that there was no greater crime in Melbourne than to be eccentric, which was a bad lookout for my family. One "society" girl took up sculpture, and was asked by a friend: "But surely you don't want to do it *well*?" The idea being that this might imply a need to earn money.

The Ryans were both keenly interested in the arts, and one of my pleasantest memories of the Grange is of when they came over to Sunday supper, and drove Colin down to Melbourne afterwards.

A few years ago a young woman, in the peevish and censorious tones of modern criticism, wrote an article on my "double alienation". I am not conscious of this myself as regards England and Australia, which are both Anglo-Saxon countries. My problem as regards them is no more psychological than that of, say an eighteenth century relative in County Mayo, who would have liked to spend part of the year in London, but was deterred by the expense and discomfort of the journey. My inner division, if I have one, is the age-long one of the European, between the Mediterranean and the north, the Classic and the Gothic worlds.

I was perfectly at home at the Grange, and what duality I had was satisfied by the old world interior of the house, and the external Australian landscape, so beautiful in those parts. If I could have had in the neighbourhood half a dozen of my best English friends and those Australian friends living in other States, I would never have wanted to leave.

There were times when the division of the hemispheres was healed, notably when the Chomleys came up to luncheon. As I have said, I had known them, with two or three long gaps, since the cradle, when Eileen told me that as a little girl she had been reproved for taking me out of it and jogging me too violently on the steps of Glenfern. We knew the splendours and miseries of each other's families, which largely overlapped, and almost identical conditions had given an individual flavour to our appreciations of the social world. The recipe for this was a basis of Irish Protestant Ascendancy; grandparents who had settled in Victoria before the gold rush; and a life spent for long periods in both England and Australia. In an Australian country house of the early days we were in our most congenial setting.

Our conversations were incredibly snobbish, though none of us was snobbish in personal associations; but "Melbourne Society" had an almost scientific anthropological fascination for us, and also provided us with a lot of fun.

When they complained of the inadequate status of a new governor, I said that I had heard the king was responsible for his appointment. They said: "I don't think the king understands Melbourne Society."

We agreed that it was less humiliating to have relatives who had gone down in the world, than it would be to have some who had come up. In support of this theory a friend told me that she saw one of my impoverished relatives standing with his children waiting for a country bus. She said that they looked terribly poor, but with an air of wild distinction, like the exiled princes of some savage tribe.

The Chomleys had various connections in the Irish peerage and one of their aunts had been a Marchioness of Salisbury. They were plaintively amused that this brought them no prestige in Melbourne, compared with that of rich Australian girls who had married into grand English families. We decided that in a society where money was the supreme value, a titled relative was not a status symbol unless he had been paid for in cash.

This kind of snobbery is more fun than that of today. There is probably none greater than that which the intellectual displays toward someone who is ignorant of existentialism or the latest abstract painter. I have even known a Communist intellectual to cut someone who was shabbily dressed, and one of this type described herself as belonging to the "intellectual aristocracy", in the same way that Mrs. Carruthers called herself "upper middle class". I never heard the Chomleys refer to anyone as belonging to any class. They only poked fun at them as individuals and never with any real unkindness of feeling, but rather with gratitude for the amusement they provided.

In contrast with this sort of conversation my life was largely that of a peasant, spent out of doors in clearing away the rank growth of ten years. It gave me great satisfaction to see order gradually emerging.

I planted all the scented fruits and flowers which would not grow in England—passionfruit, guavas, persimmons and daphne, and six orange-trees along the old handmade brick front of the house. I also went to nurseries and bought rosetrees of the same varieties I had had at Plumstead. But like Moses with the Promised Land, I never reaped the fruits of my efforts.

The borough council took away my one outdoor worker, and then sent a man to threaten me with the law if I did not clear up the thickets of blackberries, which like rabbits and foxes had been introduced in the early days to make Australia home-like, and were its chief pests.

I was told of a new spray which destroyed them without the heavy labour of hacking the thorny canes and grubbing out the roots. I bought this stuff and enjoyed the easy work, but in a few days I was disgusted with what I had done, seeing the beautiful young shoots not fallen to the axe, but hanging sick and poisoned. It seemed a crime against nature.

My only companion for most of this time was a golden labrador, which we called Dudley after a comic character in a wireless programme. When he was little more than a puppy I took him for a walk, and we came to a pond. This was the first time he had seen any expanse of water and he stared at it intently. Then he went down to it and touched the water with his foot, recoiling immediately and rushing round in a circle. Then he went back to the water and repeated the performance. A sort of flirtation began between the dog and the water, he was full of delight and excited, and finally plunged into it, swimming round, again in a circle. Labradors have long been trained to retrieve in water, and this was one of those recognitions to which I have

referred, of the same nature as my own to plainsong, or
Greek sculpture, or renascent Italy.

Someone told me contemptuously that animals have no
reasoning or moral qualities and no affections. A dog's
loyalty to his master is only because he feeds him. Dudley
was fed by the housekeeper, yet he sat with me and slept
under my bed of his own choice. He had a good deal more
moral and religious sense than many young intellectuals I
have met. He obeyed absolutely the laws of nature, which
are those of God. When a man of evil character came to the
house, though he was of mild aspect, Dudley growled at him
furiously. When the Perceval children came to live at the
Grange he was their constant companion, and would have
protected them with his life. They all had yellow hair and
their mother, Mary Perceval, Merric's daughter, said that
she never knew whether she had four children or four dogs.

Sometimes on turning from the Prince's Highway towards
the hills of Harkaway, I would sing "Ai nostri monti
ritorneremo", at which Dudley would put his chin on my
shoulder.

Yet animals like this, with their vocal chords removed so
that their cries will not disturb the sensibility of their torturers, are daily being cut up alive. Rabelais's prophecy, already
quoted "when Science becomes divorced from the conscience
of mankind, mankind is doomed", seems horribly close to
being fulfilled at the moment. There is, in fact, only one
problem for "modern man", and that is to recover his
conscience, or he will soon be merely an old-fashioned corpse.

My happiest time at the Grange was my last six months,
when the Percevals came to live there. Mary's husband John
Perceval was, and is, a painter, and they both made pottery.
It pleased me to have this kind of activity in the house, while
the children filled it with life and fun, and also some
dramatic moments, as when Dudley chased a possum into
their room just after they had gone to bed, and the

pandemonium was unique. In the evening after their bath, the children or dogs used to scamper up the passage into the drawing-room to say good night, usually pretending to be lions or some form of wild beast.

However, in spite of my enjoyment of this life, I still wanted to see my English friends, and I decided to go back for a year's visit. Before this I went over to Yarra Glen to see the two of the Ross family remaining at Kincraig. It is strange that seeing how much Yarra Glen filled my imagination, and how often my thoughts returned to it while I was in Europe, I only went there once in the three years when I lived less than thirty miles away. When I did go and came into the last straight mile or two of road before crossing the river into the township, I felt as if I were returning to the true home of my spirit, though I knew that I could never live in it again. It was perhaps the one place where I had felt absolutely at home in the world, and this sense of belonging lasted for the two days I was there. Whether it would have remained if I had settled in our old home, instead of at the Grange, I do not know.

Kincraig had been burnt down for the second time, in the raging bushfires which broke out shortly before the war. The great avenue of pines had been destroyed. I have never understood why people plant these inflammable trees near their houses in Australia, a country of bushfires. I was once burning off a patch of grass in the middle of which was the stump of a pine-tree, sawn off like a table. This flat surface burst into flames which it was difficult to extinguish, so full of resin was the wood. The green leaves of a deciduous tree, on the contrary, would act as a firebreak.

From Kincraig, on a promontory of the hills, I could see two miles away on the river bank the home of my schooldays. All the trees in the grazing land between the road and the house had been cut down. I did not know the present owners, so did not call there, but sat on the Kincraig veranda looking down like Moses at the promised land in which I might not dwell.

When I was first told this story of Jehovah's vindictiveness, I repudiated it with every fibre of my being. This may not have been due only to my hatred of injustice, but because my essential self knew that it was an omen of the pattern of my life.

I departed from Kincraig not knowing that this was my last visit to Yarra Glen, as I had not then decided to return to England; and even if I had, it would not have been my intention to stay there.

A few weeks before I did leave, I had a conversation with the retired head of a vast business concern, with branches all over the world. He said how very happy he was now, living in a country house in a pleasant neighbourhood. He said: "I have three evenings of bridge a week, and a delightful garden. By the way, what are we going to do with those 400,000,000 Chinese? We'll have to poison 'em off. Well, I have three evenings of bridge a week, and the best antirrhinums in the district."

This reminded me of Austin Chamberlain's autobiography, in which after revealing how much he had done to pave the way for Hitler, having refused any concession to the pacifist Germany of the 'twenties, he ends up saying how happy he is with his antirrhinums in Sussex.

At about the same time Tristan Buesst brought Salvador de Madariaga up to luncheon. He had made a broadcast on arriving in Australia in which he praised our good wines. This provoked a letter to a newspaper, saying that we did not want foreigners coming here teaching our people to drink. He was justifiably very indignant at this crudity, and showed me the cutting immediately he arrived. The drunkeness in Victoria is due to the absurd rules about closing time, which is at 6 p.m., so that many people rush to fill up before that hour. There is no closing hour in Italy, and in my eight years here I have not seen one drunken Italian.

Don Salvador gave discerning appreciations of the house, and seemed reluctant to return from the country to Melbourne. One thing he said is fixed in my mind: "Reform is always necessary. Revolution is always wrong."

I sailed from Melbourne early in June 1951, and left the ship at Fremantle to see Mim, and my sister Helen whose husband had been appointed Resident Naval Officer in Perth. Dudley stayed with the Percevals, and became a familiar figure at artistic reunions. I spent a happy fortnight in this pleasant city, still small enough to have an individual human character, and with its suburbs spread along the wide reaches of the river. I went for a country excursion with Mim, and walking along the bush road between the saplings, we might have been at Warrandyte, forty years earlier. When I arrived in London I met a man who had just been round the world. He did not know I was an Australian, but he said: "If I could live anywhere I liked, I would choose Perth in Western Australia."

Here I had better finish the story of the Grange. After a year in England, for reasons I shall give in a following chapter, I decided to sell it. My lawyer wrote to me that there was a slump, and advised me to sell it for half the price I could have got when I left. He had a purchaser, a member of an old and titled Scottish family. I thought: "Well, anyhow, they'll keep it up well, being used to nice houses" and I let it go. Within four years the purchaser died, and his widow sold the place for three times the price that I had accepted. This was mortifying, but the tragedy from my point of view was that it was sold to be a quarry. The lovely hill which sloped from the house down to a wood, where Dudley and I had walked in the quiet evening, was gashed into one huge open wound; the house was abandoned, and wandering louts smashed the windows. Arthur's murals

245

remain in this desolate wreck. The family home, which I had spent three years trying to save, I had ruined. This purchase had put our modest house into *Burke's Peerage*, but only to earn it a sad epitaph, such as I had overheard in my childhood: "Cousin Coo was knighted and died."

I do not feel that I have done justice to this time in Australia. It was full of activity and a sense of purpose in life, and I renewed many friendships with relatives, school-friends and others I had known in the past. A period of life may be extremely enjoyable, and yet one cannot pick out any definite occasion to record, while one remembers some silly rudeness or comic contretemps. This is a fault that I acknowledge. It is a disease of our time, and is called realism, though the good is the only reality.

THE ABHORRED SHEARS

ON LEAVING THE SHIP at Marseilles I went straight through to Cambridge, where I stayed with Miss Ursula Somervell from Westmorland, a friend I had made while still at Plumstead, and who had much the same attitude to Cambridge as myself. Her house, one I had formerly coveted, was open to undergraduates of every country, and the scene of many lively parties, and much volatile argument. I was very fortunate to be able to go straight to this pleasant home, so that I had no sense of "alienation" which seeking admission to an hotel might have given me. Life was for delight from the moment of my arrival.

Cambridge had recovered all its enchantment. The summer days were perfect, and the gardens truly seemed apparelled in celestial light. The pinnacles of King's, seen above the trees of Clare, were like illuminations of a mediaeval paradise. This enhanced condition was partly brought about by the fact that the Festival of Britain was in progress, and there were concerts and pageants in college courts and all kinds of cultured fun, their enjoyment shared with reunited friends.

I went to evensong in King's College Chapel and there in the choir was my chorister of the passionate years, returned as a choral scholar. I knew that I should see him, but to him my presence was a surprise. He told me afterwards that when he looked up and saw me it gave him a psychological jolt. A young man of twenty-two is not the same animal as a boy of fourteen. Seeing me in that place reproduced for him exactly the conditions of eight years earlier, when he was a different species. After this we remained articulate and unromantic friends, though that earlier relationship of the spirit gave, I think, an enduring quality to our friendship.

In September I went with Alan on a holiday to France, one of the best we ever had. I cannot remember any of his *obiter dicta* on this tour except that he said that something had happened to me in Australia because I didn't fuss about catching trains any longer. This may have been due to my psychic trauma at the Grange, on the rainy eve of the party.

We went to Troyes, Chatillon, Avallon and Vézelay, all in a region new to me, and awaking new recognitions. We bathed in streams and browsed in churches, and in the evenings we had delicious meals and good wine, of which we drank a comfortable amount. At Nuits-sur-Ravière, after a reasonable consumption, Alan told me the story of his emotional life, which I remember whenever I pass this station in the Rome express.

But through all these golden days I was as it were fluting a wild carol ere my death, which according to God and nature should have happened a month later. One night, after dinner with my chorister friend, who would have been a suitable companion for my last supper, I was taken suddenly ill, and the next day underwent a major operation which was nothing compared with a visit to the dentist.

Afterwards they gave me various drugs, which made me sweat pints in the small hours. I would ring the bell, murmur "wet and sweat" and the night nurse would change my bedding. One day a scientific don visited me, and asked, "Why was it wrong for Adam to eat the apple?" I gave what

I thought to be the correct theological explanation, and he asked: "Is there any literature about that?"

That night my temperature rose to 104°, and I believe I was dying. It was not a disagreeable sensation, but unique in my experience. I felt that I was dividing painlessly into two. They gave me some drug which cost eleven pounds, but would not tell me what it was, and it remained nameless on the chemist's bill.

I rather enjoyed the weeks of my convalescence, except that as I recovered my appetite the food became worse. I became strong enough to take walks in the passage where I met the widow of a former master of a college who lived in the nursing home. She was dressed in bloomers and a superb Edwardian garden-party hat, all flowers and feathers. She asked me the way to the lavatory, which she ought to have known by then.

It was very pleasant to have no responsibility, and instead of having to trail out in search of company, to have my friends visit me, bringing carnations and pots of cyclamen. I felt like a woman in the village at Eversden, who lived in bed in the best room of her son-in-law's cottage, while he kept a garden blooming outside her window. I asked Mrs. Jakins what was wrong with her. She said, "Nothing. All that family go to bed at forty."

The drugs besides making me sweat, made me coarse and aggressive. I dreamed that I was punching people's noses. In this mood I began to write *The Cardboard Crown*, which I had tentatively begun before my illness. I put my new crudity into the mouth of Cousin Ted, disguised as "Uncle Arthur". About this time I read C. P. Snow's *The Masters* which repelled me by its lack of any grace in any character, but if I put it down, I had to pick it up again in a few minutes to see what happened next. When I went to London, George Kinnaird asked me to dine, to meet Snow, having first told him what I thought of his book. I tried to explain that although the characters had not charmed me, I was engrossed by the story. But he did not seem to mind much what I said as long as I talked about it.

At the beginning of January, still semi bed-ridden, I set out for Rome with Elliott Howes. We had forgotten that it was necessary to go through the Customs at Dover, and we went on board, leaving our luggage with a porter, who took it to the Customs. We did not see it again for a fortnight, when some of the contents were stolen. Fortunately I had picked up a small case containing my traveller's cheques and the incomplete manuscript of *The Cardboard Crown* together with some personal essentials. Elliott had insisted before we left that one must have an umbrella in Rome, and for two weeks that was all he did have.

I went to Rome partly because I had only seen it before from a perambulator, but also to verify the Roman scenes in *The Cardboard Crown*. After two months I thought I had now seen Rome and quite enjoyed it, but had no particular wish to return. I went back to London and took a small furnished flat in Dover Street, glad to have my own front door again.

When I came out of the nursing home I said, "In the course of nature I should have died, but modern science has cheated fate. Therefore I have no responsibility for the rest of my life. It is like a bonus from a share, and I can spend it as I like."

Although I said this flippantly, there was some feeling of the kind in my attitude for the next few years. I was no longer strong enough to cope with the problems of the Grange, and as none of the family wanted to take it over, I decided to sell it. Having failed to establish my life there, I felt that I had no positive obligation to anyone. Without putting it into so many words, my intention was to live for pleasure. But God is not mocked.

In London I saw a good deal of George. He had a black

servant called Ojo, an African of strong individual character. When waiting at table, he was apt to mutter incantations against untoward omens. He believed it was discourteous to leave guests alone, and when Lady Kinnaird was staying with George, while he was out, Ojo came and sat with her, and she spent an uncomfortable hour with this child of the jungle glaring at her from the corner of the room.

When George took him to see a film of the Mau-Mau, he uttered shrieks of delight every time a white man was slaughtered. He stole cigarettes from a kiosk, but George explained that this was not a felony as the man had been rude to him, and he only took them to satisfy his honour, which shows a nice sense of moral theology. Finally when he knocked the porter of Brooks's Club over the head with an umbrella for refusing to take a message to his master, it was decided that Ojo must go. But before this *dénouement*, looking noble in African robes he had attended a reception to the Emperor Haile Selassie in the House of Lords, and had sat in a box with the Duchess of Kent, to whom George was host at a Billy Graham meeting.

In the summer of 1952, with the chorister undergraduate, I went to the south coast of Brittany. It was a lively and amusing holiday but slightly blemished by poisoning from mussels and theological argument. Twenty-seven years earlier I had gone to Brittany with one of the Oxford undergraduates from Batcombe, a holiday which also was ruffled by theological arguments. This seems a strange recurrence of circumstances, and suggests something incorrigible in my nature, or it may be due to a recurrence of planetary aspects; or to both interrelated. I have known two or three remarkable coincidences, which if put in a novel, would provoke criticism of its absurd unreality.

A few years ago I was with two women friends on the Campidoglio from where we walked down to the 90 bus stop at the foot of the Aracoeli steps. Suddenly one of them was taken ill. It was six o'clock in the evening, and I dashed about in the whirling traffic of Piazza Venezia trying to find a taxi for a distressed lady sitting on the marble seat by the bus stop.

A year later I was with Hertha and another friend walking towards the same 90 bus stop, which recalled the incident of the previous year, and of which I told her. She was mildly interested and then suddenly cried: "Shelagh!" There was our friend, lying on the footpath, having sprained her ankle. It was six o'clock in the evening and I dashed about through the whirling traffic of the Piazza Venezia, trying to find a taxi for a distressed lady, who was sitting on the marble seat by the bus stop.

Someone suggested that I should experiment again with an unwelcome acquaintance.

Once at Lee Priory before the war while we were waiting for dinner, Mrs. Ramsay was telling me of a Lady Gough who had been staying with them. (A coincidence within a coincidence was that there were then four Ladies Gough in London. Once they all arrived at a party in succession. When the fourth was announced everyone laughed, and she went home in a huff.) This Lady Gough had confessed as they waited in the drawing-room before dinner, that she had always been afraid of choking to death. Mrs. Ramsay expressed mildly sympathetic interest and they went into dinner, where Lady Gough had the most terrible choking fit she had ever seen. I expressed mildly sympathetic interest and we went in to dinner, where Mrs. Ramsay had the most terrible choking fit I have ever seen.

In the summer of 1952 I discovered that owing to some legislation of 1948, I had lost my citizenship. Until then I had a British passport, but when I went to renew it, I was told that because I was born in Switzerland I was a New Zealander. The explanation of this imbecility was that my father was born in New Zealand which he left in early

252

childhood and never returned. If I secured various documents from Switzerland, Dunedin and Melbourne, I might be granted a passport as a favour. I wrote to the High Commissioner for New Zealand asking if he would let me have a passport. He wrote back apologetically saying he was not allowed to do this unless he too saw all the documents. The anomalies under this law were and still are grotesque. A man of the purest English blood, who was born in India, then British territory, where his father was serving his country, can be, and often is, told when applying for a new passport, that he is a Pakistani. A Latvian refugee can get a British passport in a fortnight. A large building in Holborn is occupied by a hive of civil servants engaged in making British subjects British again. The Government has flatly refused to repeal this rule.

The recruiting posters might read "Join the Army and lose your children their citizenship."

At last in 1957, having been recognised as a "British subject without citizenship" I was granted, as a gracious favour, a British passport.

A new regulation is that Australians arriving at Dover must go through the aliens' barriers. I wrote to Sir Robert Menzies, to protest against this affront to my countrymen, though I have a British passport. I had a reply from a secretary, saying he was sorry I felt offended, but the British had a right to make their own regulations. They have no moral right to treat as aliens people of their own blood, who have twice come to their immediate aid, in wars which were not of their making.

If I had one clear aim after I was ill, it was to live in the sun. I did not like the idea of returning to Australia, without possession of the Grange, which had been a kind of moral stronghold to me. (I hope my readers understand that when I use the word moral I am seldom referring to sexual morality.) I decided to settle in Provence, to which my thoughts had often turned through long English winters, and where I had spent a few weeks on my way back from Rome. Compared with Melbourne, it was a negligible distance from London and Cambridge friends. I did not like to go alone, and I engaged a manservant, who advertised for a position of this kind in *The Times* and gave excellent references. He was a pleasant spoken young man, with an educated voice, but he turned out to be schizophrenic. This condition was brought about by a tragedy of his childhood, his father's sudden dismissal from a lucrative post by Beaverbrook, and his resulting suicide and his family's plunge from a well-found Wimbledon establishment into poverty. At times he was light-hearted and very amusing with a lively wit. Sometimes he would go to bed in good spirits only to appear the next morning scowling and evil. In a rational mood he explained to me that he would imagine a thing that might happen. This would provoke the resentment which he would have felt if it actually had happened, and which was usually directed at myself. He had a passion for domestic cleanliness and made a little altar on his dressing table, of detergent flanked by polishing brushes, arranged on a yellow duster.

Cassis itself had changed. There were now, instead of the Bloomsbury birds of paradise, only four English-speaking residents; Jean who was unwell at Fontcreuse; a retired man, who had had a stroke; the widow of a former resident, and an Australian woman Communist, who said that Stalin had done a splendid job. Peter had died only a day or two before I returned from Australia. Jean told me that while he was in his last agony some of those "friends of friends" who had consumed so much of their wine, sat drinking in his bedroom.

While I was there the parish priest celebrated a Requiem Mass, which I attended, for Peter, a Roman Catholic who died "in sin"; for the husband of the widow I have mentioned, an Anglican; and for an American painter, an atheist, the lover of the Australian. In the front pew sat, by invitation, the three relics, Jean, the Anglican widow and the Communist. This must be the most extreme example of oecumenism on record.

At last my schizophrenic servant left me to take employment with a Hungarian nobleman in Nice. At first he wrote with pride that everyone who came to the house was a prince or a duke, but in a few weeks he found the Hungarian too exigent, and he fled back to London with only a few francs in his pocket. He must have had demonic strength of mind, as he forced a Paris taximan to drive him and his baggage from the Gare de Lyon to the Gare du Nord for nothing, simply repeating, "But I have no money, you must take me."

I returned to England at about the same time. Provence had died on me, and I have never been there since. I spent a dislodged and undecided summer, staying at an hotel on the river bank in Cambridge, and wondering where to live. I had bought a nice Georgian house overlooking the park at Greenwich, and about half a mile from Noël and Bernard Adeney, who had a beautiful seventeenth century manorhouse on Croom's hill. I had let my own house to my nephew David. Finally, I decided to go to London where I took a small service flat in St. James's Place. It was convenient, if cramped, and had the additional advantage that all the letters I wrote to *The Times* from this address were published.

Here I continued writing *A Difficult Young Man* which I had begun at Cassis. First the conversation of my manservant there, and now the worldly influences of my surroundings, made this book very snobbish, and I dislike it, though I think it contains some of my best writing. When it was finished I was at a cocktail party at Gordon and Kitty Waterfield's, and complained to their daughter Harriet, the daughter-in-law of Charles Morgan, that I did not know what to call it. She asked, "What is it about?" I said, "A difficult young man." She said, "Well, why don't you call it that?" So I did.

My eighteen months at St. James's Place was rather like an orchid stuck in the buttonhole of a tweed suit, beautiful but arbitrary. I made various ephemeral contacts, but also was close to other friends, such as George, Helen Harben, Arthur and Anne Hay, Alan, and the Ells with whom I lunched every Sunday. These were about the liveliest and also the best meals I have ever had. As soon as we sat down to the table something sparked, especially if their daughter Pam was there; and these Sundays at Westminster Gardens are a bright and clear entry on the credit side of my balance with life.

Once they lunched with me in the hotel at Cambridge, where the conversation was inclined to be hushed and academic, and we provided the overtones. Afterwards an elderly don came up to us and said wistfully, "I wish I could have been at your table. You did seem to be enjoying yourselves." Now, when I have no Aunt Chomley and no Lee Priory, the Ells still provide me with an anchorage when I am in London.

One day in the spring of 1954 Alan came in and said, "Will you come to Rome with me?" I said, "Very well. I've been there, but I don't mind seeing it again." We arrived in May. I had been before in January and February, still convalescent; staying in bed till lunch-time, and enjoying a few hours of tepid sunshine before tea. The population seemed all brown and grey in overcoats.

Now the sky was blazing blue, the Aventino was breathing with scented shrubs, the young population, lithe and free and lightfoot, with bright shirts and flowered shirts and Leonardo faces and their arms around each other's necks were moving jewels in the street. The impact on my heart and mind was forcible.

On this holiday Alan first developed his powers of evoking what he called "Catholic Privileges", by which he meant any spectacular religious ceremony. We went into St. Maria sopra Minerva, and immediately two rows of Dominicans came out from behind the altar and sang the Salve Regina. We went into the cathedral at Perugia and found a crowd of children pelting a priest at the altar with flowers. A year later at St. Margherita Ligure, it was he who insisted on my going down to the harbour to see the water illuminated for a mile with floating candles, which I describe in *Much Else in Italy*. When I returned from this holiday, Italy was in my blood.

A few months later I again went to Brittany with my ex-chorister, but this time simply to act as chaperon to his girl-friend whom he was taking for a holiday. I scrupulously left them alone together all day, expecting to enjoy a little talk and laughter at dinner-time, but the young lady, who had a large nose, resented any attempt I made to enter the conversation. My mother had once said to me, "If you don't want to be bossed, don't marry a girl with a big nose." My friend evidently discovered the truth of this in time, and later married very happily, I hope and believe, a more docile bride. However, like the infant Russell, there is nothing which enrages me more than being gagged, so I left them to control their own passions and went off to hear plainsong at Solesmes, and to look at the tapestries at Angers, which lifted one into a mystic world.

While at St. James's Place I became more friendly with George's parents, whose London residence was now in Smith Square, overlooking the leafy ruins of the Wren church.

One day I was there to luncheon, when Hugh Gough's daughter, a delightful young girl, came in and affectionately greeted her grandparents. This gave me a sudden nostalgia for the family life of which I had seen so little of recent years. It was an echo of Lee Priory, and perhaps of even more distant times, of Wilton and Glenfern. I said something of this kind to George, which he repeated to Lady Kinnaird, and she sent me a message, inviting me to come often.

The atmosphere of this household was very sympathetic to me, possibly because of its composition. Lord Kinnaird was a Scot of early mediaeval family, and Lady Kinnaird an Englishwoman of deep religious feeling. Mr. and Mrs. Ramsay made the same combination, and so more remotely did my parents. Whether or no it was due to this correspondence, on the Australian farm or in the great English and Scottish country houses, the recognitions were the same. My mother once said to me that though she and my father were different in so many ways, where any principle was involved, their views were identical.

I think it was this feeling of basic goodness that made me feel an affinity with these two households. Although I liked surroundings of richness, nobility and pleasure, I found that without it they were hell, which is why I have made no whole-hearted effort to move in exalted circles. Lady Kinnaird once admitted with wry amusement that she did not care much for the text that "not many noble, not many rich" would enter the Kingdom of Heaven.

Hugh Gough, then Bishop of Barking, was one of those instrumental in bringing Billy Graham to England, Lady Kinnaird asked me if I would like to hear him. I did want to but I hated crowds, and was glad of the opportunity of doing it de luxe. We had sherry at Smith Square and the bishop drove us to Harringay, where we had an excellent dinner with roast duck, in the company of an air marshal and his wife, though the only item on the wine list was Coca-Cola.

Billy Graham spoke forcibly—he was said to thump eight bibles to pieces every year—but his emotion was more that of a lawyer arguing a case from a given premise than that of a revivalist preacher, or of the Bishop of Zanzibar whom I heard in 1923, almost chanting in a voice full of tears: "Come up, come up into the Sacred Heart of Jesus."

On the way back the bishop's daughter asked him what the air marshal was doing now, and was told that he was at the Air Ministry, but was anxious to get back to the Woomera rocket-range. It struck me as odd that no one seemed to think that salvation and preparation for mass-slaughter were strange bed-fellows; except myself quasi-agnostic and as self-indulgent as my circumstances allowed.

One day Alan came in, seething with indignation. He said that he had been to the most contemptible play he had ever seen, one that jeered at all the basic human decencies. I thought it was an isolated event, but it was the first drop of that rain of poison, in books, plays and wireless programmes, which for the next ten years was to pour on the supine heads of the people of Great Britain, and was also to drive me again off the literary map.

At this time I seemed to be gathering up the motifs of my London life, as composers do with the last movement of a concerto.

I went down to Eastry to see Mrs. Aubrey Waterfield, who was then writing *Castle in Italy*. She was disgusted with D. H. Lawrence, who had spent an apparently enjoyable time with them, but afterwards had written disparagingly of Mr. Waterfield because he was a gentleman.

While there I met Edward Rice of Dane Court, who asked me to come over and see the improvements he had made to his family seat since re-taking possession of it many years earlier. I was very pleased to see again after nearly a third of a century this house where I had spent such happy times during the 1914 war; but what struck me most was unconnected with that period.

Long before this I had read Harold Nicolson's *Some People*, in which he describes having to take some official document to Lord Curzon who was unwell. He was received in his bedroom, a poky apartment with a cheap chest-of-drawers. Nicolson was unable to conceal his surprise, and Curzon said, "I can assure you that my wife's apartments are of unexampled magnificence." I wondered what they were like, but thought, "Well I'm no more likely to see the Marchioness Curzon's bedroom than to become President of the United States", and I put it out of my head.

However, at Dane Court when Mrs. Rice, who was Lady Curzon's daughter, was kindly showing me round the house, she casually opened a door and said, "This is mother's room." There in the middle of this pleasant country house bedroom glowed the most resplendent bed I had ever seen, certainly unexampled in my modest experience.

In the autumn of 1954 I went with George to stay with his parents at Rossie Priory in Perthshire. Half of this Wyatt Gothic palace had recently been pulled down, to make it a more manageable country house than when it needed twenty-three servants to run it; but it was still large enough to house the magnificent collection of pictures by Rembrandt, Van Dyck, Tiepolo, Parmigianino and other famous artists. To have tea in the drawing-room was like having tea in a room in the National Gallery. In this evangelical household there were inherited piquant contrasts, such as the statue of an ancestor, a friend of Byron's, in the costume, or rather absence of costume, in which at the age of twelve he went as Eros to a fancy-dress ball. Even at Smith Square, grace before meals was said sitting on chairs which might have come from Madame Du Barry's boudoir. I very much like the atmosphere in which all things comely are reconciled.

Mrs. Ramsay once said to me that Mr. Ramsay only began to breathe when he had crossed the border into Scotland. It was probably because in Scotland, as in Ireland, there is a pervading sense of common humanity. The people speak to each other, low to high, poor to rich, with a freedom which is not offensive because it is perfectly natural and without any conscious familiarity. In England nowadays the insolence of railway porters and bus conductors, except the West Indians, is a denial of common humanity.

One of Lord Kinnaird's duties as Lord Lieutenant was to meet the queen as she passed through Perthshire. He had just performed this function, which was reported in the papers. The next day he was on the Dundee ferry, where the captain said to him, "I see you've been making yourself conspicuous." One day we drove up the east coast to Dunottar Castle, a romantic fortress on a rocky promontory. When we arrived at the entrance, a Celtic face, almost Slavonic in its vitality, appeared on the ramparts and yelled directions at us. Its owner again showed neither subservience nor insolence, but was like a boy directing three others of his kind.

Another story of slightly exaggerated common humanity is of the days before the telephone. In one Scottish mansion the housemaids had to sleep in the family's beds to keep them aired while the latter were in London. The elderly owner with his wife returned unexpectedly. They had just gone to bed and put out the lights, which apparently was a signal, when a hefty and amorous young gardener leapt in between them.

We drove on a still sad autumn day to call at a house in a remote part of the country. We entered a drive a mile or more in length, bordered with golden trees alternating with sombre evergreens, but returning to a wild state. The house was an old castle with renaissance extensions, a place that seemed reeking of history. Our host lived in this huge house with a blind sister and one servant. The first of his line had been whipping boy to one of the Stewart kings, and had earned the estate in the same way that the public schoolboy, according to my undergraduate friend, earns his social position. This added to the general feeling of melancholy which I had in this, my farthest and probably last penetration into the backcloth of my childhood.

While I was at Rossie the ashes of George's aunt, Margaret Kinnaird, who had died some time earlier, were brought there for burial. I had met her long ago as a young girl in her first London season. I did not want to intrude on this family occasion, but George said his parents would like me to come. The interment was by a mediaeval chapel, the family burial place in the park. Just as the small coffin was laid in the grave, lined with laurel, the midday bell tolled from the house, and a flight of wild geese flew overhead. It was easy to understand how belief in omens, linking human life with the natural world, grew up among people of vivid imagination. There also seemed to me a poetic sadness in my standing at the grave of someone I had briefly met as a young girl, full of delight in life, almost a lifetime since.

The tranquil circumstances of the rite increased this feeling and also made one believe that she was truly at rest.

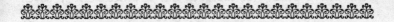

PHYSICAL COMFORT

IN THE EARLY SUMMER of 1955, David and his family
returned to Australia, and the Greenwich house was available.
But I decided that English winters were death to me, and
that I wanted to live in Italy. I sold the house for a quarter
of its present value, though for a reasonable price at the time,
and gave up the flat in St. James's Place.

In July I set out for Rome, and Dagnall came with me
for two or three weeks' holiday. It was suffocatingly hot, and
we preferred bathing at Fregene to seeing historic monu-
ments. It is said that the oppressive heat on the Mediterranean is in July and up to the tenth of August. After that it
is hot but healthy. I have found this to be true. When Dagnall had left I began a tentative search for an apartment, but
it was not an agreeable occupation in the heat. While I was
beginning to feel pessimistic about any success, I had a letter
from Miss Somervell, saying that a flat she formerly occupied at Trumpington Hall was vacant, and would I like it.
Under the present blazing skies the thought of the peaceful
English countryside was bliss, and I replied that I would.

On the way back I stayed a fortnight at St. Margherita
Ligure, where Alan joined me. He at once began to evoke
Catholic Privileges. As soon as we set foot on the piazza of

Nozzarego, a festive procession came out of the church. We dined in a garden restaurant, and a procession of seven enormous crucifixes edged with gold filigree came through the square, dipping under the electric wires, while the orchestra stopped playing dance music, a rather bizarre intrusion into the musical comedy scene. It was on this occasion that he compelled me to come down to see the harbour covered with floating candles.

Trumpington Hall belonged to the Pemberton family. A rule of succession was that if it went to a female, she must take the name of Pemberton. The result of this was that Mrs. Pemberton, to whom it belonged, though she had only been married once, had changed her name four times. She was born with her father's name. Her mother inherited the estate and she became Miss Pemberton. She then married and became Mrs. Wingate. She then inherited Trumpington and became Mrs. Pemberton.

The house was much bigger than she needed, living there alone, and she turned one wing into three flats. Mine was on the top floor. The sitting-room windows looked on to the forecourt and up the avenue, the kitchen and bathroom windows on to a side court with a walnut-tree from which the rooks stole the nuts, and the bedroom windows down across the sloping park to the river, and beyond that to the tower of Grantchester church. There was always boiling hot water in the taps, and the central heating was excellent. There were only four rooms in my flat so I could use the pick of my furniture from the Grange, and the result was much admired. Mrs. Pemberton was the kindest of landladies, and for about the first time in my life I was ideally housed, with all the amenities of country house life, but none of the responsibility.

However, I only stayed there for eighteen months. In the next year I went to Italy for two months, to collect material for a book, and again felt the lure of this country. But I doubt if I should have left for that alone. I found that in spite of the superlative comforts of Trumpington I could not keep well in the English winter, and after the second, I decided firmly to go to Italy and stay there, which I did.

I cannot remember much of interest that happened in those eighteen months, except that I wrote two books, *Outbreak of Love* and *Much Else in Italy*, both rather bad titles. It was a pleasant existence, of tea parties and meals with friends, but with one terrible fortnight, made worse by the ray of hope with which it began, the resurgence of the Hungarian people against their alien tyranny. Then came the incredible folly of the side-show of Suez, which distracted the attention of the whole world from the demonstration of Communism in action, and which made Khrushchev exclaim: "If God existed I would thank Him." Then came the returning Russian tanks which even the children fought against with bare hands. Some moronic Leftist thug told me I was "sentimental" to object to their massacre. All the sensations of Munich and the fall of France returned, that the ship in which one was journeying through life was heeling over.

Otherwise this was a kind of quiet evening of my English life, for I do not expect ever to live there again. As I have now come to the end of that part of my existence, I shall go ahead for a few years to sound again two of its major motifs, but gone into a minor key, like that of the Rhinemaidens after Alberic had stolen the gold. They occurred in the last four days of a recent visit.

On the first day I met my cousin Frances Knight by the Marble Arch. She was the daughter of my Aunt and Uncle Chomley, the only one of their four children to have remained in England. She had been at the Grange as a child, and was one of my Wilton playmates. She had been a friend of the 1914 war years and had also been on the Sussex coast. We often met in London during the 'thirties and she had visited me at Plumstead.

We went into the Cumberland Hotel and had some coffee, but a man insisted on sweeping the carpet with a noisy machine, so we went out and down a subway, coming up on to a sort of island. There with the traffic whizzing and whirling around us, we sat on a stone step, revolving many memories.

The next day I went down to Lee Priory. Mr. and Mrs. Ramsay had both died soon after the end of the war and the house had remained empty, as their surviving son had inherited a place in Scotland. After some years it was sold, and the purchasers began to pull down this splendidly built house, a mania of today.

They had to blow up part of it, so strong were the walls. They destroyed the fine Georgian rooms and the delicate Wyatt Gothic fantasies; but when they reached the kitchen wing, for some reason they stopped, and converted it into four pleasant terrace houses, so that it looked something like an old Normandy manor. Lady Boucher, formerly Margaret Ramsay, one of the little girls who had played in the impromptu orchestra at Dane Court, bought one of these houses, returning to a part of her former home which she had never entered before. Somehow, in this hitherto unknown region of the original house, the old ethos still survived, and outside the drawing-room windows the lawn still sloped to the tennis courts. I was now going to stay there on my way to Dover.

Eager to recreate the conditions of pre-war days, I had asked that Pearce, the former chauffeur who had so often met me of old, and was still a family friend, might do so once more; but it was Sunday, and Margaret herself met me at Canterbury. It was strange to turn in from the park, beneath the lime-tree so well remembered, and to see flower beds where formerly we had sat down to dine.

Dorothy and Helen, her sisters, were waiting at the door, and when I arrived they said, "Welcome home." In these two words were echoed all the wonderful friendship and hospitality I had been given here during three decades.

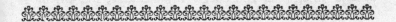

EXPATRIATE

ALAN CAME WITH ME TO ROME, but wanted to go to Venice on the way. When I was young my brothers had teased me, saying that if I returned to the country of my birth I would be conscripted into the army. This gave me a physic trauma which had prevented my ever going there. The direct route from Calais to Venice was through Switzerland, so in the cause of friendship I agreed to risk being dragged out of bed at the frontier and being imprisoned as a deserter. However, I woke up free in Italy, and had traversed my native land without seeing a square inch of it.

After an amusing three weeks, sprinkled with Catholic Privileges, Alan returned to London, and I went down to Formia for two months of Mediterranean life, before settling in Rome for the winter. Here a man in the hotel introduced me to some Italians who, like myself and the rest of the holiday population, spent the morning on the beach. One of these, a boy called Luciano Trombini, was learning English, and would sit under a blue umbrella and ask me to recite to him the paradigms of various English verbs.

Soon I was visited with that complaint which attacks those who do not adapt themselves gradually to food cooked in oil. I spent a night in agony. Luciano, not finding me on the beach, came to my hotel in the morning, found a doctor, acted as interpreter and bought my medicine, and anything else I required. I told him he had saved my life. On returning to Rome he repeated this to his friends, but he told them he had done it by saving me from drowning, because, he explained to me, it sounded better.

We went for a walk on the hill. He led me up ragged rocky slopes, through thorny scrub and barbed wire. When I protested he said: "Oh sir, this is a very comfortable road."

Before Christmas, walking past a wine shop, I asked him what he would like for a present and suggested a bottle of brandy. I did not mean it seriously but he accepted the offer, saying: "It would please my father." I doubted this, but we went in and bought it. Coming out he said: "We will always drink brandy." This turned out to be true, though I managed to keep the consumption moderate.

For the next seven years he lunched with me every Saturday. His parents lived in the country about ten miles out of Rome, and he used my apartment as a foothold in the capital. When I returned from a visit to England he always met me on arrival.

This gave me a feeling of belonging, of having a link with the community which was invaluable to me at the time, obviating the sense of exile and "alienation" from which otherwise I might have suffered; as well as bringing the vivid interests of a growing life into my home.

He not only was doing brilliantly in physics and electronics at his school, but he wrote poems with a sensitive response to the natural world. He was at the most advanced scientific school in Italy, but following the strong Italian sense of civilisation, the boys also studied the Christian religion, Dante and the great literature of their country, so that here science was less likely to be divorced from the conscience of mankind. Luciano could also discuss an abstract idea, and had an individual wit of the kind I enjoy. He also brought me presents of my onomastico, the feast of my patron saint; a large bunch of flowers, or a pot plant and a sumptuous cake. This was a new experience, as for over sixty years my relatives and friends had ignored this opportunity for generosity. He now has a wife and daughter, Carla and Flavia.

I had vaguely thought that coming to live in Rome, I would be entering a sort of Maurice Baring world of immense culture and distinction; or be like Mrs. G. who spent her ten years here talking to princes. I do not know whether this would have been possible, as I did not present the few letters of introduction I had. I do not believe that men over sixty like going to parties. Walter Savage Landor said that it was barbaric for more than two people to dine together. I would increase the number to four, possibly, among old friends, to six. Anyhow, when I may have had the chance of entering a society which thirty years earlier I would have thought dazzling, I no longer had the inclination for it.

My chief human interest was in Luciano and when I wanted the society of my own countrymen I could go to the English Centre, where I met people of every sort, some of whom have in time become my good friends.

But this time in Rome has been unrelated to all that had gone before, which fact slowly and subconsciously has had the effect of enabling me to see that previous life with complete objectivity. The result of that detached vision I hope to give in the final chapter. Here, as the excuse for my autobiography, apart from ordinary human evidence, is the fact that I am a writer, I shall give a short review of myself in that capacity.

Everybody's literary career begins at school, but with the majority of people it ends there. I wrote verses for the school magazine, *The Mitre*, and for my last two years I was its editor. But many other boys also wrote verses as good, or better than mine. Once when we were studying *Pride and Prejudice*, the headmaster pointed out how Jane Austen, instead of describing her characters, conveyed their reality by their actions. I had no idea then of being a novelist or any kind of writer, but this remained in my mind as the essence of good fiction, and I think has influenced the intention of all my novels. This was only brought into my conscious mind two years ago, when I read an essay on my work by Doctor Leonie Kramer of the University of New South Wales. She writes of my "highly original method of depicting" my characters; and of my "chief interest—the description of character in the making".

After the war, disturbed by the loss of and separation from friends, I wrote some poems in the style of Rupert Brooke, but this was chiefly to express my feelings.

Again, when I left Batcombe, I wanted to express my feelings, and this time I did it in a novel, as I have related. When this was accepted by Constables, I naturally wrote another, and when this was also accepted I considered myself a novelist. I was not anything else. Constables accepted yet a third book *The Montforts*. All these books were published under a pseudonym, but lately *The Montforts* was republished under my own name, like the belated recognition of an illegitimate child. The other two and the pseudonym I wish forgotten. Completely unknown as I was, Constables gave me more generous terms for these than I have had for my latest books. I had to deal with Michael Sadlier, who was helpful and courteous, while Otto Kyllman, the then chairman of the firm, came out and gave me encouraging words.

But I am not exclusively, or chiefly a writer. At one time the phrase "life and letters" was often used. With me life comes a long way before letters, and I believe that life is for delight. If some phase of life or some incident gives me this, or if it evokes a sense of its pathos, or a repudiation of cruelty or injustice, I want to perpetuate that in writing as clear and vivid as I can make it. When I have done so, I do not want to go on writing until I have a new impulse, not as a man goes on making wheelbarrows, though if he is a good craftsman he will have some feeling for his wheelbarrows.

I have heard literary people talk about "new ways of using words" as if this was the whole purpose of "contemporary" writing. This is putting the symbol above the reality, like putting money above the goods it represents, which in the Myth is the Idolatry of the Golden Calf. Idolatry is usually thought of as a rather foolish but harmless veneration of images. It is something much more serious, a corrupt attitude of mind, which in public life is almost universal today.

It is the quality of a man's imagination, his sense of values and his powers of observation that make him a good writer, and he must have an adequate command of words to express himself. But the most brilliant ability to arrange words in new patterns, without these three things, will not make him good. The greatness of a novel depends on its content of humanity.

A Melbourne critic not long ago wrote that I was an amateur. She stated this as one of my failings, but as when the young man in Sussex told me I had the face of a mediaeval peasant, I was very pleased at her censure. Some of the greatest novelists have been amateur. Tolstoy was a soldier, a nobleman, and a peasant, not a professional writer. It was his powerful imagination and sense of humanity that made him great. Flaubert struggled for six years to produce *Madame Bovary*, his only real achievement. He did not sit down and write it straight off with professional competence. Proust was obsessed by the society of the Faubourg St. Germain. It set his essential self purring creatively. Its rich twilight glows and fades through the pages of his great novel, but it is full of technical faults that a professional writer would have avoided. They do not matter.

The above critic wrote of "the capacity for hard work" as one of the marks of a good writer. It may be of the professional, but not of the truly creative writer. He does not work, he functions. He cannot do this until his essential self, the Holy Ghost in him, begins to purr. He cannot produce by cerebration alone, however hard he tries.

This has a correspondence with the difference between talent and genius. These two things are different in kind not in degree, as Dallas Kenmare has shown in *The Nature of Genius*. The talented writer can turn on the tap of his ability at any moment, the genius has to wait for the spark from heaven, or rather for the dynamo of his essential self to function. The merit of his work depends on the quality of his essential self alone. It is not necessarily better than that of a man of talent. It is possible for it to be worse.

A few days ago I walked into an exhibition of paintings. They were inspired, but they were hideous and depraved. The colours were cold blue-grey and black. A naked woman, her body covered with huge black sores, was getting into bed. Two men, who looked the personifications of intellectual cruelty, filthy torturers, were seated motionless at two tables. One felt one was in hell. They were the work of an evil genius, and they were bad. The critics assume that because works like these I have described provoke a powerful reaction, they have great merit, but it is only the same reaction as when one sees the decaying corpse of a dog in the gutter. It does not need a work of art to produce it. In writing any fool can produce a bad character, and evoke vividly a scene of filth. He is merely stimulating a physical reaction to squalor, and in time giving weak characters a taste for it. It needs far more skill, with sympathy and subtle observation to portray a good character, or to make a scene of beauty vivid.

The truly great work of art of course must have genius. Talent alone cannot produce it. The old saying that genius is the capacity for taking infinite pains is nonsense. The genius lost in creative frenzy is not consciously taking infinite pains. He is merely allowing his essential self to function, which may involve the infinite pains.

However, perhaps it is enough to repeat what is often said, that the novelist must be a poet in his apprehensions. The true critic must also have those apprehensions. Though he lacks the ability to use them creatively, he can recognise them in the work of another, and share in the act of creation by helping the reader to do the same. Such critics are few. The modern idea that literary critics can be "scientifically trained" is resulting in grotesque absurdities. Last week I read in the first paragraph alone of a review in a highbrow weekly the following phrases:

"alienation from modern assumptions";
"The essence of the novelist's art is the quotidian";
"The wound-and-bow psychological theory";
"methodological inferences".

It must be great fun concocting this jargon, but it has no connection with the poetic intuition which is essential to the criticism of works of art. Apart from this pretentious clique, there was up to about ten years ago a large body of conscientious reviewers, competent to deal with the bulk of newly published fiction. I am now coming to how this affects my own story.

Up to about that time I was nearly always treated fairly and sometimes very well by reviewers. If I had an unfavourable review it was a rational judgment, not an outburst of spleen. Since then a large proportion of my reviews have been quite unprincipled. I give some examples:

A reviewer, a Roman Catholic, in a leading London newspaper dismissed my book, *Much Else in Italy*, with an insolent snarl. The book showed much sympathy with Roman Catholicism, but also contained some sharp criticism. I protested to the literary editor, who gave as sufficient excuse that the reviewer "was irritated by something written in the blurb" which I had not written!

Another writer of a malicious review gave as sufficient excuse that he "was temperamentally opposed to me".

While writing a passage in the above book, I thought: "If anyone liked to lift this out of its context, he could make me look a complete fool. But I don't suppose anyone would be so low as that." But a reviewer in a leading Sunday newspaper was so low.

Since then I have had reviews of extraordinary guttersnipe abuse. Other present-day reviewers have developed a technique of supercilious belittlement, which can be applied to any work, great or trivial. Here is how one of these might review, say, *Romeo and Juliet*:

"This is the saccharine tale of a couple of Italian teenagers suffering from erotomania, whose respective parents have had a row, which prevents the pair from getting into bed together. There is every sort of cheap stage device, moonlit balconies and the rest. The play wades drearily through moanings and murders, until we end up practically in a morgue. It has, I suppose, a few lines of lyrical adroitness, which I must admit set my teeth on edge, but which may titillate the palates of those over sixty."

This method can be used on anything, as a typhoid germ can destroy equally a man of the finest intelligence or a half-wit. My last two or three books, whether good or bad, were submitted to a proportion of reviews of this kind.

Many of the reviewers are also publishers' readers, and so are in almost complete control of the literary world. It seems to me that a high proportion of these are intellectual delinquents, while the remainder support the Establishment. To neither kind am I acceptable.

Living in Italy, I did not quite realise what was happening until about five years ago. I had a letter from my agent telling me that "fiction today" must be "violent, outspoken and crudely sexual". To say that fiction today must be anything except what the author chooses to write about, and present with his individual vision, struck me as odd, but to tell an author of established reputation that in his middle sixties he must begin to write filth astonished me. I replied that I preferred to fade out than to trade in pornography and that practically finished my literary career.

I should have realised earlier what was happening. C. P. Snow had said to me, referring to some novelist: "Fiction isn't going that way." I remember a vague feeling of surprise that fiction should be regarded as a mass-produced commodity, and "go" in a certain direction, like the design of motor cars.

While I was at Trumpington, George, who was literary adviser to Murrays, came down for occasional week-ends, bringing me beautiful bottles of *Château Mouton Rothschild*, and suggesting that I should submit my next book to Murrays. C. P. Snow had also told me that when he changed to Macmillans his sales went up by tens of thousands. I thought that Murrays were the same kind of old-established publisher, and would have the same effect on me. I also heard that they were very gentlemanly, and I imagined that they were one of those mythological firms who, having taken an author, would back him up in his characteristic work, even if it brought in little money. So I gave them the manuscript of *Outbreak of Love*. They told me on the day I signed the contract, that it would not be published for a year, and they refused my next book, *Much Else in Italy*. I heard later from an outside source that it was thought to be extremely blasphemous. When it was published by Macmillans, but without the effect enjoyed by C. P. Snow, it was given in the *Church Times* two columns of the highest praise I have ever had. I decided to avoid very gentlemanly firms in future. But I had no future.

My next and last novel *When Blackbirds Sing* had a

strange history, due I think to its subject, but I shall leave the reader to judge.

My aim was to show the awakening of a young man, caught in the 1914 war, to the reality of what he was doing, and to spotlight the essential act of murder; but I wrote to appeal to the minds and not to the glands of the reader, which is expected in war fiction today. As this is the most important negative preoccupation of my life, I wrote with all the cold intensity of which I am capable, suppressing any impulse to be witty or irrelevant.

My agent was evidently delighted with the manuscript, and wrote to me enthusiastically, addressing me as "Dear Boyd" dropping the "Mr." which is a sure sign that an agent or publisher thinks a book is going to pay. When *Lucinda* was so successful I had a pink and personal Christmas card from my then agent—the first in fourteen years of association.

When the book at last was published, one of the best critics in England wrote to me that it was the "most real and compelling book I had written" and that it had "the stark necessity of a Sophocles tragedy". A university lecturer, a Litt. D., wrote to me praising it highly, and saying it was my best book. Olivia Manning, reviewing it in the *Sunday Times*, wrote of "my power of conveying emotional profundity" and said that "when time had sorted things out" I would have "an enduring place among the writers of my time". An American reviewer wrote that just as he was beginning to despair of modern fiction, a book would come along to restore his faith, and *When Blackbirds Sing* was one of these. I had several letters of appreciation from friends who had never written to me before about my books. Last year over eighteen months after its publication, I saw it in two public libraries and took it down to see how much it had been read. It had been out steadily every fortnight since it had appeared, while works of the best known authors on the same shelves had only been out half a dozen times.

Very well—it seems odd that a book with these appreciations should be so bad that it could not find a publisher. Yet this is what happened for about five years. It was refused by nearly every leading publisher in London, not one of whom gave a genuine reason for his refusal; and I happen to know that it had had some excellent readers' reports. Finally it was taken by a small American firm, who took four months to give a decision, and a further year to publish it. Their terms were far below those given me by Constables for my first novel.

It seems clear that the theme of the novel was the reason for its rejection. One critic said to me: "No one could go to war again after reading that book."

But on its publication an even more curious phenomenon occurred. I had been used to having sheaves of reviews. My last novel had been praised in every leading paper, and I was recognised in England, if not in Australia, as one of the two major novelists of the latter country. If I had written a very bad book, it was a matter of literary interest and an item of news; but except for the *Sunday Times* review, which somehow slipped through, *When Blackbirds Sing* was received in dead silence. A man in the literary world told me that this must be a deliberate conspiracy, I did not see how this could be possible, though I had other evidence that it might be. Anyhow, I accepted that England was no longer a country where "a man may speak the thing he will". This present book I hope will prove that I am wrong.

Shortly after this, I received my agent's request for pornography and gave up what no longer seemed to me a reputable profession. All this killed the Langton sequence, which I had intended should cover one hundred years.

In 1961 I took to drawing and painting, and last year held an exhibition of my work in Cambridge, risking the accusation hurled at any of my relatives who does this, that I was cashing in on my nephew Arthur's success.

The impulse behind my painting was to show man living untrammelled in delight in the natural world. There were boys riding on dolphins; Europa on the bull; a series of donkey boys escaped to freedom, eating the golden apples of paradise and meeting the goose girls, overcome with hilarity; Spartans dancing; and Children of the Sun.

Friends told me that entering the gallery with all these golden brown bodies in graceful antics round the wall, gave them a feeling of great cheerfulness.

The vicar's wife said they were disgusting.

THE SICK COUNTRY

THERE ARE TWO ATTITUDES OF MIND that lead to a contented old age. One depends on ourselves, the other on the condition of our times. The first is to look back on the good things we have known, the delight of youth, and the capacities of manhood, not with regret, but with satisfaction, regarding them as an asset of memory.

The second is to realise that those assets are not lost forever, but will be enjoyed by others through centuries to come. When a young man of a thousand years ahead feels delight, the delight we felt is immortal. When he feels the same response to a girl's face, or to an orchard in bloom, or to an aspect of truth, to that extent, apart from all theological speculation, we continue to live. Therefore our personal happiness in our later years depends partly on how far we think present conditions are conducive to the perpetuation of our own experience. I do not mean that art forms or social habits or games must be the same, but that man's essential self must cherish the values which the good men of every known civilisation have held to be eternal.

However it is useless to speculate on millenniums ahead. What we may be concerned with is how the young people we know, and possibly their children, are to achieve the conditions for a good life. Old men are proverbially inclined to view the world as going to the dogs, so I shall try to regard present tendencies objectively, and see truthfully how they help to give me the second attitude of mind.

There are two things which seem to threaten the immortality we have in the survival of our values. They are the myths of the "atomic age" and "modern man". I have seen a review which condemned a book for affirming traditional standards in "this atomic age".

About a dozen men have gone into space in a Sputnik. The remaining hundreds of millions of humanity either go to work by bus or train, or plod across the fields, and the groceries are still delivered by a boy on a bicycle. They do not come whizzing into the store cupboard by atomic energy. None of these millions are affected in any detail of their lives by the "atomic age" and their interest in the man in the Sputnik is rather less than that in the divorce of a filmstar or the price of vegetables. As Archbishop Fisher said, these flights "have not solved one human problem". No discovery of science, no rocket into outer space, can alter in any way the laws of our essential being, or of our obedience to the forces of good. The only effect the atomic age has had on man has been to give him an underlying sense of nervous apprehension, which also must have been felt during the Black Death, and by the Christians under Diocletian.

"Modern man" is another myth without meaning. There is no such thing. The young Italians playing football on a vacant piece of ground near my room are identical in every emotion and shout and gesture with the boys who sixty years ago used to play impromptu football at Kew, while waiting to go into school.

The man who goes up in a Sputnik is identical with the one who fifty years earlier hacked his way through ice to the North or South Pole; and he is identical with the Elizabethan who went in search of the North-West Passage; and he is identical with Odysseus; while the unhappy refugees from modern tyrannies are identical with the Holy Family fleeing into Egypt; and when we relate them to the true Myth, they are not merely political victims, but our brothers and the eternal children of God.

The hospitals in England are crowded with people who are suffering from nervous diseases, and these may be called "contemporary". They are unique in their separation from the healing rhythms and force of Nature, but even of this Matthew Arnold wrote an hundred years ago:

> "This strange disease of modern life,
> With its sick hurry, its divided aims . . ."

In the past seven years at the English Centre I have met numbers of young English people between the ages of eighteen and thirty who have come to work in Rome for a year or two. Some of them have become my friends. They seem to share very much my outlook on life, and I find them no different in any essential way from the girls and young men I knew fifty years ago. Only one of them was "contemporary". He said he did not know what to do in life, but thought he would be an artist. I was immediately interested and said: "I did not know you could paint." He replied: "I can't, but I would do abstracts and no one would know."

I also met an enthusiast for modern art and literature. She was a maiden lady of uncertain age. When I objected to the squalor of so much of it, she said with a winsome smile: "We can also see stars reflected in the gutter."

If a man who is only modern in his disease does not manage to cure himself, he will simply be an old-fashioned corpse. He thinks he is of the future, but the present is never the future, and never has been.

However, what naturally concerns me most is how those

of my own country are likely to grow up in the conditions I have named.

Although I think of myself as Australian (and apart from the perhaps significant accident of my birth, that is what I was through my happiest and most hopeful years) I have spent most of my adult life in England, and so am more sensitive to the condition of that country, which I more easily understand.

A young Australian of purely English origins, who arrived in Rome yesterday, said to me: "I don't want to go to England. It's a sick country." Ten years ago this would have provoked from me an angry repudiation. Today I could only give provisional assent.

It is a fact that the majority of English people who come here on holiday or on a visit, say that England is in a terrible state of decadence. I hear this word applied to it over and over again. If it is true, it is due partly to the inept governments that have been in power for most of forty years, who prolonged one war and created conditions for another, prolonging that until they had achieved the disruption of Europe. From this disruption it was inevitable that a miasma should arise, infecting the wounded civilisation. Its carriers are the intellectual delinquents, those who think and reason in a moral vacuum.

I shall take as an arbitrary symptom and symbol of the disease, and of the puritanism which weakens the defence against it, the tolerance of the practice of artificial insemination, which interferes with human life at its source. In a recently published book by advanced intellectuals, a sort of blueprint for the future social pattern, it was advocated that this practice should be the only lawful means of reproduction. At present a woman who wants a child which her husband cannot give her, instead of finding, if she has no moral objection, a fine specimen of manhood, and conceiving in the full-blooded passion of the natural world, submits to this obscene medical attention. The diseased puritanism which informs most of the intellectuals, gives her the assurance that as there is no beauty or pleasure in the act, she is still virtuous. A commission of leading doctors, psychologists, and lawyers issued a report that "the evils inherent in this practice are so great that it should immediately be made punishable by law". But the Government took no action, as there was no money involved.

The depravity of much modern art is also due to the diseased puritanism dwelling in the mind of the artist. His sexual impulses still are joined to a sense of guilt, but being divorced from the natural world, have a hothouse intensity to which he must give expression; so like the woman committing adultery with a syringe, he paints, instead of with the lovely non-sensual eroticism of the Renascence, hideous deformed creatures, naked women covered with sores, and so he satisfies his lust.

One of the most highly praised modern painters sets out to create disgust. He painted a Deposition, and said in a newspaper interview that he tried to make the body of Christ like "a great worm slithering down the Cross".

A woman who likes to keep up in the "art race" as it has been called, took her sixteen year old daughter to an exhibition of this man's work. She gave one look round the gallery, clapped a handkerchief over her daughter's eyes, and rushed her out into the fresh air of Bond Street. The paintings were not obscene in the ordinary sense of the word, but their effect was to make man disgusted with his own existence, which is the vilest crime one can commit, to deprive young people of their delight in their first love, and to drag it down far below honest animalism. I may mention in this connection the number of crimes against children reported weekly in the English press. In Italy these crimes are unknown. There is no puritanism in the children's upbringing, of which another consequence is that a psychoanalyst cannot make a living here.

Their children are suffocated with kisses for the first six years of their life, and seem to thrive on it.

I heard an English intellectual say: "My little girl's head is covered with golden curls—revolting!" He had completely reversed the meaning of disgust. He would presumably prefer his child's head to be covered with a crop of poisonous caterpillars.

On my last visit to the Tate Gallery, I saw a new purchase, an old sack dipped in tar, torn and roughly mended and hung in a frame. Puritanism had arrived at its logical end—death. The very latest artistic movement is called "Anti-Art".

I could give hundreds of similar examples, but the above is enough to show that in England the artistic world is half rotten with hoax and imbecility. The same thing has happened in other countries, but here the Venice Biennial Exhibition of this sort of stuff is greeted with derision.

It is surprising that Australia, a new, clean, virile country priding itself on its independence, should tamely submit to infection from this purely European disease.

In the literary world, especially in fiction, the decadence is even more evident. My agent's request for pornography is almost sufficient proof of this. During the last five years or so, I have noticed that the novels dealing with violence and sexual depravity are nearly always put at the head of the list of reviews. One friend who lives in the country wrote to me that it was almost impossible for him to find in the county library one that was not depraved. Over and over again I hear people say: "I wish I could find a novel to read that is not filthy."

This again links up with puritanism. A publisher recently charged with producing an obscene book, said in defence that it was highly moral as it disgusted people with sex. He too was depriving young people of the rapture of first love, the bridegroom "who sees his true love on her naked bed" and feels that he is at the gate of paradise. The attempt is to reduce his feeling to that of a hungry man looking at a porter-house steak.

One of the worst evidences of the pervading "sickness" is the existence of a "Theatre of Cruelty". Surely the dregs of humanity are those who take pleasure in the cold-blooded watching of inflicted suffering. Yet a writer in a newspaper did not hesitate to identify himself with these dregs, and asked: "There is a theatre of kindness. Why should there not be one of cruelty?" Here is a pure example of a moral vacuum. One might as well say: "There are fountains of drinking water. Why should there not be fountains infected with bubonic plague?"

The effect of wireless and television programmes in stimulating crime is now established. A doctor speaking at a meeting of the British Medical Association stated that venereal disease among children between twelve and fourteen years was due to sexual television programmes. In America, Congress has threatened to take action if the broadcast authorities do not modify their crime programmes.

A man and a woman were beaten up on an English beach, while about fifty people, sitting about on the sands, made no attempt to protect them. This has been attributed to tele-vision, which produces in people the condition of watchers, and largely watchers of crime. A mother of two young sons told me last summer that she lived in dread of their being turned into criminals by watching these programmes, and that most of her friends had similar fears. In two weeks this year, I read of three trials in which the accused said he learned how to commit his crimes from watching television. A government official stated: "We must show our children films of crime and violence so that they will not grow up in a fantasy world." The soldiers of 1914 did not show less courage because their childhood was not spent in the sewer and the torture chamber.

Even more disturbing is the move of education into the

moral vacuum. A few months ago some parents of Oxford undergraduates sent a protest to the university authorities against dons "who conceive it to be their duty to shake their pupils to their intellectual and moral foundations, without giving them anything in exchange".

A professor of London University, in a newspaper controversy with Bertrand Russell, who had stated his objection to cruelty, tried to establish the moral vacuum as a condition of our times. I entered the controversy with the following letter, which I think answered his argument. He did not attempt to reply to it.

"Professor Eysenck appears to question the validity of all moral and spiritual belief, because it can be conditioned in the same way as salivation in dogs. But can he, by passing human beings through a similar degraded hell to that in which Pavlov tortured his dogs, condition them to write something equal to the Gospel of St. John, or an ode by Keats, or give them the enduring intellectual clarity and courage of Bertrand Russell? If he cannot, he has not yet disproved the influence of the Holy Ghost, and it seems he can only condition them to become the unresisting slaves of despotism.

"He is prepared to deal 'a grievous blow to our conception of human worth, ethical responsibility and religious free-will'.* That this, were he really able to do it, would produce a state of moral anarchy, does not trouble him."

There are many symptoms of the sickness of which the young Australian complained—the gratuitous racial problem which is being allowed to grow; the historic centres of London being disfigured by the vast glass boxes which put the whole city out of scale; the turning of the noble city of Oxford into a sort of manufacturing suburb; the steady diminishing of human rights, and the submission of humanity to financial interests; the poisoning of the soil and the air. It is impossible to deal with them here; I only indicate their

* These are the professor's own words.

existence, as they affect my human evidence. Must I accept that my particular world is dead? In my own sphere, roughly that of the writer and the artist, it seems at least defeated. The intellectual delinquents appear daily to gain more power to deny the individual value of the human soul. They deny all that has nourished the mind and heart of mankind from the beginning of history. In the art of every civilisation —Chinese, Greek, mediaeval, Renascence, down to the French Impressionists—there is a common element of beauty, which is denied by the majority of modern painters. To them it is "tiresome romanticism" as it is to the teachers and writers. They refuse to be present in all ages and are marooned on an infinitesimal island of time.

They deny the ancient wisdom of the East: "As a man's mind is, so he becomes."

They deny the prayer of Socrates: "Grant that I may be beautiful in the inner man, and that what I have of outer things may accord with those that are within."

They deny the teachings of Christ, that the Kingdom of Heaven is within them.

They deny the saying of Wordsworth: "The mind of man becomes a thousand times more beautiful than the earth on which he dwells."

They even deny their own idol, D. H. Lawrence, who wrote: "The Holy Ghost is the deepest part of our consciousness; if we go counter to our deepest consciousness, we destroy the most essential self in us, nonentity is our portion."

They are dead teeth, stuffed with amalgam instead of the living nerve. The whole of history damns them.

There are two protests against sickness—the negative gutless one of giving up and dying; and the positive one of fighting back to health and life. Theirs is the Protest of Death.

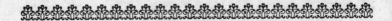

OUR IMMORTALITY

THE PRESENT IS NEVER THE FUTURE. It may leave bad legacies. It always does, but action and reaction are equal and opposite. Last summer in Cambridge the wife of a don said to me: "Everyone is sick of it." She was speaking of the sour humour, the endless denigration, the depraved writing and distorted art. Even periods of the greatest creative genius go out of fashion. It is certain to happen to our own. The only painting and literature that will survive is the fraction that contains something of the eternal. This morning as I went out, two beautiful girls came running down the lane. One had a perfect Leonardo face; and because of Leonardo my delight in this moment was present in all ages.

The danger to our values does not lie only in the harm that depravity and hoax are doing now, but in the nature of the reaction they will provoke. There is a form of primitive brutality, allied to the instinct of animals, which destroys what this instinct tells simple men is mad and degenerate. It cannot discriminate, and when at last aroused into action by the "sickness" of today, it may turn against all liberal thought, "every shade of pink", against all genuine creative freedom in painting, and all literature that is not Fascist.

Not only the lunatic content of the Tate Gallery will be thrown into the Thames.

So the preceding chapter is not the last word. Much harm has been done by the evils I have listed, largely because they have been given disproportionate publicity.

One wretched youth, interviewed in a newspaper, said that he wanted to do something worth while, and that to kill a woman was worth while. This is appalling, but there is probably not more than one in ten thousand of these evil morons among the millions of adolescents. Yet because of them the press spreads abroad the picture of a country sinking into moral chaos. It is true that the English who come to Italy say that their country is in a state of decadence; but the disease is at the top, among the politicians without stability or principle; the intellectuals living in a moral vacuum; the publishers of obscenity and sadism. The evils seep down, but the bulk of the population is still uninfected. I meet no one from England who does not repudiate it, except a few frustrated women who so sweetly see stars in the gutter.

Also in Cambridge, I was standing one evening on a bridge over the Cam, when a punt came along in which were three of the long-haired youths who are supposed to be the symptom of our decay. I thought: "Here come some of these brutalised little thugs." But as the punt floated under the bridge, one lifted an innocent face and said: "It's good to be young, isn't it, sir?"

Further along some of the same kind were diving from a footbridge near the rollers, up which a man and a girl were trying to pull a heavy punt. The divers ran towards them. Having read the newspapers, I thought that they were going to kill the man and rape the girl, but they helped them pull up the punt and then returned to their diving.

In the market square I saw a "mod" or "rocker" in the get-up of his kind. Again I thought: "Horrible little assassin!" But he took some silver from his pocket, counted it carefully, and bought a pot plant, most likely for a present for his mother.

I passed three more in Trumpington Street, and the only fragment of their conversation which I overheard was: "They would think we were undergraduates reading mediaeval history."

Last year, Christopher Geering, my godson, went with a small dramatic company of his contemporaries touring in a van through Europe, to help to create friendship between different nations. Many things of this kind are done by the young. In England some adolescents undertook to help old people who were too feeble to look after themselves. Others have formed a league against foul literature, determined to protect themselves from corruption, if the Government and the Church will not do it.

And is it not better to see them on a holiday, riding out of London in their bright shirts on their blue and yellow bicycles, than as they would have been in the dirty decade, dressed in their fathers' cut-down clothes, grey, half-starved and smutty at the street corners?

Much has been made of the violence in seaside towns, but little is reported of the above activities. There is the usual demand for the birch and the gallows, which may occasionally be justified, but the rioting is no new phenomenon. It has been going on for centuries in the universities between Town and Gown instead of "mods" and "rockers". Future lord lieutenants and cabinet ministers smashed windows and wrecked rooms. One of the latter burned the furniture in his tutor's study, including a manuscript which was the result of ten years' research. No one suggested flogging. Others drowned a fellow student in the Cam. No one suggested hanging. Less than ten years ago, on Guy Fawkes night, I saw undergraduates in the market square trying to overturn motor cars in which women were driving. These savageries conducted by young men who have had the best education the country can provide are condoned as merely due to youthful high spirits.

Unfortunately many of those who would agree with what I have written in the preceding chapter, think that the remedy is more conscription and preparation for more war, instead of feeding the imagination of these lively and potentially creative young people. At the moment there seems small hope of the higher authorities realising this.

C. P. Snow, now Minister of Technology, a peer, and with a son at Eton, said that we needed managers for forty million people. This hints at the social pattern envisaged by the Left—a new ruling class, still titled and Etonian, managing the millions in the factories. It does not sound like the sort of place in which the values we have cherished will survive, or in which humanity itself will survive, divorced from all contact with the natural world. It is stated that now more boys want to do classics than technology. That would throw a large spanner into the works, or rather not enough spanners. Are they to be ordered into the factories, like the man who shouted "Heil Hitler" in 1945?*

The long-haired boys and the marchers are regarded as symptoms of our decay. On the contrary they are signs of life and our greatest justification of hope. They are sick of death. Their long hair is not meaningless, it is not something they have bought as a joke from the wig-maker, it is part of their natural life and growth. Short hair came in with the puritan Roundhead, and was passed on to the convict and the conscript, and the slaves of the industrial revolution. It is part of the reduction of a man to a functioning machine.

An Australian, interviewed by the press on his speedy return from England, said he could not bear the long-haired youths in the streets. He would also have returned quickly from the England of Raleigh and Drake, of Shakespeare

* The political, as well as the human answer to all this is to switch the focus of our livelihood back to agriculture; if food cannot be sold it can be eaten. The people cannot eat a glut of motor cars or refrigerators.

and Chaucer, and of Richard Coeur de Lion. He would have handed the scissors to Delilah.

The long-haired boys and the marchers know either consciously, or with only vague awareness, that their fathers and grandfathers have been senselessly butchered, in wars that were inflamed by lies and fed with the fuel of their bodies. They know that between the wars those who survived, promised "homes fit for heroes", lived in slums and rotted on the dole. They know that owing to the unbelievable folly of their rulers, the second war ended in a situation as dangerous as that with which it began. They know that another war would bring their annihilation. They are sick of death.

At Christmas 1914 the German and English soldiers dancing together between the lines realised that the quarrel was not theirs, but was forced on them by their rulers, who preferred to butcher them, than to use their own brains. They knew that every European war is a civil war. It has been since Charlemagne. But an English colonel fired into the German lines and these bloody Abrahams destroyed half their seed, and hope died.

In Ireland during the second war, the interned English and German soldiers were put into the same camp, and were on friendly terms, going out together on leave. Again their enmity had been forced upon them from above.

Now with a new generation, hope is reborn and the long-haired boys and the marchers no longer intend to pay with their living bodies the price of these old men's stupidity. They say: "We won't be had for mugs."

They know that if the heads of the half-dozen great nations were gifted with even average moral intelligence, they would meet together and say: "The threat to all humanity, not only to our generation, is so great, that we shall not leave this room until we reach agreement." But they meet like suspicious little boys exchanging a top for a penknife.

They know too that there is no salvation in politics. They agree with Lord Attlee, who after forty years' experience, admitted they were "a dirty game". Their Protest of Life is beyond politics. The best political system can be corrupted by bad men, the worst mitigated by good.

The politicians themselves destroy their mystique. They try to preserve it with elaborate obsequies for their defunct fellows, but every day brings them further discredit. A former Minister has claimed that the lie is a legitimate political device. It was certainly used by the Air Minister to Archbishop Temple. Early this year, when Parliament met after a brief interval, the two parties, ignoring the Speaker, shouted abuse at each other across the floor of the House. *The Times* in a leading article, asked how adolescents could be expected to keep from crime, when Parliament set them this example.

However, negation is not enough. The exclusive use of weed-killer has been the blight of this century. If the adolescents will not be had for mugs, they must turn in some new direction.

Revolution is always bad, even though it is always the fault of those who provoke it. The revolution now stirring may be different, not led by intellectuals or vindictive proletarians. It is a Protest of Life from a new generation, and need not be disruptive, if the old bottles can hold the new wine.

In spite of Freud, and the dreary swarm of his dupes, we are the noblest and most glorious animals placed in this world. Of all living creatures we alone have the power to adorn it, to raise a Parthenon or a Sainte Chapelle. The mind of man can become a thousand times more beautiful than the earth on which he dwells; and this is because it can receive the direction of the Holy Ghost, not only of instinct.

In his own subconscious the adolescent knows this is true, but when nothing is done to release this knowledge into his conscious mind, in his frustration he may smash the windows of a seaside town. Yet his potentiality is God-like if his lively energy is admitted to all the kingdoms of the heart and mind.

Lowes Dickinson wrote that art, religion, music were "age-long secretions in the soul of man". These secretions form our myths. In the Western world they are Greek and Christian. For our physical life the Greek myths are enough; but our physical life must be redeemed, or it will destroy itself by its own violence.

The intellectual delinquents pretend that all this is "out". Yet on the day of the most spectacular beach riots of the year, an equal number of adolescents packed St. Alban's Cathedral on a pilgrimage. Across the road from where I live is a church teeming with life every day of the week. It is crowded with young and old at the frequent Masses. They know as well as any Huxley that the Virgin Birth is a normal biological impossibility, but they also know that the spiritual truth of the Myth transcends it. Albert Schweitzer saw in Christ the incarnation of "the Cosmic Will-to-Love", but one cannot say that to simple people. One must use the Myth and the Symbol.

> "A second Adam to the fight
> And to the rescue came."

Those arid dexterous minds which are trying to "demy-thologise" the creeds and the liturgy are destroying the religion which it is their function to preserve. Some children, having read a newspaper article by one of them, asked their parents: "Why should we believe in God when the bishops don't?"

In spite of the sickness at the top, new hopes are rising everywhere today. If our rulers are not again seized with the madness of Abraham, the future may be better than anything

294

that man has yet known, and one part of our immortality assured. To the young all things are new, and if their minds are not injured by their upbringing, they respond with wonder and delight to what is eternal in the beauty of all kingdoms.

For the rest, I can only quote the last recorded words of the greatest scientist of our time, those of Einstein: "Man's chief need is to reconcile himself with God."

THE BOYD FAMILY

Arthur Merric Boyd sen. The founder of the Boyd artistic dynasty was born in Dunedin, New Zealand, in 1862 and moved to Australia in 1886. He was principally a watercolour landscapist. He visited Europe in 1891-93 and exhibited at the Royal Academy in 1891. He was the father of Penleigh Boyd, painter; William Merric Boyd, potter; Martin Boyd, writer; grandfather of Arthur Merric Boyd, painter; Guy (Martin), potter and sculptor; David, potter and painter; Mary, painter, former wife of John Perceval and now married to Sir Sidney Nolan; Lucy, painter, wife of Hatton Beck, potter. Arthur Merric Boyd, who died in 1940, has works represented at the National Gallery of Victoria and the Geelong Art Gallery.

E. M. (Emma Minnie) Boyd. A painter of landscape and *genre*, whose work ranked with that of her husband, Arthur Merric Boyd sen., E. M. Boyd was the grand-daughter of Sir William a'Beckett, first Chief Justice of Victoria. She exhibited with her husband at the Royal Academy in London in 1891.

William Merric Boyd. Born in Melbourne in 1888, he died in 1949. The father of Arthur, Guy, David, Lucy and Mary. Said to be Australia's first ceramic artist, his pottery decoration was based on Australia's plant and animal motifs. He later made many primitive studies of plant and animal life in coloured crayons. Established the Boyd family pottery kilns at Murrumbeena, a Melbourne suburb, in 1911.

Doris Gough Boyd, born in Melbourne in 1888. The wife of William Merric Boyd, her work is represented in State collections and the Australian National Gallery, Canberra, as decorated Merric Boyd pottery. Her paintings are also represented in many private collections.

Theodore Penleigh Boyd, born in England in 1890 and died after a motor accident in Victoria in 1923. The father of architect Robin and pilot and airline executive Pat. A painter and etcher, he was celebrated for his lyrical drypoints of tree subjects and paintings of wattles. He held a successful exhibition in Melbourne at the age of nineteen, and left for England where his work was exhibited at the Royal Academy. He is represented at all Australian State and many provincial galleries.

Martin a'Beckett Boyd was born in 1893 at Lucern, Switzerland. He was educated in Australia and studied architecture before serving in the First World War. In 1924 he began writing novels, the best known of which are *Lucinda Brayford* and the four novels of the Langton Series—*A Difficult Young Man, Outbreak of Love, The Cardboard Crown* and *When Blackbirds Sing.* His novels were mostly built around his family background, and the Anglo-Australian society in which they moved. A bachelor, he lived in Rome in his later years and died there in 1972.

Arthur Merric Bloomfield Boyd. A celebrated painter, and also a potter and ceramic sculptor, Arthur Boyd II was born at Murrumbeena, Victoria, in 1920, the son of William Merric Boyd and Doris Gough, painter. First exhibited impressionistic landscapes in Melbourne. After the war his work moved through phases of psychological expressionist pictures, a 'Brueghel' period of crowded landscapes, a religious phase, a series of renowned landscapes of northern Victoria and the Wimmera, and the celebrated Half-caste Bride pictures. He is represented in all Australian and many provincial galleries, and in many overseas collections.

Guy Martin Boyd. Second son of William Merric Boyd and Doris Gough, born in 1923. Sculptor, designer and manufacturer of successful art pottery. Made sculpture a full-time career in 1965 and is represented in many galleries, including the Australian National Gallery in Canberra, the various State galleries and the Australian Embassy in Washington. He was commissioned to do a large bronze sculpture for the National Sports Complex in Canberra in 1984.

David Boyd. Born in Melbourne in 1924, the third son of William Merric Boyd and Doris Gough. Potter and painter, his talents were first expressed in his non-utilitarian pottery, which gave vigorous impetus to Melbourne pottery standards. Later he turned to painting and has successfully exhibited in Australia and London. His ceramics, and paintings, mainly large panels with social themes, are represented in many State galleries. Lives in the South of France.

Hermia Boyd. Wife of David Boyd, she was born in Sydney in 1932. Her paintings are represented in the Australian National Gallery, Canberra, the National Gallery of Victoria, as well as many private collections.

Lucy Boyd. First child of William Merric Boyd. Ceramic artist and painter. The wife of potter Hatton Beck. She and her husband took over family pottery at Murrumbeena and held a successful exhibition there in 1961.

Mary Boyd. Fifth child of William Merric Boyd. Painter and ceramic decorator. Former wife of Australian painter John Perceval and now married to Sir Sidney Nolan.

Robin Gerard Penleigh Boyd. A celebrated architect and author, Robin Boyd, the son of Penleigh Boyd, was born in 1919 and died in 1971. His books included *The Australian Ugliness, The Walls Around Us* and *Design for Living*. He was a partner of Romberg and Boyd, a major Australian architectural firm, member of the National Capital Development Committee and designer of the Australian pavillions for the Montreal Expo 1967 and Osaka, 1970.

INDEX

INDEX

INDEX

INDEX